CW00550400

TIGRIS GUNBOATS

TIGRIS
GUNBOATS

The Forgotten War in Iraq 1914–1917

Vice-Admiral Wilfred Nunn

New Introduction by
Sir Jeremy Greenstock

CHATHAM PUBLISHING
LONDON

This edition first published in Great Britain in 2007 by
Chatham Publishing
Lionel Leventhal Ltd,
Park House, 1 Russell Gardens,
London NW11 9NN

First published in 1932 by Andrew Melrose Ltd

British Library Cataloguing in Publication Data

Nunn, Wilfred
Tigris gunboats : the forgotten war in Iraq 1914-1917
1. World War, 1914-1918 – Campaigns – Iraq 2. World War,
1914-1918 – Naval operations, British 3. Iraq – History –
1534–1921
I. Title
940.4'15

ISBN 978 1 86176 308 2

Printed and bound in Great Britain by T J International Ltd, Padstow

INTRODUCTION

THE truth of war rarely emerges from a broad or distant overview. It is built up from stories of action in the sound and smoke of gunfire, or from first-hand accounts of the private deliberations and arguments of political leaders. This book is a splendid tale of military endeavour on its own terms, explaining how during the First World War the British Army and Navy combined to break the Ottoman hold on Iraq. It was a resourceful but agonising operation, which started from the Gulf port of Basra in September 1914, recovered from the disaster of Townshend's surrender at Kut in April 1916 and ended in the capture of Baghdad in March 1917.

Tigris Gunboats also illuminates for us a typical experience of British forces in the imperial age, an assignment to a remote corner of the globe with little apparent relevance to the defence of the homeland and its immediate interests; where men suffered from appalling afflictions and deprivations, saw their comrades dying in unforgivingly empty territory and yet found a way to adapt themselves to the circumstances and deliver what they had been asked to do. As Naval Commander in the theatre of operations, Vice-Admiral Nunn's matter-of-fact approach to the business of war disguises the pain and the courage of the individual, but enables us to understand the soldier's and the sailor's heroic acceptance of the necessity of war, the global nature of the struggle which had overwhelmed their lives and the ultimate importance of the force of arms.

The defeat at Kut was significant. More often than not in the military history of the British Empire, enemy numbers and hostile terrain are somehow absorbed and dealt with. Kut proved to be an outpost too far. As Nunn says: 'What ill-wind had blown us to this shore – to this dreary, inhospitable country, the home of the treacherous Arab and cruel Turk? In summer hot even for Indians, to the English cold in winter, even the elements had fought against us, as we struggled through mud or barren desert.' Getting to that point, still more than a hundred miles short of Baghdad, had cost 40,000 casualties, including nearly 12,000 captured at Kut, 4000 of whom then died in captivity in very unpleasant circumstances. Regrouping and pushing through to Baghdad risked the same over-extended lines of communication and could have led to an even greater failure. But good generalship, extraordinary teamwork between the Army and the Navy and countless examples of individual bravery reversed this setback. Kut made the capture of Baghdad seem all the sweeter.

The victory of March 1917 also represented a substantial achievement: it ended for good any Turkish prospect of holding on to Mesopotamia and contributed to the momentum and morale of the British and allied forces more widely as they began to drive the Ottomans out of the whole of the Middle East. Yet it left the British owning the territory of Iraq after the war, bringing them many years of trial and distress in trying, first through colonial occupation and then through intrusive diplomacy, to stabilise a nation that has rarely in its history remained both united and peaceful.

Is it too churlish to ask whether the leaders of a more modern administration might have profited from studying this experience? It now transpires that many individual American officers did try to learn from Iraq's earlier history. But other considerations closer to home were weighing on the top-level decision-makers; there was little delegation of real authority to those in the theatre who could see what the local conditions required; the different parts of the military and civilian systems were out of tune with each other; and the limitations of the use of force were poorly understood.

That meant that a sense of common purpose was missing after the ousting of Saddam Hussein, which was not the case nine decades earlier. Although the combined operation lay under the responsibility of the imperial government of India and communications between India, Cairo and London over Middle East operations were occasionally contentious, the commanders and their troops knew how their success or failure might feed into the larger picture of British wartime objectives in the Middle East. The availability of a mass of information and the shortening of distances with modern technology do not necessarily generate a clearer perception of the task in hand. The context in this book of a war for national survival makes a difference, but imaginative leadership is also a vital ingredient.

Neither the British Government in 1917 nor the Coalition in 2003 really understood what they were taking on when they assumed control of Baghdad. The city stands as one of the great capitals of history, at various times in the past a cosmopolitan centre of commerce and political authority and a powerhouse of scientific and religious teaching. But its sprawl of streets and buildings fails to present an image of imposing dignity. 'Of course, there are some fine mosques in the city', says Nunn, 'but the Government buildings and the arsenal were rather shabby-looking edifices. Otherwise Baghdad seemed to contain only rather shabby, tumbledown houses, straggly narrow streets, and many wonderful smells.' Perhaps clues could be found there to the chaotic nature of Iraqi politics and culture and the dissonance between rulers and their subjects over the ages.

Yet it is the rivers which represent the character of Iraq. The Tigris and the Euphrates carry water from the mountains of Turkey and Kurdistan through the Iraqi and Syrian deserts to the Arab/Persian Gulf. Like the other great desert rivers, the Nile and the Niger, they pass through long tracts of empty wasteland without nourishing more than their own banks. It is an evocative experience to fly along these wandering channels of liquid life and see, from one horizon to the other, the stark contrast of glinting blue water and dry brown sand. But as they begin to come together south of Baghdad, the silt plain builds up and broader expanses of agriculture start to take shape. Eventually, a few dozen miles short of Basra, the two streams join in a great marshland system which expands and contracts with the seasonal flow of water, leaving the river traveller endlessly guessing the navigability of the next bend.

Within the Arab World, only Egypt and Iraq possess these ingredients of a stable agricultural civilisation. The sharp differences in culture and sources of livelihood between the peoples of the river and the desert mean that a powerful political structure has to be in place to combine them in one nation. The Egyptians, benefiting from the size and dependability of the Nile and their distance from any other base of settled civilisation, developed such a structure over long millennia of uninterrupted control. Mesopotamia never established that independence except when the ruler at the central point in Baghdad was oppressively strong. So the tribes along and to the side of the two rivers evolved their own separate and often incompatible traditions as the changing characteristics of the land imposed their compelling force. It is hard to think of any period in Iraq's history when the government at the centre enjoyed the ready loyalty of the whole people of the territory it controlled.

In *Tigris Gunboats* the native population of Iraq barely features.   Two foreign forces slug it out across their land as they watch almost helplessly from the margins. Occasionally a band of marauding Arabs causes a minor problem for a few hours; or a local sheikh aids or hinders the passing army with a short-term intervention.   But they are small-part players.   No wonder a deep xenophobia has built up over the centuries amongst the people of Iraq, a habit of bending with or against the next stranger who passes by with some overwhelming if temporary advantage, but who is fundamentally unwelcome when true feelings can be shown.   The silent witnesses of this Great War drama expressed their sentiments more directly when the British became their rulers from 1919 onwards; and that memory was fresher in the minds of Iraqis in 2003 than it was in Western capitals.

SIR JEREMY GREENSTOCK

January 2007

ACKNOWLEDGMENT

I DESIRE to acknowledge with gratitude the great help that I have been given in the arrangement and writing of this book by Lieut.-Commander E. Keble Chatterton, R.N.V.R., and by Mr. Leonard R. Gribble.

I also desire to express my thanks to officers who took part in the events described and have assisted me with information, verifying details, etc., from time to time, particularly Rear-Admiral C. R. Wason, C.M.G., C.I.E., Commanders C. H. Heath-Caldwell, D.S.C., and I. M. Palmer, D.S.C., Lieut. H. P. Baylis, R.N.V.R., and Lieut.-Commander G. E. Harden, D.S.O., to whom also and Commander A. G. Seymour, D.S.O., I am indebted for many of the illustrations which are reproduced from photographs taken by them at the time, sometimes whilst under fire.

I have referred to and quoted from the official records and dispatches throughout, a number of the Naval dispatches amongst which I originally wrote myself. I have also consulted and am greatly indebted to the Official History of the War entitled *The Campaign in Mesopotamia*, 1914–1918, compiled by Brig.-General F. J. Moberly, C.B., etc., also *My Campaign in Mesopotamia*, by the late Major-General Sir Charles V. F. Townshend, K.C.B., D.S.O., and *The Navy in Mesopotamia*, by Conrad Cato, and *The Long Road to Baghdad*, by Edmund Candler. To all the above I wish to express most grateful acknowledgments and thanks.

WILFRID NUNN.

July 1932.

PREFACE

IN the following pages I have written an account of the
Naval co-operation with the Expeditionary Force in
Mesopotamia from the time of our arrival in that
country in 1914 until shortly after Baghdad fell into
our hands in 1917, during most of which time I had the
honour of commanding the Naval forces.

These operations in the land of the great rivers Tigris and
Euphrates have particular interest in that they were largely
of an amphibious nature ; most of the important operations
occurred near the rivers because of the facilities these
afforded for easy transport through the deserts. A series of
combined operations resulted, in which the Navy, Army,
and Air Force co-operated, often under conditions when it
was difficult to determine where the responsibilities of one
service ended and those of another began. Indeed, both
those onboard the specially built shallow-draught gunboats
—which, however, frequently grounded on the sand-banks
of the shallow lakes and rivers—and the troops floundering
their way through a foot or so of water in the low levels of
the desert quite agreed that there was usually too much
water for the soldiers, but not enough for the sailors.

In view of these conditions, therefore, and as an aid
toward clearness, it has been found convenient in certain
instances to summarize the published Military dispatches ;
only so much as is essential for the continuity of the narrative has been introduced.

The outbreak of war found my ship, H.M.S. *Espiègle*, on
the Naval East Indian Station. After rounding up as prizes
some German merchantmen off Ceylon, and patrolling

the trade-routes in the vicinity, we were ordered to the Shatt al Arab, where the Turks were already creating a difficult situation.

The *Espiègle* and others of her class were selected for this duty on account of their requiring only about thirteen feet of water in which to move ; and, although of an antiquated design, they carried an armament of 4-inch guns, which for many months were the only heavy guns larger than 16-pounders with the Force. The efficient wireless equipment of these gunboats was frequently the only communication between the Force and the outer world.

To be in the East at that time was a great disappointment to all in the Force. Most of the soldiers were wishing themselves in France, while our hope had been, in common with that of every one else in the Navy, to be present in the North Sea at the delivery—long prepared for and expected—of a rapid *coup de grâce* to the German Fleet.

However, we were destined, as the narrative shows, to an exciting time in the Asian deserts, our little corner in the World War. Most of us arrived back home eventually, to be scattered to other scenes of the struggle—the North Sea and Mediterranean, the Red Sea, the White Sea, and, for all I know, the Yellow Sea ; to Dover and the Q-boats and P-boats. Some were present at Jutland, and some were among those who in the destroyer *Shark* so gallantly gave their lives for their country.

This book has been written neither with the intention of provoking controversy and anger, nor of attacking and criticizing the actions of men often placed in positions of great difficulty ; nor am I hoping that it will wound the feelings of the unsuccessful, or add bitterness to the sorrow of those for whom its pages bring sad memories. Herein is a plain account of our doings in that campaign far away from home, comfort, and civilization.

My only desire has been to present an account of the

PREFACE

Naval activities of the " Tigris gunboats," and to testify to the gallant deeds, the cheerful endurance of hardship, and the good comradeship of the officers and men of my small and happy command, who ever faced the difficulties and dangers of the campaign with spirits as gay and carefree as might be conjured in one's mind by the name of their little leader, the *Espiègle*.

W. N.

CONTENTS

Book I

OPERATIONS LEADING TO THE CAPTURE OF BASRA AND KURNA

Book II

OPERATIONS LEADING TO THE SURRENDER OF AMARA

Book III

FROM THE CAPTURE OF NASIRIYA TO THE INVESTMENT OF KUT

CONTENTS

Book IV

OPERATIONS FOR THE RELIEF OF KUT

Book V

OPERATIONS LEADING TO THE CAPTURE OF BAGHDAD

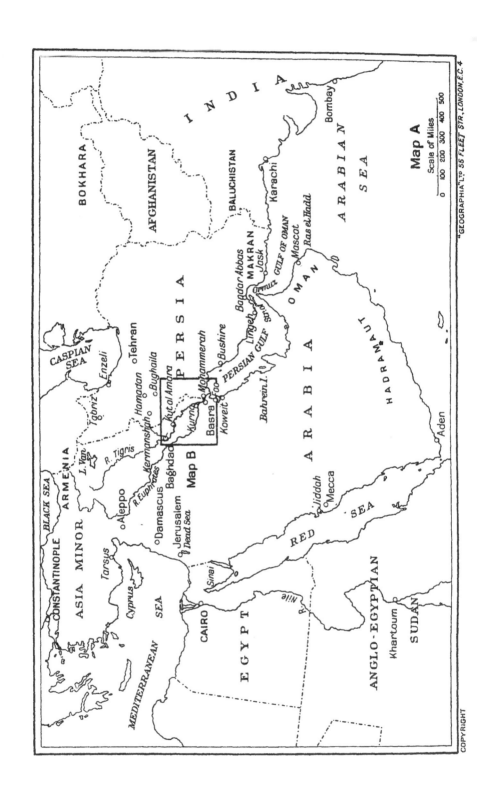

Map A

Scale of Miles
0   100 200 300 400 500

"GEOGRAPHIA" L.TD. 55 FLEET STR., LONDON. E.C. 4

COPYRIGHT

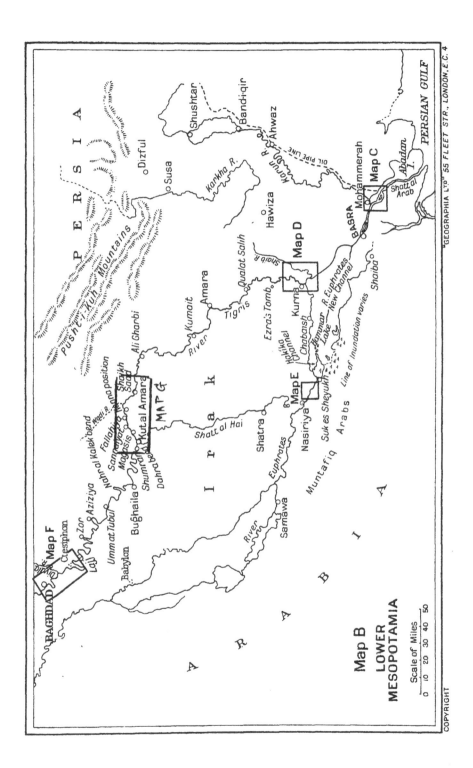

Map B

LOWER
MESOPOTAMIA

Scale of Miles
0 10 20 30 40 50

COPYRIGHT

"GEOGRAPHIA LTD" 55 FLEET STR., LONDON, E.C. 4

CHAPTER I

WAR WITH TURKEY COMMENCES

ORDERS to proceed to the Shatt al Arab reached me on September 12, 1914, at Colombo, where I was in command of H.M.S. *Espiègle*. Leaving next day, we called at Maskat for coal, and, proceeding up the head of the Persian Gulf, arrived in the early morning of the 29th at the entrance of the river, where we met the *Odin*, a sister sloop, and I took over from Commander Cathcart Wason the duties of Senior Naval Officer.

As the reader is doubtless aware, the Tigris, Euphrates, Karun, and other smaller streams flow through the Shatt al Arab and its deltaic channels into the head of the Persian Gulf. The important and ancient town of Basra, the home of Sinbad the Sailor, nearly seventy miles up the Shatt al Arab, is, and has been from time immemorial, the head of sea navigation. At the time of which I am writing vessels drawing over twenty feet could get there at high tides.

About fifty miles above Basra the Shatt al Arab divides into the Tigris and Euphrates. Baghdad, about 600 miles farther up the Tigris, is the principal market of a vast area, and a great converging point of caravan-routes, whence merchandise destined for the outer world has been coming down the river to the port of Basra for generations. Indeed, a modern writer conjectures that the well-known lines in the Psalms, " These men see the works of the Lord and His wonders in the deep," were elicited from the Prophet when, on a visit to the port, he saw for the first time the crowded shipping, the thronged streets, and the wharves with their strange arrivals from overseas.

A few words as to our position and interests in the Persian Gulf and Mesopotamia at that period just before the War will be of interest. The Navy had policed the Gulf—in which we exercised some small protectorates—for years, and to a certain extent, with the approval of the Turks, the Shatt al Arab, in order to protect the Indian trading *dhows* from piracy during the date-export season.

Moreover, we enjoyed certain extra-territorial rights in the country, and our Consul-General at Baghdad was allowed several unusual privileges, such as a guard of Indian infantry at Baghdad and a small armed vessel of the Royal Indian Marine for a yacht.

For a long time the only steamers on the Tigris were those of the British company of Messrs. Lynch ; but British commercial interests up and down the rivers were considerable. At one period not long before the War, and before the advent of the Young Turk Party, we might have had the country for the asking. The Turks were never able to control the unruly wandering Arab tribes, and frequently there was fighting, in which the Turkish troops were often worsted. Sniping continued without pause, and steamers in the upper river, which had to pass through the marshes, were usually fitted with special bullet-proof plating.

The two powerful neighbouring sheiks of Mahommerah and Koweit were also afforded our protection and they were in many ways practically independent of other rulers.

It will be seen, therefore, that the British enjoyed privileges in which other European nations did not share. To these were later added an immense interest in the Persian oilfields, whose pipe-line led to their refinery at Abadan, on the Shatt al Arab, just below the junction with it, at Mahommerah, of the Persian Karun river.

These interests acquired by Great Britain had, as previously stated, grown up before the revival of the authority of the central Turkish Government. There was, it seems rather naturally, much latent jealousy on their part. More latterly signs had not been wanting that the control of the Turkish authorities was being tightened, particularly since the arrival of the Young Turk Party, which the Germans in the background used as a tool in their plan to exploit Turkey and Turkey in Asia. Numerous German plots to establish themselves in the Gulf by means of concessions had been thwarted by the British. As a part of this scheme to establish German, and undermine British, supremacy the Baghdad Railway and the Hamburg-Amerika line of steamers to the Persian Gulf were important factors.

Very soon after the outbreak of the War it became apparent that Turkey might be drawn into the vortex on the side of Germany, and British local interests jeopardized thereby. With Turkey hostile, moreover, enemy interest and propaganda would soon spread throughout Persia ; thence to Afghanistan and the unruly tribes of the Indian North-west Frontier. Again, the possibility of Basra becoming a hostile port, improved by the Germans and connected to Central Europe by the Baghdad Railway, which might very well convey the material and *personnel* for a submarine base, from which our Indian sea communications could be preyed upon, would not bear contemplation.

Commander Wason had a good deal to tell me at our meeting, and informed me of many difficulties which were arising with the Turks locally. Their leaning towards the Germans was well known, as were their objections to our presence in the district ; and the rumour of their intention to block the river—a step which could be directed only against British interests—was an indication of which way the wind was blowing in Turkish politics.

Early in August it had been reported that the Turkish gunboat *Marmariss* at Basra was showing unwonted activity, and that the Turks had requisitioned the stocks of coal and oil of Lynch's local British shipping company. Information was also received that the German crew of the Hamburg-Amerika liner *Ekbatana*, which had taken refuge at Basra, were filling disused vessels with sand preparatory to sinking them in the fairway.

The *Odin* had been waiting in the Shatt al Arab since September, in order to prevent any move of this nature, which, if carried out below Abadan, might have made it impossible to send oil fuel out of the river. This vital necessity of preserving the flow of oil from the Persian hills to the refinery at Abadan, thence by tankers home, to ensure essential supplies to the great fleet in the North Sea, became more and more insistent ; and the likelihood of the Turks attacking or damaging this refinery prompted the suggestion that a small land force should be sent from India to protect it. This suggested land force is the first we hear of the expedition, which later grew in size and objective until eventually it became the army which conquered Mesopotamia as far as Mosul.

Wason had also received information from the British Consul, who was still at Basra, that the Turks had placed a battery to command the river narrows ; that strong reinforcements were coming down river from Baghdad ; and that formidable earthworks were being thrown up in other places commanding the river channel. The Vali of Basra also protested against the presence of the *Odin* in the river, and on September 19 sent an officer aboard requesting her to leave and to cease transmitting wireless messages until outside. The Turkish officer was politely informed that the request would be referred to the British Government. This episode occurred on a steaming hot day, and there is an amusing story told regarding the visit. The commander of the *Odin*, determined not to fail in traditional Naval hospitality, but at the same time fearing to hurt Mahommedan susceptibilities by offering alcohol, ordered the preparation of a sherbet. The only " sherbet " obtainable was some " Eno's Fruit Salt," a large glass of which, mixed with iced soda-water, the Turk gratefully accepted—with somewhat disastrous results !

The next move in the game was when the British Government informed the Porte that our ships would remain in the Shatt al Arab as long as Turkey ignored her obligations of neutrality in Europe. At the same time the *Espiègle* and the *Dalhousie* were sent to reinforce the *Odin*, and the small R.I.M. paddle-steamer *Lawrence* was prepared and armed at Bombay in readiness to join them. The Expeditionary Force was mustered in India, and left Bombay for Mesopotamia early in October.

Our meeting with the *Odin* occurred outside the bar of the river, nearly out of sight of the distant low-lying shores of the entrance to the Shatt al Arab river highway to Mesopotamia, where the events chronicled in this book took place.

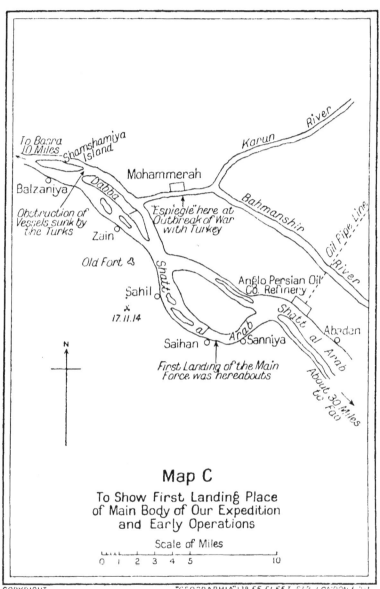

Map C

To Show First Landing Place
of Main Body of Our Expedition
and Early Operations

Scale of Miles

0 1 2 3 4 5   10

"GEOGRAPHIA" L? 55 FLEET STR LONDON E C 4

After our conference the *Odin* steamed away, and we entered the river, communicating at the entrance with the Turkish station at Fao, where it was thought that we were the *Odin* returning. Care was taken that they were not undeceived.

On arrival I anchored the *Espiègle* off Mahommerah, in Persian water. However, indignant protests from the Turks still continued to arrive. They culminated in an ultimatum which was delivered by a Turkish officer who set out towards us one day in an armed patrol-boat.

The document he presented to me was a curiosity. It stated in the queerest admixture of fluid Turkish and very ungrammatical English that the entire river belonged to Turkey, that battleships (*sic*) belonging to the belligerents were not to enter, and it concluded with the underlined words : " *Please you leave the Shatt.* " In reply I told him that I would confer with my superiors. Upon being notified the Admiralty ordered the *Odin* to proceed outside the three-mile limit, and so we remained stationed in the Persian waters of the Karun. The Vali later sent a further message to say that any attempt to pass out of the river after eight days would be prevented by armed force. The Turks then erected a small battery on Dabba Island, which enfiladed the Karun ; but our native interpreter, Mahommed Salim, went over in disguise and thoroughly examined these manœuvres.

The Turks were now showing a considerable activity up and down the river. One ominous sign was that they had placed a small camp opposite the oil-refinery at Abadan. A small gun hidden in the vegetation thereabout might have done immense damage.

Rumours circulated to the effect that mines for laying in the river were being sent *via* Baghdad, and also that there was a possibility of the *Emden*, which later became so notorious, coming up the river to be sold to the Turks. Certainly, if she had come, she would have proved an ugly customer, for her 4·1-inch guns far outranged the old 4-inch guns of our sloops. She could easily have disposed of the *Odin* and ourselves without our getting a shot into her ; and, making her way into Basra, she would have made

A.3

Baorah   7/10/1914   بسم الله الرحمن الرحيم
تعبذ

Dear sir

I am sorry to information you that I recei- ved an ordre to day from my Gouvernemat; Turky being nature and from Fao to the all river *Shatt* be- long to Turkey, from this reason any battle ship be- long to the Gouvernemat at war " Les États belligérants " can not entre from Fao into the Shatt.

Please you leave the Shatt before 24 hours.

I remain your faithfully

Acting commader

C. Shukry

considerable difference to the opening of the campaign. In fact, the stiffening afforded the Turks by her fine, tried *personnel* and heavy guns would have made the landing of our expeditionary force a very different affair from the easy manœuvre it actually proved to be.

Looking back over a period of years, one wonders if this move was ever intended for the *Emden* ; such rumours in those days were very definite, and at about this time she did appear in the Laccadive Islands, which are not far from the entrance to the Persian Gulf. Both her venturesome captain and the German Admiralty must have realized that her lease of life as a cruiser was becoming short. This suggested enterprise would have been a method of utilizing her guns as well as her stores, of getting officers and men home overland if required. Reports also came through to us that German and Turkish Naval officers and men were on their way out overland to reinforce her crew. I accordingly asked if a more powerful ship than the little *Odin* might be sent to the mouth of the Shatt al Arab to prevent the German cruiser from entering. The reply directed that the old battleship *Ocean*, which was convoying the transport of the first brigade of the Expeditionary Force now on its way from Bombay, should remain with us. Meanwhile, in case the *Emden* put in an appearance, we were directed to manœuvre into such a position, by utilizing the bends of the river, as would neutralize the extra range of her guns, by forcing her to engage within our range. This direction read quite simply in the telegram, but how it was possible of being carried out was more than any of us could discover !

However, with the small amount of material at our disposal, we prepared an amateur minefield, and hoped that it might serve to frighten an approaching enemy. As the river-banks near the entrance to the Shatt al Arab are flat and low-lying it is perhaps just as well that we never had to tackle in grim earnest the problem of neutralizing the extra range of what was a much faster ship, although a successful solution of the problem would doubtless have proved of considerable interest to students of naval tactics.

The first brigade of the Expeditionary Force (designated Indian Expeditionary Force " D ") had been packed into transports at Karachi, and these steamed away in company with a number of others under the impression that they were all bound for France. Having reached a certain stage in the journey, however, Captain Hayes-Sadler of the battleship *Ocean*, which was leading their section, opened, according to instructions, a sealed envelope, and learned that he was to proceed to Bahrein. Luckily his knowledge of the geography of Asia was sufficient to locate this place as somewhere in the Persian Gulf!

There was no time to consult directories or gazetteers ; in fact, a signal ordering a course to be steered towards the new destination had to be made forthwith. Very soon the strings of bunting were imparting what was a good guess at the new course. The transports of the Expeditionary Force parted from the remainder of the convoy on a northerly course, while the heads of affairs took occasion to find out where Bahrein really was.

The Force eventually learned that it was bound for Mesopotamia, to make history there, and, due to secrecy well planned and kept, a brilliant *coup* resulted. However, there landed on a river-bank in Asia soldiers who had been filled with expectancy of trenches in France. They found themselves instead in arid desert sands, lacking the artillery and medical and other stores with which a self-contained force should have been provided, but which could not be supplied without betraying the fact that their destination differed from that of the remainder of the convoy from Karachi.

Bahrein had been chosen as an advanced rendezvous on account of its being an island in the Persian Gulf over which we exercise a protectorate. The Force arrived on the 23rd of October, to await the outbreak of hostilities with Turkey. The time between the landing and then was usefully spent in practising landing operations, and similar manœuvres. Shortly after landing the *Odin* and some armed launches joined the *Ocean*.

Meanwhile affairs in the river were becoming more and more serious. Activity on the part of the Turks was already more pronounced, and they sank vessels across the river narrows just inside the border-line of their territory.

The *Espiègle's* means of communication with the outside
world became increasingly difficult, owing to the idiosyn-
crasies of the Persian telegraph line, on which for a while
we had largely to depend, as the distance between ourselves
and the Admiralty was too great for our wireless. It was
almost a relief when, having made every preparation and got
most of the English steamers out of the river, news arrived
of the Turks' attack on Russia in the Black Sea, and of the
dispatch of the British ultimatum.

The preparations referred to above included, among
other things, the placing of sandbags round all vital points
on board. As the sloop did not possess a conning-tower we
contrived one with sandbags and iron plates, and very glad
we were afterwards, for we were frequently within easy
rifle-range of the river-banks. Another important item was
providing every one with a suit of khaki ; at that time there
was no Naval uniform of that colour, and, with the weather
still blazing hot, we had only white clothing to wear.
White, of course, was out of the question, as it afforded
much too easy a mark for snipers ; so we adopted the
expedient of dyeing our white clothing in a weak solution of
permanganate of potash. This turned it into a degraded
sort of khaki colour and served its purpose, although I must
confess I have rarely seen such an awful-looking collection
of pirates as we appeared when wearing these garments.

Whenever possible—with due regard, of course, to
necessary secrecy—I tried to keep everyone on board
informed of what was happening, and generally described
what was intended to be performed at operations. At the
critical period before the outbreak of war with Turkey, for
instance, I told the first lieutenant to ask all the officers into
my cabin, so that I might explain the state of affairs. He
hurried them in, and I thought they seemed rather disturbed,
fidgeting while I was speaking, and I wondered what was
the matter. That evening some one confided to me that
they had been cutting for a round of cocktails, and had
only the last dice to throw when the first lieutenant had
hurried in and sent them aft to listen to my lecture with
some impatience before the important event could be
decided.

In the early hours of November 1, a telegram even more lengthy than usual was brought on board, and when deciphered was found to order commencement of hostilities with Turkey.

The *Espiègle* was instructed to protect British interests up-river ; the *Odin* to await the Expedition off the mouth and to accompany it in, dealing with the Turkish battery near Fao, a few miles off, which commanded the entrance. I also received instructions that the Sheikh of Mahommerah was to be reassured and told that we had no quarrel with either him or the Arabs. Khazal Khan, the Sheikh of Mahommerah, a most loyal ally of ours, to whom the Expedition was much indebted, was at that time subject to the Persian Government, but, in effect, he was the independent ruler of Arabistan. As will be seen later, he was of great service to us on many occasions, and one particular instance of his loyalty at this critical time became known to us only afterwards. The *Espiègle* was lying a little way inside the Karun River, not far from its entry into the Shatt al Arab, where it was so narrow that there was only just room in which the ship could swing round. We were overlooked by a row of high, flat-roofed houses, whence the dour-looking Arabs could almost peer down upon our decks.

However, as I have said, it was afterwards, when the papers of the Vali of Basra were found at the capture of Kurna, that we read of the pleasant surprise he had wished to give us some still, hot afternoon, but had been prevented by the Sheikh. Among the papers was a copy of a letter to the Sheikh with a proposal that the latter should allow a large body of Turkish troops to be concealed on the house-tops on each side of the Karun River where the *Espiègle* was lying. It was arranged that when the *Espiègle* was engaged with the battery on Dabba Island this force on the house-tops should fire on the gunners. " Thus," the letter proceeded, " there will be an unexpected slaughter "—and at the short range of a few hundred yards this would indeed have been the case—" and when no one can defend the gunboat they will board it, killing every one they can find, and seizing the gunboat." The Vali took the occasion to point out that this was an excellent opportunity for the Sheikh to perform a valuable service for the Turkish Government.

It was well for us on board the *Espiègle* that the Sheikh's loyalty remained unshaken, and that he would have nothing to do with the scheme.

In order best to protect British interests it seemed advisable to move into the Shatt al Arab and to take up a central position between Mahommerah and Abadan, whence one could be in touch with either, and, in addition, be able to watch the main stream and side-channels for enemy craft.

For several reasons it was expedient at this time to avoid engagement with the Turkish battery commanding the entrance to the Karun River and the reach in which we were lying. For one thing, any of the enemy shells which went over the *Espiègle* would probably have crashed into the offices of the oil company, and have done a great deal of damage. Also an engagement with the battery would have given the enemy an excuse to infringe upon neutrality rights, and to wreck our properties at Mahommerah before the Expedition could arrive on the scene.

So we slipped out in the middle of the night without any disturbance, and when the Turkish gunners woke up next morning the Infidels had vanished. *Kismet!*

We steamed down-river, and on the Turkish bank near Seihan, landed a party who cut the Fao–Basra telegraph line, which at this point passes close to the river-bank. I suppose this was the first hostile act on our part in the campaign.

We may now turn to the doings of the Expeditionary Force, which in the transports *Varela*, *Umaria*, *Umta*, *Berbera*, and *Masunda*, convoyed by the battleship *Ocean*, remained for some days off Bahrein, before coming to the head of the Persian Gulf and anchoring off the mouth of the Shatt al Arab. The Force was joined at various intervals by the armed Indian Marine ship *Dalhousie* and the armed launches *Mashona*, *Miner*, *Carmsir*, and *Sirdar-i-Naphte*, which I had sent down from Mahommerah.

A strong southerly wind was heaping up a swell on the bar, delaying considerably the business of preparation, and it was not until the evening of the 5th of November that the next move could be made, the Senior Naval Officer, Captain Hayes-Sadler, directing operations on board the *Odin* from the Naval viewpoint in co-operation with General Delamain, commanding the troops. It was arranged that the *Odin* should precede the transports into the river, silence the Turkish battery near the entrance, and safeguard a landing near Fao in the vicinity of the enemy post and telegraph station.

CHAPTER II

THE LANDING IN MESOPOTAMIA

AT daylight on the sixth day of November, 1914, the *Odin* accordingly weighed anchor and steamed up the Shatt al Arab, preceded by mine-sweepers, followed by transports and small craft. The historic Mesopotamian Expedition had begun.

Shortly after ten o'clock the battery guns opened fire on her, and a brisk action ensued, in which large bodies of enemy riflemen took part. The *Odin* was hit several times, but after a sharp engagement of forty minutes the enemy guns were silenced. The riflemen having been dispersed with a good dose of shrapnel, the transports *Umaria* and *Varela*, the armed launches, and the *Ocean's* steam-boats, towing the landing-party, came steaming up the river.

This landing-party consisted of some 600 infantry, including some of the Dorsets and the Indian regiments, and a hundred Marines from the *Ocean ;* bluejacket maxims and beach-party, and a section of Mountain Artillery. All were soon got ashore near the telegraph station, and the men occupied the enemy position practically unopposed. The transports meanwhile proceeded farther up-river before anchoring for the night.

We in the *Espiègle*, however, who were some twenty miles farther up the river, had also experienced a somewhat exciting time. In that part, down to its mouth, the Shatt al Arab runs between Persian territory on its eastern bank and what was then Turkish on its western. Thus, an outpost on the enemy frontier, and some way from support, we were rather what would be described in military parlance as *en l'air*. Reinforcements were known to be coming down the river from the Turkish Army Corps headquarters, at

Baghdad, and from the neighbouring country, so that our assigned duty of protecting British interests at Mahommerah and Abadan might, but for the supineness of the Turks, have proved an impossible one.

I made arrangements for obtaining information from either quarter, and remained between them in a more or less central position, from which any vessel going up or down the river could be observed The only suspicious craft we saw, however, was a small white motor-boat flying the Turkish flag, who was soon brought to by a few shots fired across her bows—especially when, owing to the movement of the ship and the vagaries of our three-pounders, the shot fell pretty close to her ! I learned that the alarmed occupants were agents carrying messages from our ally the Sheikh of Koweit to the Sheikh of Mahommerah. The Koweit flag at that time was the same as the Turkish. When this was pointed out to the agents they were greatly impressed by the need for some distinction. The outcome of the incident is the present flag of Koweit, which has white Arabic lettering on a red ground, and looks something like an amateur outline drawing of a duck.

I moved down to Abadan in the *Espiègle* on the 6th, having received from the *Odin* a wireless message that she was approaching the entrance to the river leading the transports. Warning had previously reached us that this advance would be the signal for an enemy attack on the Anglo-Persian oil-refinery at that place. We had received frequent warnings that such an attack was impending, and in view of the enormous damage which could be done an attack was only to be expected.

There was known to be a force of enemy entrenched opposite Abadan, and we saw some signs of them as we passed that place and anchored in a position where any of their shots that missed us would not harm the oil-tanks. Shortly afterwards they opened fire, and the whole ship seemed to ring with the noise of the impact of bullets on our funnels and plating. A brisk engagement ensued, which our sailors enjoyed immensely. At last, said they, the War had begun. The guns' crews of the disengaged side and others were given rifles and soon we were firing off pretty well

c

everything we had got—4-inch and three-pounder guns, Maxims, and rifles. The enemy were in trenches, behind mud walls, and in thick scrub and reeds on the river-bank, which in places was only about 500 yards away. They were heavily punished. Their fire slackened after a while, and eventually died away. After this we moved up, enfiladed their trenches, and searched the vicinity with shrapnel, completely silencing their fire. It was ascertained afterwards that they had sustained heavy casualties as compared with our good luck in having only two wounded in what we always referred to later as the battle of Abadan.

The *Espiègle* remained in this vicinity, and during the night, which passed quietly, was in telephonic communication with Mahommerah. On the following day, November 7, it was a relief to sight in the distance the *Odin* and the transports of the Expeditionary Force coming up-river. So that, as it chanced, we not only took part in the expedition to Mesopotamia, but were actually there when it arrived.

When coming down-river in the *Espiègle* we had noticed, a short distance above Abadan, a section of the river that was lined with a firm, moderately high, steep bank ; deep water ran close up to it ; and this place was selected, on my advice, for the disembarkation which commenced immediately the transports came up, and continued, undisturbed by the enemy, during the 9th and 10th.

It is surprising that no interference was attempted by land or water—another example of the Turk's habitual lethargy and lack of enterprise. The disembarking was allowed to proceed without interruption at a time when formidable bodies of Turkish troops were being massed in the vicinity.

Between superintending the operations of the launches watching the river and observing the patrols of cavalry watching the desert approaches, we were kept much on the *qui vive*.

I remember being roused early—about 1.30—on the morning of the 9th by a signal from the senior officer, directing me to proceed to intercept hostile motor-launches, a report of whose presence in the locality had been received from Major Trevor, our Consul at Mahommerah. Two enemy craft were reported to have been seen in the channel behind Abadan Island during the previous evening, and it was thought that they might have remained in the vicinity, meditating an attack on the transports.

The *Sirdar-i-Naphte* and the *Ocean's* picket-boat (commanded by Lieutenant-Commander F. S. McGachen) were sent to the southern end of the Abadan boat-channel at the same time, with orders to drive any enemy craft they might find there out at the northern end, where the *Espiègle* took up position (near Harta) at about 2 A.M. However, as no enemy launch was discovered, I proceeded at earliest daylight to examine another boat-channel behind Dabba Island, a little farther up-river, which I thought might have been meant in the first instance. It seemed more probable to me that some such craft might be caught napping in this channel. As it grew lighter and the hazy outline of the shore was revealed more clearly, we gradually became more visible. Suddenly a sharp round of rifle-fire opened on us from the Turkish police-station on the bank. Troops in other fortified positions and in a mud fort to the southward of the police-station joined in. We stayed long enough to reply briskly from all guns, and I believe considerable damage was effected.

Shortly after, as we steamed up-river, the boat-channel south of Dabba Island opened before us. There in the steely half-light we made out a Turkish patrol-boat hiding behind the island. We at once engaged her. She replied with her pom-pom, but we had all the advantage of being prepared. Several of our shots raked her badly, and it was not long before she filled and sank. Our first victim! So, having accomplished the object of our excursion, I dropped back, and returned down-river to the anchorage. Throughout the brush we had been under heavy rifle-fire from the Turkish troops, who by this time had come down to the right bank in large numbers and taken shelter behind the date-palms and undergrowth which thickly lined it. The ship was hit many times, especially when we had to turn in the shallow water, and during several unpleasant moments while we were aground. The Turkish riflemen appeared to have found our range with surprising accuracy. Even behind our improvised defences of sandbags and iron plates on the little bridge, they managed to make our work decidedly " warm." The standard compass was hit, and a bullet smashed through the middle of the chart-house clock ; but luckily there were no other casualties. The return to the anchorage was made without any alarming sequel. It had been chosen because from our position we could, together with the other ships, protect at the same time the transports and flank of the camp.

It was now decided that the force should make no further advance until the arrival of reinforcements, on account of the large numbers of the enemy in the district, the reported advanced of Turkish troops from Basra, and the necessity of safeguarding the oil-works.

On Monday the 9th of November the armed launches *Mashona*, *Carmsir*, and *Lewis Pelly* joined us. The *Lewis Pelly* was a small single-screw steamer which had been used in the political service in the Persian Gulf. She had been allotted a crew by the *Ocean* on the 7th, and was armed with two three-pounder Hotchkiss guns and one ·303 Maxim, and placed under the command of Lieutenant J. F. Carslake, R.N., of that ship. The armed launches were usefully employed in patrolling the river between Abadan and Fao, where a small garrison had been left, besides guarding the transports. The launch *Carmsir*, however, was soon found to be unfit for this service ; so the Naval crew was withdrawn and she was disarmed.

Captain Hayes-Sadler at this time moved from the *Odin* to the *Espiègle*, and from this time until his departure I assisted him in the direction of the Naval operations.

Reconnaissance on the 9th and 10th failed to discover any enemy in the vicinity, but on the evening of the latter day the Sheikh of Mahommerah further increased our indebtedness to him by informing the General of reliable news he had received : that Sami Bey, with a strong body of Turkish and Arab troops, had arrived from Basra at a point opposite Mahommerah, with the intention of making a night attack on our camp.

At 3 A.M. on the following morning he again sent us word. This time that his spies reported the Turkish force to have started on its march towards our camp. Due precautions were taken. Troops stood to arms, and outposts were strengthened. The enemy was given a hot reception when he delivered his attack, at 5.30 A.M., on our advance post, which was held by a double company of the 117th Mahrattas, with two machine-guns. The Turks advanced to within fifty yards of the post, but there faltered, and were driven off by a counter-attack made by the 20th Duke of Cambridge's Infantry, with the support of the 23rd Peshawar Mountain Battery. The straggling enemy retreated across the desert, suffering heavy losses in the retirement. When the grey dawn brightened the mountain guns and the guns of the sloops opened fire with devastating results. That completed Sami Bey's night attack.

Lieutenant-General Sir A. Barrett arrived to command the Force on the 14th of November, bringing with him the 18th Indian Brigade and Divisional Troops. The disembarkation was made as rapidly as possible. The infantry for the most part rowed themselves ashore in the transport boats ; but the landing of guns, wagons, and horses in small lighters (obtained from the Anglo-Persian Oil Company) and *dhows* presented considerable difficulty. Our steamboats assisted, and bluejackets were lent to coxswain the transport boats, but the lack of steamers and tugs was felt in the strong river current, for we had not as yet obtained the use of Messrs. Lynch's river-steamers. Several of these were lying in the Persian Karun, quite near ; but, owing to the question of Persian neutrality, they could not be made available until about a week later, when, owing to the victory of Sahil, a further stretch of the Shatt al Arab River up to above Mahommerah fell into our hands, uncovering the mouth of the Karun.

Fortunately the place chosen made things fairly easy, the bank being " steep to " and about three feet above the river. Mainly for this reason, and through the excellent work of the sappers, who used the hatch covers of the transports as gangways, the inevitable difficulties incidental to landing a large body of troops on the muddy banks of a river, where neither wharves nor piers existed, were overcome.

On November 15 a reconnaissance in force was carried out by General Delamain to reconnoitre and dislodge enemy forces who were gathering near Saihan, about four miles west of our camp at Saniyeh. The *Odin* co-operated, steaming up-river parallel to the advancing line of troops, and was later joined by the *Espiègle*. The fire of the two vessels, however, was much restricted, owing to the difficulties of observing the effect of the shells, which were directed over the thick belt of date-palms lining the river-bank. Our force on shore had some heavy fighting, but the men rushed two Turkish positions, inflicting considerable damage to the Turkish camp. A return to Sanniya was made in the evening, and the ships returned to an anchorage nearby.

A general conference was held on the next day. It was decided that an advance should be made the following day at daylight, as most of the force would have been landed by then ; and it was considered advisable that no time should be lost in showing our ability to make headway against the Turks, as the attitude the Arabs would adopt depended largely upon the impression we made at this stage.

H.M.S. *Lawrence* joined us the same day. She was an armed paddle-steamer of 1130 tons, mounting four 4-inch guns and four six-pounders ; before the War she had usually been employed as the yacht of the Political Resident in the Persian Gulf, and had been manned by the Indian Marine. She now flew the White Ensign, and was under the command of Commander (Acting) R. N. Suter, R.N. The armed paddle yacht *Comet* also joined us at this time. She arrived from Mahommerah.

At daylight on the 17th—that is, that day following the conference—the advance began in the direction of Basra, the troops having their right flank on the river covered by the *Espiègle*, the *Odin*, the armed launches *Sirdar-i-Naphte* and *Lewis Pelly*, which kept abreast of their advanced parties.

General Barrett's force consisted of a wing of the 23rd Light Cavalry ; the 63rd Battery, R.F.A., three guns of the 76th, 23rd, and 30th Mountain Batteries ; the 16th and 18th Indian Brigades, the 17th Company Sappers and Miners ; the 48th Pioneers ; and pack transport, ambulances, etc.

Information had been received to the effect that a force of the enemy would probably be met with near Sahil and Zain, while the main body was believed to be in a position at Balzaniya. At the time of the advance, however, the whereabouts of the Turkish Naval forces was not known. Our intention was to turn the enemy's right flank, and drive them towards the river, so that the gunboats moving up level with the advance could co-operate.

Recent rain had rendered the going very heavy ; the desert was a veritable sea of mud. A persistent downpour during the forenoon entirely obscured the front for some time, but the enemy position was sighted by the advance guard of our army at about 8.50, and soon after the Turkish guns opened fire. Our two brigades advanced to engage, leaving a space between them to allow the artillery to come into action ; the cavalry moved up, covering the left flank and the wide spaces of the desert, while the men-of-war covered the right. These manœuvres continued steadily until about 11.45, by which time the opposing forces were heavily engaged along the whole front.

As the key to the enemy position appeared to be a mud fort on his left, General Delamain now moved to turn that wing and attack it, while General Fry, with the 18th Brigade, engaged the enemy's right and centre. The movement was skilfully carried out ; and our troops pressed on steadily, despite the treacherous nature of the ground. The enemy wavered, finally abandoning their entrenchments and fleeing. Our force pursued, doing considerable execution. Both prisoners and guns were captured.

Owing to the banks of the river being thickly fringed with date-palms, as I have already explained, and to the shallows and islands preventing a close approach to the Turkish shore, the operations could not be seen from the decks of the ships, but a clear and uninterrupted view of the action, together with the Turkish forces and position, could be obtained from our mast-heads. From one of these an officer controlled our gunfire by megaphone directions, with excellent results. Several of the enemy guns were seen to leave the open and to take shelter on account of our too-close attentions. In order to steady the ships in the river current

—thus ensuring a more accurate fire—we anchored from time to time, and it was during these intervals that we were also kept busy by enemy riflemen sniping from behind the trees and scrub along the bank. However, by means of such manœuvring we succeeded in shelling and setting fire to the enemy camps, which the officer directing our fire could see beyond the expanse of trees.

We had to anchor soon after 3 P.M., when, after being engaged with a Turkish patrol-boat, a very heavy sandstorm came on, blotting out everything from view. The storm blew violently for some time, raising a nasty sea, which swamped two *dhows*—containing supplies, R.F.A. wagons, etc.—alongside the transports. This equally unforeseen and unfortunate incident resulted in the loss of several lives.

After the battle our troops encamped in the vicinity, the transports were brought up, rations, stores, etc., disembarked, and the wounded put on board.

At this battle of Sahil the British casualties were 54 killed and 430 wounded, the enemy, under Bimbashi Ali Bey, having lost nearly a thousand, with some prisoners and guns.

Our troops remained in camp for a few days, while supplies were landed and reconnaissance of the enemy's next defended position was carried out. That position was at a place called Balzaniya, a little farther up the river past the islands opposite Mahommerah, where the river was blocked by vessels sunk abreast of it.

The entrance to the Karun being now open to us from the Shatt al Arab, the *Espiègle* went up to Mahommerah, and sent down all the available steamers and lighters which had been lying in the Karun. These comprised several shallow-draught river-steamers, the property of Messrs. Lynch, which were at once found to be of great value in working as ferries between the heavy-draught transports and the shore. They were placed under the orders of the Transport Officer of the Expeditionary Force.

We also found a quantity of abandoned Turkish stores, as well as ammunition, at the southern end of the Dabba boat channel, and here we obtained confirmation of the report that the Turks were going to make their next stand at Balzaniya. General Barrett was informed of this by wireless.

On the 19th, two days after the advance, the *Espiègle* made another reconnaissance to examine the enemy position at the north-west end of Dabba Island, and the block-ships were sighted. A Turkish motor patrol-launch which we surprised in a creek on the other side of the block-ships was soon destroyed and sunk.

The Turkish gunboat *Marmariss* was also dodging about on the other side of the next island upstream, and a few shots were exchanged with her, but she quickly retreated up-river, having, as we heard later, been hit and somewhat damaged by one of our shells. A boat which had kept alongside her was sunk. Altogether we had rather a lively time, as we were also engaged by the battery at Balzaniya, on the right bank. Our landing-party a few days later, when we occupied the place, had the satisfaction of finding the base of one of our 4-inch shells in it. From this closer view we came to the conclusion that the river was not completely blocked, and that there was a narrow passage between the steamer *Ekbatana*—one of the craft sunk by the Turks—and Dabba Island, with possibly room for the passage of the sloops.

On our return to the anchorage off the camp a conference was held, at which it was decided to make a further advance early on the 21st ; the armed launches were to go by the boat-channel, the sloops and the *Lawrence* proceeding down the main river channel, to support the right flank of the army, engage the Balzaniya position, and, if possible, to pass the obstruction. However, the whole situation was altered by news received late in the evening of the 20th from the Sheikh of Mahommerah, who, accompanied by Major Trevor, came down in the Consulate steam-launch, bringing information that the Turks had fled from Basra, were making for Amara with all their forces, and had evacuated the Balzaniya position.

Next morning at daylight the *Espiègle*, the *Odin*, and the *Lawrence* proceeded up-river and confirmed this report, meeting with no opposition. The battery at Balzaniya was found to be deserted, the cavalry discovering the same fact from the land side. We anchored just below the obstruction in the river, off the north-west corner of Dabba Island. Here Lieutenants Harden and Curry were sent forward to examine a narrow channel that we had noticed between Dabba Island and the bows of the steamer *Ekbatana*, the only place appearing to afford a likely passage.

These operations were rendered very difficult by the numerous eddies and small whirlpools, caused by the strong tide and river current rushing like a mill-race round the bows of the *Ekbatana*. While at anchor here a steam-launch came down the river and joined us. She had on board some of the principal British residents of Basra, and the Mayor. The leading British citizens, after the outbreak of hostilities, had been treated as prisoners by the Turks, but had been liberated when the latter retreated. These British gentlemen informed us that the Turkish troops had evacuated Basra, and that the Arabs, who were looting the town, had already set the customs house on fire. They strongly urged the immediate necessity of a force being sent up to occupy and restore order in the town.

By now we had ascertained that the passage round the bows of the *Ekbatana* was clear, so it was decided to endeavour to negotiate it, and to push on to Basra with the ships in company. The General was informed of our decision by wireless, and he asked whether the ships could go on and ascertain the situation, if not too risky, and, if possible, render help. Thus it was decided that two light-draught river-steamers should be sent up to join the men-of-war and proceed to Basra, while the General marched with the remainder of his force that evening.

When it appeared to be nearly slack water, at 2 P.M., we weighed. Although the tide was found to be still running hard, accompanied by strong eddies, with some difficulty, and after several attempts, we successfully negotiated the passage between the island and the bows of the *Ekbatana*. The other craft followed the ships, eventually anchoring opposite the Balzaniya battery, which had been evacuated, and parties were sent ashore to dismantle.

At about 3.30 P.M. there was no sign of the river-steamers with the troops, but a cloud of smoke, evidently from burning buildings, could be seen in the direction of Basra. It was decided that the *Espiègle* and the *Odin* should continue, in order to reach there before dark. Both ships arrived off Basra just as dusk was falling, about 5.30 P.M., and anchored off the customs house, which had been fired in several places and swarmed with Arabs, crowds of them fleeing across the river in their *mashufs* (the local canoes), which were loaded with loot. After firing a blank charge, to frighten them, we landed an armed party from each sloop, to do what we could to save the customs house. I went in the leading boat. We pulled into Ashar Creek, and ran alongside the steps to the jetty, which, like the burning customs house, appeared to be crowded with Arabs bent on pillaging. The jabbering crowd fell back, however, as we came up the steps ; the sight of bluejackets with fixed bayonets was enough. One old man, wearing the customary fez, came up and shouted : " Do not shoot, sir ! Do not shoot ! They will all run away ! "—which they did very quickly when they saw that we meant business.

Proceeding from the jetty, we found the customs house blazing fiercely. Nearly all the contents had been removed. One dead Arab was lying in a corner, his throat badly slashed. Some one must have owed him money ! There was little we could do, and it was considered advisable to withdraw for the night, as both the town and country round about appeared to swarm with armed Arabs, and we were, of course, unaware how far off might be the Turkish troops. During the night we heard sounds of continuous rifle-firing in the town, which was in a state of disorder—usual in the interval between the retreat of one lot of owners and the arrival of another ; but the next morning we sent in parties from the sloops, took possession of the Turkish barracks, the customs house, arsenal, the Turkish commodore's house, and the German Consulate, and placed the German Consul and his staff under restraint, for it was known that they had been instrumental in the attempt to block the channel.

The Turkish barracks were empty and very dirty. Piles of torn papers and records lay strewn on the floor of almost every room in the place. In the dockyard was an odd mixture of things : old and new guns, ammunition, quantities of stores and coal, etc. We used the coal later, and at the bottom of the largest heap some very serviceable anchors were disclosed. A strange place to keep them— but probably not unillustrative of the efficiency of the Turkish Naval machine. There was also an unfinished graving-dock, for the construction of which, I was afterwards told, large sums of money had been expended—on paper. When Constantinople had become curious about it a framework imitation of a gunboat had been constructed in the dock, and a photograph sent to the Turkish Admiralty !

Pending the arrival of the troops, we placed a few blue-jacket sentries over the Government buildings, which were pointed out to us by members of the local firms.

The river-steamers, carrying a British and an Indian battalion, under Major-General Fry, arrived about 9.30 A.M. The men were landed, and took over the posts from the bluejackets. We were very glad of this, as the few men that could be spared from the sloops were dangerously insufficient for looking after the evacuated Turkish establishments. The Arabs, however, remained quiet as far as we were concerned, and the houses of the English merchants had not been attacked or disturbed. Indeed, we found that the English Club had neither been entered nor looted, although during the past few days the Turks had held the British residents prisoner. I suppose the Young Turk- and German-implanted ideas had not permeated far enough for the crowd to pillage the old-established club, that had been sacred to the English for as long as they could remember. Anyhow, while I was being shown round the evacuated Turkish Government buildings we passed the club, and, looking in, found that nothing had been disturbed ; so we rested from our labours for a few minutes, and drank some very acceptable lager beer.

Next day Wason carried out a reconnaissance up-river in the *Odin*, and landed some troops at Messrs. Lynch's yard at Margil, without sighting any enemy. No damage appeared to have been done to the premises ; but a large quantity of material intended for the Baghdad Railway was found, and this proved very useful.

On the afternoon of the 23rd of November General Sir A. A. Barrett made a ceremonial entry into the town at the head of the troops. The Royal Navy was represented in the procession by Captain Hayes-Sadler, myself, and Major Temple, R.M.A., and it also provided a guard of honour under Lieutenant Singleton, R.N.

The foreign Consuls and notables were presented to the General by Mr. Bullard, who had recently been our Consul there ; and the Chief Political Officer, Sir Percy Cox, then read a proclamation in Arabic on behalf of the General Officer Commanding. The Union Jack was hoisted on a conspicuous house on the western side of the town, and near the entrance to the Ashar Creek, the *Espiègle* firing a salute of thirty-one guns and the troops presenting arms. Then three rousing cheers were given for the King.

After the occupation all was quiet at Basra, and the inhabitants seemed fairly well disposed and friendly to us, although occasionally there was some sniping on the outskirts of the town at night. But probably that was an infrequent practice merely continuing from the days of our predecessors.

CHAPTER III

THE KURNA OPERATIONS

HAVING established ourselves at Basra, the advisability of securing our position by occupying Kurna soon became apparent. Kurna is a town about forty-five miles farther up the river, at the principal situation where the Tigris and Euphrates combine to form the Shatt al Arab. It is thus a place of considerable strategic importance, and also comprises a natural outpost for Basra.

The question of occupying Kurna was discussed at length by a conference presided over by General Barrett, held at General Headquarters during the early days of our stay at Basra. It was decided to ask the Indian Government to approve this step. At the present time, after all the recriminations which have since taken place, it is interesting to recall that at that meeting the question of supplies, river-steamers, etc., necessary if an advance were made to Baghdad, was clearly put forward and debated, and the necessity of a railway emphasized ; but, as it was not intended then to go farther than Kurna, nothing was done in these matters. It will be seen later how heavily we were to pay for the lack of due provision and preparation for which these changes of policy were largely responsible.

Approval having been received from India, it was decided to carry out a preliminary reconnaissance. The sloops and armed launches left Basra in the early morning of November 25, and no signs of any enemy were seen until, when about six miles from Kurna, the Turkish gunboat *Marmariss* was sighted a long way off, retiring up the river Tigris. Now, about three miles below Kurna the river takes a sudden sharp bend. It was immediately after rounding this bend

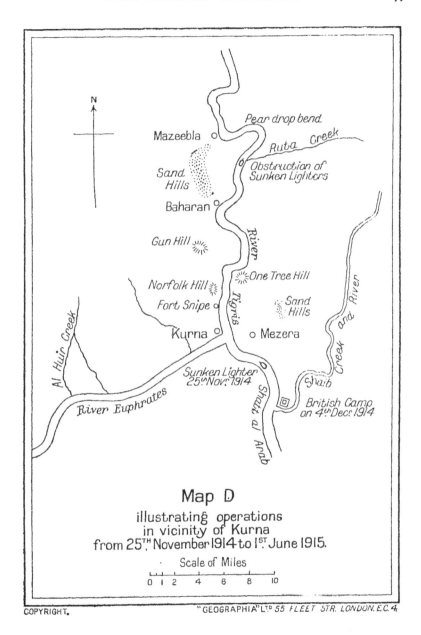

N

Pear drop bend

Mazeebla

Ruba Creek

Sand Hills

Obstruction of Sunken Lighters

Baharan

River

Gun Hill

One Tree Hill

Norfolk Hill

Sand Hills

Fort Snipe

Tigris

Kurna

o Mezera

Creek and River

Al Huir Creek

Sunken Lighter 25ᵗʰ Novʳ 1914

Shaib

Shatt al Arab

River Euphrates

British Camp on 4ᵗʰ Decʳ 1914

Map D

illustrating operations
in vicinity of Kurna
from 25ᵀᴴ November 1914 to 1ˢᵀ June 1915.

Scale of Miles

0 2 4 6 8 10

that the ships came in sight of the town and its fortifications. Our approach was the signal for a welcoming round from two or three guns placed before Kurna, with an *obligato* of rifle-fire from the near-by trenches. However, almost as the guns opened fire the ships ran into shoal water which prevented them continuing farther forward.

The *Odin* now reported that she had struck some submerged obstacle in the river, and had badly buckled her rudder, the *Mashona* had also run foul of something, damaging a plate, but luckily she sustained no material harm. As a result both these ships were sent back to Basra for examination and repair.

About 2 P.M., when things were fairly quiet, Lieutenant Harden was sent in the steam-cutter to sound the river and to see if there was a navigable channel through the shallows. He found less than two fathoms beneath his craft, but perhaps a more important discovery was that a steel lighter had been sunk close to the left bank, as an obstruction to our advance. It was against this that the *Odin* had struck.

At the time we had only an old rough sketch-map of the river, showing no soundings, and affording very little information except for the soundings taken by Lieutenant Harden. It was only afterwards, when we occupied Kurna, that a more detailed and accurate survey could be made. Examination of that survey shows that in the widest part of the Tigris in this neighbourhood—that is, from about seven to fifteen cables south-eastward of Kurna—there is a shallow bar, which in the low-river season is covered by only about eight or nine feet of water ; in some places by only six feet. It was in the shallowest part of this stretch of river that the lighter had been sunk.

The Tigris varies considerably in height according to the time of the year ; the difference is dependent largely on the melting of the snow in the Caucasus Mountains. Therefore, as we were at this time only a month past the usual period of the lowest river-level, there was very little more water than the depths stated above. Later in the operations, however, we found that a small rise and fall of tide is experienced as far up as Kurna during this low-water season, and were able to take advantage of the fact. In the high-river season—

viz. from April to July—the river would rise from six to eight feet above these depths ; then the rise and fall of tide would be unnoticed, and the tidal current even below Basra would be absorbed in the strong river current.

From these few tidal facts one can readily appreciate the difficulty experienced by the sloops, each drawing about twelve feet, while manœuvring in the shallow waters. Luckily the bottom of the river is entirely composed of mud —there is no rock in these lower reaches of the Tigris and Euphrates—or else the ships would have been considerably more damaged, and certainly unable to take the risks they did. Even so, we had some very awkward moments at times, when practically unable to move, and under shellfire from the enemy.

However, now that the object of the reconnaissance had been attained, we returned to Basra. An examination was made of the *Odin's* rudder, and, as it was found impossible to repair it locally, it was decided to send her to Bombay as soon as the Kurna operations could be concluded, for a definite decision had been made that Kurna should be occupied by our forces.

Meanwhile the passage through the obstruction in the Shatt al Arab between Mahommerah and Basra had been buoyed ; a number of transports had managed to come through to Basra at slack water, and troops (including the 17th Brigade, supplies, etc.) were expeditiously disembarked, in spite of the great lack of such facilities as wharves, landing-piers, etc.

Preparations were now hurried on apace, and, for use in the shallow water, the *Shaitan*, a small, light-draught tug, was fitted out in place of the *Sirdar-i-Naphte*, and placed under the command of Lieutenant-Commander F. J. G. Elkes, R.N.R.

On the afternoon of Tuesday December 3, the *Espiègle* and the *Lawrence*, with the armed launches *Lewis Pelly*, *Miner*, and *Shaitan*, proceeded up-river. They were later rejoined by the *Odin*, which had been sent on before because of her difficulties in manœuvring with her damaged rudder.

The military forces detailed to take part in the operations were also dispatched from Basra on the evening of the 3rd,

D

in the four river-steamers *Mejidieh, Blosse Lynch, Malamir,* and *Salimi.* The forces consisted of two eighteen-pounders of the 82nd Battery, R.F.A., one company of the Norfolk Regiment, and a half-company 3rd Sappers and Miners, the 104th Rifles, and 110th Mahrattas, all under the command of Colonel G. S. Frazer. The *Mejidieh* and *Blosse Lynch* each had also two eighteen-pounder Field Artillery guns, manned by their own officers and men, mounted on the forepart of the deckhouse, to be placed at the disposal of the Senior Naval Officer as soon as the landing of the troops had been completed.

Colonel Frazer was ordered to land at a spot on the left bank of the river a few miles below Kurna, selected by the Senior Naval Officer, and, acting in concert with the Naval force, to clear the enemy off that bank as far as Kurna ; after accomplishing this he had a free hand to decide whether to cross the river and attack the town of Kurna, or to hold on and await the arrival of reinforcements.

At 5 A.M. in the morning of the next day, the 4th, the river-steamers with the troops having arrived, we proceeded to Shaib, a position about three miles below Kurna on the left-hand bank, just south of the Arab village of Umrash, in the bend of the river. Shaib had been selected for the landing because it was out of sight of Kurna, and was farther round the bend I have mentioned, it was also, as judged from our reconnaissance, out of gun-range from Kurna.

At this place there was a good steep-to bank for landing. It was situated, too, on the side nearer to Kurna of a stream called the Shaib, which, of considerable volume and depth, runs into the Tigris in this vicinity, and would have proved a difficult proposition to bridge or to transport troops across. There was another but much smaller creek between the camp and the village of Umrash, across which the sappers threw a bridge.

The foregoing, of course, describes the locality only during the time that these operations were carried out, when the river-level was low. At the greatest height of the river— which would be some months later—the site of this camp, together with a large surrounding tract of desert, would be under water, and the Shaib greatly increased in volume and flow.

In order to cover the landing, the *Espiègle* and the *Lawrence* continued a little farther upstream, rounding the bend of the river and coming in sight of Kurna itself. The Turks promptly opened fire from the guns mounted in the vicinity, and very soon we were all heavily engaged. Both ships were hit several times.

The river-steamers drew alongside the river-bank at the place selected, and disembarked their troops, who immediately prepared to advance, an advance base being speedily formed. The *Odin*, which, of course, could not manœuvre without difficulty, and the armed launches remained near Shaib to guard the camp.

From the small adjacent Arab villages white flags fluttered timidly. They were still fluttering when, at 9.30 A.M., the advance commenced. It had been delayed somewhat by small creeks and marshes.

The river-steamers, after landing their troops, reinforced the *Espiègle* and the *Lawrence*, and speedily opened an accurate and telling fire on the enemy position from the eighteen-pounder field-guns mounted in their bows. Their shrapnel burst with admirable accuracy directly over the enemy positions. It was soon discovered that the enemy were entrenched along the edge of the date-palms near the village of Mezera, with guns mounted both there and at Kurna. Consequently we in the ships divided our fire in order to support the advance, beside engaging all the enemy guns, the heavy fire from which being in this manner diverted from the advancing waves of troops, who cleared the village and assaulted the trenches with only slight casualties.

The enemy fell back through the date-groves, where the ditches afforded them considerable cover. But they were routed out and driven down to the Tigris—here some two to three hundred yards wide—over which they were ferried. Our troops, pursuing, penetrated to the bank, only to find themselves, however, under a heavy fire from Kurna, and with no means of crossing the river.

It was impossible for the sloops to move up farther, owing to the shallow water, and the armed launches, which were, of course, comparatively small, poorly protected craft, were held up on attempting to approach the town by the heavy fire. They were all hit many times, and the *Miner* was holed by a shell which penetrated her engine-room at the water-line. If her commanding officer, Lieutenant Heath-Caldwell, had not managed to run her aground near the *Espiègle* she would have sunk in deep water. In fact, it was only through the bravery of Stokers Jones and Lacey, who, although both wounded, stuck to their post in the engine-room, which was rapidly filling as water poured in through the hole, that the engines were kept going long enough for this to be accomplished. Once in shallow water, the *Miner* was out of reach from the enemy guns. I am glad to say that both men, Jones and Lacey, afterwards received well-deserved decorations.

Our small force being now held up by the Tigris from reaching Kurna, and the sloops by the shallow water, and Kurna being held by a greater force than had been expected, Colonel Frazer decided to fall back on the Shaib camp and ask for reinforcements. The retirement commenced shortly after 2 P.M. As soon as we in the ships became aware of it, we redoubled our bombardment of the enemy positions, to cover it, drawing on ourselves a good deal of the enemy's fire. As the troops retired towards the camp the other vessels also were ordered to drop back. But darkness descended before the *Miner* could be repaired sufficiently to float and be towed downstream. The *Espiègle* was still aground, and we had to remain some time longer in this unpleasant position, until, the tide having risen a little, we called up the *Lewis Pelly* to assist in towing our bow round. She proved very unmanageable in the river current, however, and while this was proceeding the moon rose suddenly over the desert wastes, illuminating the river scene with an eerie, silver half-light, and the Turks again opened fire. Lying there motionless, lit by a clear stream of liquid moonlight, the *Espiègle* presented a splendid target for the Turkish gunners. I hurriedly rang down again for " Full speed astern," and this time, owing to the river having slightly risen—possibly also to the encouragement given the engine-room department by the shrill whine of a Turkish shell—the ship shuddered her way slowly astern into deeper water. Soon, little the worse for the trying experience, we were dropping back to the camp.

Talking over this episode with one of the officers some time afterwards, I remarked that I thought at the time we were in rather an awkward predicament. He agreed, but added that it had been even more exciting than I had known, because, just before we moved astern, the *Lewis Pelly*, in an effort to cross our bows, had been set down by the river right across our stem. Our bowsprit had passed between her masts, and if by the merest chance we had not gone astern at the moment we did, at least her masts and funnel would have been taken out of her !

The British casualties throughout the day had been slight. As two guns and seventy prisoners had fallen into our hands, and considerable loss had been inflicted on the enemy, the advance had not been entirely unsuccessful.

General Barrett, who had been kept informed by wireless of the course of events, now sent up General Fry with the remainder of the brigade and four more field-guns. These much needed reinforcements arrived early on December 6.

Reconnaissance now disclosed the fact that the enemy had reoccupied his old position at the village of Mezera, placing there some more guns, which exchanged shots with the *Lawrence* during the forenoon ; and we received a surprise when, early in the afternoon, the enemy, about 500 strong, were descried from the *Lawrence* advancing with guns across the plain.

Reinforcements had reached the Turks from up-river, and it is probable that they had exaggerated our retirement of the previous day into a serious reverse.

Our outposts were now promptly reinforced, and the *Espiègle* took up a position to protect the north-west angle of the camp. With the *Odin* and the *Lawrence* she opened on the Turks with shrapnel. The *Espiègle* was hit several times by shells, but no serious damage was done. Upon our Field Artillery also coming into action, however, the enemy was soon forced to retire, with considerable loss.

Spies informed us that the enemy had been considerably reinforced since the action on the 4th, and their strength was now estimated at between 1200 and 1500 around Mezera, with six guns, and about 800 in Kurna, with four guns. Further, the enemy's movements in the afternoon had shown the desirability of attacking Mezera as soon as possible, and clearing the left bank of the Tigris ; but it was realized that this manœuvre might, like the former, be rendered ineffectual unless we were prepared to remain in possession of the captured ground. It was decided, therefore, that the opening of a short line of communication from such an advanced position to the Shaib camp would be essential to the success of the advance, and arrangements were made accordingly.

General Fry's plan of attack was for the 2nd Norfolk Regiment and the 120th Infantry to attack the village of Mezera and the trenches south of that place, while the 110th Light Infantry, on the right of the Norfolks, were to carry out a turning movement against the north of the village, the 7th Rajputs and 104th Rifles being held in reserve.

The section of the 82nd Battery was to support the left, the 76th Battery the right, and the 30th Mountain Battery—which had just joined us—was placed between the field batteries.

This operation commenced on Monday morning December 7, when the *Espiègle* proceeded up-river to the north-westward of Umrash, with the *Lawrence* placed astern, the launches and the *Odin* to the south-eastward. The troops meanwhile moved out of camp, advancing in formation over the level and bare sandy plain. The second drive was now fully launched.

On seeing the ships, the enemy at once opened fire with the guns at Kurna and Mezera, but we were not slow in replying with lyddite—an effective answer ! The *Blosse Lynch* and the *Mejidieh*, with their R.F.A. guns co-operating, also took up positions on the *Espiègle's* port side, shelling the enemy's trenches and effectively covering the advance of our troops. The accuracy with which the soldiers burst their shrapnel over their objective was openly admired and applauded by the bluejackets.

Shortly afterwards our Field Artillery on shore opened fire, the dull, reverberating boom of the guns rolling in short echoes across the desert plain. The enemy responded impetuously with *staccato* bursts of rifle-fire from the village, the trenches covering it, their two guns at the north end of Mezera growling a more sullen challenge. These latter, however, were silenced after a few rounds by the Field Artillery, and were subsequently captured intact.

The *Espiègle* was able, by dragging through the mud, to move a little farther up-river about noon. The other ships followed, and were successful in co-operating with the 82nd Battery on shore to counter some enfilade fire from the enemy's right, under which our troops were advancing.

All this time our infantry were steadily pressing forward, well supported by the artillery, and shortly after noon they carried the village of Mezera at the point of the bayonet, a vigorous pursuit being carried out through the palm-groves. The shore artillery then moved round to the north of the captured village, and observed and shelled a large body of the enemy—estimated at from 1000 to 1500—who were seen retreating northward with two guns up the left bank of the Tigris. Unfortunately we had no cavalry with which to pursue. One gun had been placed in position on the northern edge of the palm-groves, and this raked the river-front of Kurna at a range of 2300 yards.

Later on the *Espiègle* managed to move a little farther still up the river, and, as there now came a lull in the firing, Lieutenant Harden preceeded to examine and make soundings round about the sunken lighter, so as to ascertain if it was at all possible for us to get past her.

The *Miner*, the *Lewis Pelly*, and the *Shaitan* were also ordered to move up to assist on the left flank of our troops, who were by this time advancing through the date-groves. The launches were again welcomed with heavy fire from Kurna, and after they had been in action for about half an hour the *Shaitan* received a direct hit on the bridge from a gun mounted on the town front. Piercing the half-inch protective plating, it killed the captain, Lieutenant-Commander F. J. G. Elkes, R.N.R., instantaneously, seriously wounded C.P.O. Thomas Trentwith, who was at the wheel, which was also smashed, and stunned Mr. Pysey, the pilot. The *Shaitan* was safely brought out of action by Petty

Officer Vale, who dashed on to the bridge, and, finding her steering-gear disabled, brought her back alongside the *Espiègle*, steering with the screws. It was found later that one of her rudders had been damaged by a shell, and she was sent down to Basra for repairs.

The launches had a hot time under the heavy fire from the Kurna guns and the sniping from the river-bank, both of which they vigorously returned. Later it was considered advisable to recall them, as they were riddled with bullets, and had several casualties. Poor Elkes had behaved with conspicuous gallantry throughout the operations, and he was certainly one of the bravest men I have met. He was on board the *Espiègle* during the interval of leaving the launch *Carmsir* and taking up command of the *Shaitan*, and spent most of his time at the mast-head in the look-out position, keeping an eye open for a possible enemy. He was always keen, and paid us a great compliment one day by saying that he would prefer to spend the interval between these small commands on board the *Espiègle*—as she was always in it if anything was going on ! We sent his body down to Basra, where it has laid to rest in the little British cemetery of those days. I arranged that the Union Jack which had covered the body on its way down should be sent back to us at the front. It was hoisted over Kurna when finally we took possession.

Mr. Richard Gain, gunner, R.I.M., of the *Miner*, was another who received commendation for gallant conduct in remaining at his post, though severely wounded in the leg by a rifle-bullet.

The fighting in the palm-groves continued until nearly dusk, the enemy maintaining a heavy and shattering fire across the river from Kurna and along the river-bank. At last the General decided to camp for the night, and renew the attack next day, when an attempt at crossing of the Tigris above Kurna would be made. During the evening the Force bivouacked in some gardens between Mazera and the palm-groves. The night passed without any exciting incident.

The artillery duel between the ships and the enemy gun positions had continued in the meantime. The enemy fire had at times been heavy and fairly accurate. All the ships had been hit. The *Espiègle* was slightly damaged, and had several men wounded by a segment of shell, which hit the spreader of the main topmast rigging and burst over the poop. But the firing died down when darkness came on, and the ships remained in position, the enemy firing only a few shells again when the moon rose.

Early next morning attempts to get a line across the Tigris were commenced by our forces at the northern edge of the palm-groves ; while other parties covered the operation, and two regiments opposite Kurna, in combination with the Naval force, endeavoured to distract the Turks' attention.

During the morning Harden had again been away and buoyed the outer side of the sunken lighter. He had found out that there was apparently just room for the *Espiègle* to pass it. Thus we could creep yet a little nearer Kurna. Consequently at 11 A.M., with the *Lewis Pelly* sounding ahead, the *Espiègle* moved up, scraping her slow way through the clinging mud. The two river-steamers followed, and anchored to the north-west of the lighter, within 2000 yards of Kurna, with the *Lawrence* just behind them. The ships were now able to engage the guns at Kurna, and any houses which could be seen, with more satisfactory results, receiving intermittent replies from the enemy.

The *Lewis Pelly* again moved forward to reconnoitre early in the afternoon, after a considerable lull in the firing ; but upon nosing her way close up she once more met with a heavy fire, and had to return under cover of fire from the ships. She was hit many times, and sustained some casualties. It was about this time that we received information from the General that some of the Force had managed to cross to the right bank of the Tigris about three miles above Kurna, and that two battalions were following them. We learned afterwards that just before noon three Indian soldiers of General Fry's force had swum across the river with a line, followed by Lieutenant Campbell, R.E. A 1½-inch wire hawser was then hauled over, made fast to the right bank, and used for hauling a small *dhow* to and fro across the river.

Lieutenant-Colonel Frazer, Captain Cochran (G.S.O.3),

and seventy men crossed at 1.30 P.M. in spite of rifle-fire from some *dhows* downstream. The remainder of the battalion (110th Infantry) then moved across.

The Navy and troops in front of Kurna were distracting the enemy's attention successfully, for the crossing did not appear to be realized by the enemy until too late, though the advancing men experienced some rifle-fire and rather less effectual shellfire. The 104th Rifles managed to cross about a mile and a half farther upstream, in three *dhows*, which they secured from some friendly Arabs, and came up on the right flank of the 110th.

A section of the 30th Mule Battery, without mules, followed ; but, the party meeting with some opposition north of Kurna, Colonel Frazer decided that it was too late in the day to storm the town—there was the possibility of street-fighting to be considered—and decided to camp for the night on the right bank, near the flying bridge, covered by the Norfolks on the opposite bank.

This order to retire and to camp did not reach a double company of the 110th, under Colonel Britten, who entered the right of the enemy position, where they occupied three towers, enfilading the northern defence of Kurna. Later on, however, finding that they were isolated, they withdrew, and regained our camp without casualty. The troops were not disturbed during the night.

Firing between the enemy guns and the ships had continued intermittently until dark, and we could tell from the sounds of heavy rifle-fire and the rising columns of flame and smoke from the burning houses that the troops were progressing. Then the bombardment died down, and, shortly before midnight, a small steamer, with all lights showing brightly, was sighted coming slowly down the river from Kurna, blowing her syren as she approached nearer to attract our attention.

An armed boat from the *Espiègle*, under Lieutenant Harden, boarded her while some distance from the ship, and he reported that she had on board a deputation of three Turkish officers empowered by the Vali to discuss terms for the surrender of Kurna. The Turkish officers were allowed onboard ; but, as it was impossible to get in touch with the

General in time, we decided to discuss the matter at once, and they were ushered into the wardroom. I well remember the scene, and a strange sight it was : the small party of officers sitting round the lamp-lit table in the little sloop's wardroom, very dishevelled Turks on one side, and hardly less so British on the other.

After explaining their mission the senior Turk, a weather-beaten old colonel, said that the terms requested by the Vali were for the garrison to be allowed to march out with their arms and leave the town to us. This, of course, we would not permit. An angry scene followed, and it was only after we had pointed out to him that Kurna was sur-rounded, and that our guns and troops were in position to open fire at earliest daylight, that unconditional surrender was accepted and agreed to in the name of the Vali. The Turks returned to Kurna in order to arrange their side of the bargain, and we communicated the result to the General by signal through the base camp, whence a mounted mes-senger sped forth, reaching headquarters just before the intended assault.

General Fry and his staff rode down opposite the *Espiègle*, came on board during the morning of the 9th of December, met the deputation, and final arrangements were made for the formal surrender. We found that there was a slight rise of tide about 10 A.M., so the *Espiègle* again got under way. Pushing through the mud, with the *Lawrence* following, and the *Lewis Pelly* sounding ahead, she was able to steam slowly through the remainder of the shallows, but coming into deeper water near Kurna, turned back into the Tigris and anchored off the town at 10.50 A.M. The *Lawrence* hove to near-by.

The river-steamers *Mejidieh* and *Blosse Lynch* also came up. They had performed excellent service on this occasion, as on many others. Frequently under fire, they had on board, as we have seen, besides troops, the eighteen-pounder R.F.A. guns ; and, further, they had been used to some considerable extent as gunboats. Their civilian captains, Messrs. Cowley and Suzeluiski (in Messrs. Lynch's employ), afterwards received letters of high appre-ciation and thanks from the Admiralty for their meritorious conduct on this particular occasion, when working in co-operation with the armed forces of the Crown. Later they were given commissions in the R.N.V.R.

At 1 P.M. the Senior Naval Officer and officers went ashore with the General Officer Commanding, his staff, and the Chief Political Officer, Lieutenant-Colonel Sir Percy Cox. They landed near the house of the Vali, whose surrender General Fry received, afterwards returning to him his sword in recognition of his brave defence.

Subhi Bey, the Vali, a Turkish officer of considerable ability, had formerly been a Professor of Military History at the Staff College, Constantinople. He had been Vali of Basra since the beginning of the War, and after the Turkish evacuation of that place had proceeded with a force—levied largely, I believe, on his own initiative—to defend Kurna. There he had been the life and soul of the defence—providing a distinct contrast with the other Turkish senior officers, who, upon our approach, had promptly fled farther up the river.

Our troops moved into the town, pickets were posted round the walls, and a guard placed over the Turkish troops, who had " fallen in " and piled their arms in the open square at the southern corner of the town.

The Union Jack I have already alluded to was brought ashore from the *Espiègle*, and hoisted over Kurna with the usual formalities, and that night the prisoners were sent down-river in the *Blosse Lynch* to Basra.

The Naval casualties in the engagement were Lieutenant-Commander F. J. G. Elkes, of the *Ocean*, killed while commanding the *Shaitan ;* Mr. Richard Gain, gunner, R.I.M., of the *Miner*, wounded ; Edward Gibson, ordinary seaman, of the *Ocean*, died of wounds ; one chief petty officer and one petty officer seriously wounded ; and seven other ratings and one Marine wounded.

Lieutenant Mark Singleton of the *Espiègle* was now placed in command of the *Shaitan*, Lieutenant C. G. Hallett, R.I.M., taking his place in the *Espiègle*.

Major-General Fry's force on December 7 had consisted of 87 British officers and 981 rank and file ; 60 Indian officers and 2598 rank and file ; with ten eighteen-pounders, six ten-pounders, and nine machine-guns. Just over a thousand Turks were taken prisoners, while during the operations six fifteen-pounder Krupp guns, two nine-pounder Krupp guns, together with a large quantity of rifles and ammunition, were captured.

The Turkish gunboat *Marmariss* was reported to have been present on the 7th. However, she did not come within sight of the *Espiègle*, but was driven up the Tigris by our Field Artillery. A Turkish Naval lieutenant, who was among the prisoners, also reported that his armed patrol-boat had been struck by one of our shots on the 7th, and had sunk off Kurna.

The occupation concluded, Captain A. Hayes-Sadler, R.N., and Major Temple, as well as most of the officers and men belonging to the *Ocean* who had taken part in the engagement, rejoined their ship, which was lying off the bar, and departed for the Suez Canal, for another encounter with the Turks. She eventually went on to the Dardanelles, where her honourable sea career came to a sad end. A number of the *Ocean's* officers and men, however, remained with us in the launches, with their armament.

With the *Ocean's* departure from the Persian Gulf the duties of Senior Naval Officer again devolved upon myself.

On December 11 and 12 reconnaissances were carried out up the Tigris by the armed launches *Miner* and *Lewis Pelly*. They discovered that the Turks had sunk four steel lighters across the river just south of Rotah Creek, about seven miles above Kurna, and they also recovered two lighters which, in the hurry of their retreat, the Turks had not had time to sink. Up-river, curling upward over the distant flat and barren-looking country, could be seen the smoke of the *Marmariss*, but she did not disturb the reconnaissance.

What remained of that year passed fairly uneventfully.

On December 16 the *Espiègle* went down to Basra, where there was a good deal to arrange, but she returned to Kurna on Christmas Day, to relieve the *Lawrence*, as considerable trouble from snipers had been experienced in our camps at Kurna and Mezera. Arabs from the neighbouring hostile country were able to paddle their *mashufs* through narrow channels up to the very edge of the reeds, and from there fire direct into the camps.

Considerable reinforcements were now arriving in the country, and being brought up-river ; at slack water the transports and mail-steamers were negotiating the passage between the bows of the *Ekbatana* and Dabba Island without difficulty.

The Admiralty had granted permission to Messrs. Strick and Co., a shipping firm with branches here, to make an attempt to raise the *Ekbatana* with the assistance of divers from the *Ocean* and the *Espiègle*. In this attempt, however, they were unsuccessful, and the *Ekbatana* was left to sink slowly deeper in the mud, the scour of the current round her gradually enlarging the channel, until steamers were able to proceed through it at all times of the tide.

Throughout all this while communications had been improved, and by the 4th of December the cable from Basra to India through Fao was again working.

BOOK II

OPERATIONS LEADING TO THE
SURRENDER OF AMARA

CHAPTER IV

MINOR OPERATIONS

DURING the period between the landing of our expeditionary force in Mesopotamia and the end of the year 1914 we had thus secured a good foothold in the country ; after the occupation of Basra and Kurna we held the whole of the Shatt al Arab, as well as the strong strategical position at its head, at the junction of the Tigris and Euphrates. Up to this time no large engagement had been fought beyond the gun-range of the ships, the mobility of whose heavy guns had been of great advantage in the manœuvring. When, subsequently, some important battles were fought at a considerable distance from the river—notably at Shaiba, and an action was fought near Ahwaz—the heavy casualties we sustained were presumably due to the absence of our heavy guns.

Before the capture of Kurna, however, it had already become apparent that even vessels of moderate draught could not accompany the expedition much farther up the river, on account of the decreasing depth of the river. It therefore became necessary to consider the provision of light-draught gunboats.

The contents of the two following chapters cover the period from January to June 1915, during which the Turks made their first determined attempt to retake Basra and turn us out of the country, when they concentrated a large force in the desert to the westward of Basra, and at the same time threatened Kurna, on the Tigris, and Ahwaz, on the Karun. Their forces were augmented by great numbers of hostile Arabs, who, with their intimate knowledge of the country and of the narrow channels through the swamps and marshy plains, were a dangerous, uncertain, and elusive enemy.

Nevertheless, it must be admitted that the Arabs always retained a wholesome fear of the British men-of-war patrolling the rivers, especially of the *Espiègle.* In the case of the latter their distrust was partly on account of her crow's-nest for the look out, placed high up on the mainmast, the possibilities of the view from which they greatly exaggerated. With the ready superstition of a nomadic desert race they came to look upon it as a sort of evil eye which beheld their wicked deeds from afar.

The *Espiègle's* figurehead was another feature that impressed them strongly. It consisted of the head and shoulders of a lady in very scanty dress—what there was of it !—and represented, I suppose, some Naval constructor's idea of portraying the frolicsome spirit which the French word denotes. The name came into the British Navy list, like many others, with a prize captured in the Napoleonic wars, and it has been handed down to the present day through a number of ships—in spite of the difficulty found by the sailors in pronouncing it, even when quite sober ! I remember one day telling a fair Australian visitor the origin of the name, and she exclaimed enthusiastically : " How interesting, Captain ! And was *this* the prize ? "

Great care in the adornment of this figurehead was taken by the ship's painter, who considered himself something of an artist, and everyone on board interested himself in the scantily-dressed lady's appearance. One evening before the War the First Lieutenant came up to me in the wardroom, just before painting ship, and asked whether I wished any change to be made in the colouring of the lady.

" You see, sir," he said, " last commission she had brown hair, so this time we made her a blonde."

It was plain from this that I was expected to propose something clever and original—even artistic. Luckily a bright idea struck me. I said : " I've just been looking through the last mail from home, and I notice among the latest fashions that some ladies are going to dance-clubs wearing green wigs. Suppose she was given one ? "

The wardroom warmly applauded the idea ; even the dour-looking First Lieutenant seemed pleased. In fact, solely on the strength of the suggestion, I gained considerable prestige as a person of artistic tastes—and the lady was given a green wig, a pale face, and bold, black eyes that stared not in the least demurely across the deserts. As the sloop moved up the river-reaches the Arabs cowering in the marshes might very well have wondered whether a lady of the Court of Cyrus, King of Kings, returned their way again.

In the neighbourhood of Ahwaz our oil-pipe line was broken by enemy agency early in February, and hostile activity was revealed in every direction—the river above us was blocked and mined, floating mines were drifted down, sentries were knifed in horrid fashion, and there were few nights when the camps and gunboats were not heavily sniped. It was a harassing time for all.

These preparations on the part of the enemy culminated in their attack on our camp at Shaiba, to the westward of Basra, on the 12th and 13th of April, which our forces repulsed. Our troops, assuming the offensive after stubborn contest, gained a decisive victory at Barjisiya, and compelled the Turks to retreat in confusion.

I shall now describe how, consequent upon this and several successful operations executed by General Gorringe on the Karun, the Turkish plans were disorganized, and how again our forces, assuming the offensive, were enabled to defeat the Turkish troops to the north of Kurna and capture Amara.

EVENTS EARLY IN 1915

On January 1, 1915, I was at Kurna, accompanied by the armed paddle-steamer *Lawrence*, which was under Commander (Acting) R. N. Suter, R.N., and the armed launches *Shaitan*, under Lieutenant-in-Command Mark Singleton, R.N., and *Lewis Pelly*, with Mr. H. Coleman, gunner, R.N., in command. The armed launch *Miner*, under Lieutenant-in-Command C. G. Heath-Caldwell, R.N., was refitting at Abadan, and the sloop *Odin*, under Commander Cathcart

R. Wason, R.N., was at Bombay, having her damaged rudder repaired. The paddle-yacht *Comet* was armed and commissioned on January 1 by Lieutenant Irving M. Palmer, R.N., who took with him his crew from the armed tug *Mashona*, which thereupon reverted to duty as a tug, and was employed by the Transport Department in the lower waters of the Shatt al Arab, a locality more suitable to her deep draught. The *Dalhousie*, under Commander (Acting) E. M. Palmer, R.N., was at this time employed in patrolling the Persian Gulf.

On the Tigris General Fry, commanding at Kurna, was consolidating his position and receiving considerable reinforcements, who were fortifying that place and also our entrenched position at Mezera, on the opposite bank of the Tigris.

Since the capture of Kurna, on December 9, 1914, it had become evident that there were considerable bodies of hostile Arabs banded together in the plains around that town, and there had been a great deal of sniping into the camps at night, especially by Arabs in the marshes to the north-west. These elusive foes were most difficult to deal with, as they could come in their *mashufs* to the edge of the reeds, fire a few rounds into the camp, and then withdraw rapidly out of sight again. In fact, it was an effective form of desert guerrilla warfare that they were waging.

Reports had come in from our spies that there were some Turks in the vicinity of Mazeeblah, north of Rotah Creek, just south of which, and about seven miles north of Kurna, it will be remembered, the Turks had blocked the passage of the Tigris by sinking four large lighters across the river. A reconnaissance carried out by General Dobbie on the first day of the New Year established the fact that there was a Turkish encampment beyond two wide, unfordable creeks to the north of Mazeeblah. This reconnoitring force consisted of two battalions of infantry with a mule battery, with cavalry that moved up the right bank of the Tigris, supported on their right flank by the *Espiègle*, the armed launch *Shaitan*, and the *Blosse Lynch*—the latter with two eighteen-pounder Field Artillery guns mounted on the forepart of her deck. It was found very difficult to manœuvre

the *Espiègle* in the river, which narrows considerably above
Kurna, and has many sharp turns and bends ; but the ships
succeeded in getting nearly up to the obstruction, anchoring
just to the south of Rotah Creek while the reconnaissance
was in progress.   Our cavalry dispersed some Arabs from
Mazeeblah, but, being without any bridging material, the
troops were unable to do more than locate the position of the
Turks, and were forced to return to the camp at Kurna,
followed by the ships, which had not come within gun-
range of the enemy.

We found the Tigris so narrow at the place the ships had
reached that it was only possible to turn the *Espiègle* about
by backing her obliquely into the bank until her stern gently
took the mud, and was held while the river current swung
her bow round.   This somewhat delicate manœuvre had
to be performed under fire on several occasions afterwards.

The actual state of affairs at the obstruction could not be
ascertained except by diving operations, without which it
would have been impossible to ascertain with any degree of
definiteness how much the lighters were damaged, and
therefore what steps would be necessary for raising them.
It was obvious, also, that diving operations, if carried out,
would require to be protected by a force stationed in the
vicinity, and that salvage operations, due to the now rising
river-level, would become more difficult with every day that
passed.   The matter had, however, to be deferred in any
case, as the future policy of the Expedition and the question
of whether it would proceed farther up the river than
Kurna were not at the time decided.

From now onwards a daily cavalry patrol was carried out
to the north of our position, with one or more of the armed
launches supporting it from the river, and shots were
frequently exchanged with considerable numbers of banded
hostile Arabs.

It was also decided to reconnoitre the Euphrates River
and its passage into and through the shallow Hammar
Lake—that is, as far as the ships could proceed.   As the
" politicals " were anxious to secure and deport the pro-
Turkish Sheikh of Chabaish—a large Arab village among
the swamps, near the place where this branch of the

Euphrates flows out of the lake—it was arranged to send a small combined expedition from Kurna. On the 6th of January the *Espiègle,* the *Shaitan,* the *Comet,* and the *Lewis Pelly,* convoying the river-steamers *Mejidieh* and *Malamir,* in which were embarked two double companies of the Norfolk Regiment and one double company of the 7th Rajputs, with bearer sections, ambulances, etc., under the command of Lieutenant-Colonel E. C. Peebles, D.S.O., of the Norfolk Regiment, proceeded up that river for these operations.

The Chief Political Officer, Lieutenant-Colonel Sir Percy Cox, was accommodated in *Comet,* and the force left Kurna in the morning of the same day. We made a short stay at Medina, the village of a friendly *sheikh* about fourteen miles from Kurna, where the Union flag was hoisted, and then proceeded towards Chabaish, which is about another fourteen miles farther on. As the ships proceeded up the Euphrates to the westward the water, however, became more and more shallow, and the *Espiègle* was soon only dragging through the mud. I therefore went on in advance with the shallow-draught craft, leaving the *Espiègle* at anchor.

On our arrival off Chabaish, about 1.15 P.M., a message was sent ashore ordering the *sheikh* to come onboard the *Comet.* The inhabitants were quiet, and had already displayed white flags over the village, evidently fearful of a bombardment and attack by our force, and Salim Khayyun came onboard. He gave himself up without further incident. He was placed under guard, and I went on in *Comet,* with the *Shaitan* in company, to explore the higher reaches of the river, while the transports and the *Lewis Pelly* were sent back to anchorage near the *Espiègle.*

At dark we anchored near the entrance to the Hammar Lake, and next morning proceeded into the lagoon-like expanse of water ; but found it to be very shallow, with depths of only about three feet. So we were unable to proceed farther, and decided to return to Kurna.

The precaution was taken of ordering the transports to move in close to Chabaish. At about noon the *Comet* and the *Shaitan* neared the village, and all the ships were at action stations. Although large numbers of Arabs collected they were overawed by the show of force, made no hostile demonstration, and the ships passed on their way to Kurna, where they arrived during the afternoon.

On the Tigris the Arabs, incited by the Turks, were giving a great deal of trouble at this time, large openly hostile bodies being often visible from Kurna ; sniping at night was heavy, the ships and launches frequently being hit by bullets.

At this period I arranged for a sloop to be in the river abreast of Fort Snipe at the northern end of the Kurna defences, which ended some distance to the north of the defences on the eastern bank. Whether the last-named position received its name on account of the presence of these birds by day, or because of the Arabs sniping at night, I do not know. Both snipe and armed Arabs abounded. While there a ship always had men standing by the guns, and a boom was placed ahead of her to catch the mines sent floating down-river by the enemy. On most nights brisk rifle-fire and sharp bursts of machine-gun fire were frequently necessary to try to keep down the Arab sniping ; the funnel and upper works rang, every now and then, as a bullet struck them ; and each morning the First Lieutenant used to spoil his appetite for breakfast by inspecting new pock-marks in his paintwork.

For some time there used to be an occasional report much louder than the others, which the sailors attributed to an elephant gun, and it was said to be fired by " Father." When after some weeks its firing suddenly ceased, there was considerable argument among the marksmen on the lower deck as to which of them had " got " him.

From this anchorage we had during the daytime a view of the Turkish camp in the far distance, and of some sand-hills to the north, where their cavalry patrols were often plainly visible. We used to shell the latter. Numbers of excited Arabs, more martially-spirited than most of their fellows, used to come out of the marshes to the west, waving gaily trimmed tribal banners and totems, and chant the hymn of hate. To these also we spared a few shells.

Our cavalry patrols often rode down close to the ship to give us the latest news ; there was always some light refreshment handy, and we were kept well up to date in what was progressing. A military officer was attached to us to observe from the crow's-nest at our mainmast-head, which commanded a very extensive view. There was no little competition for this appointment!

As I have said before, we were on the best of terms with the Army and Air Force units. Many of the Indian regiments had not come across the Navy before, but we never had any difficulty in getting on with any of them, and found them all very pleasant brothers-in-arms.

During the early operations I had received a letter from Admiral Sir Henry Jackson in which he said how pleased he was to hear that we were getting on amicably with the soldiers. It was good reading, for Sir Henry was then working at the Admiralty under the First Sea Lord, and had charge of this and other small oversea operations.

The Naval force in the rivers was, of course, always a small affair, while the Army grew and grew to a great size. I always stuck to my designation of " Senior Naval Officer," and was therefore known in that society of initials as the " S.N.O." This concealed partially the very junior rank I held among the overwhelming numbers of Gold Hats on shore. Many of them vaguely wondered what exactly the rank of " S.N.O. " was!

One night while we were at Kurna, the G.O.C. dined with me, and a remark led to a comparison of the difference between peace and war conditions. A member of the Staff had paid my dinner an exaggerated compliment by remarking that for a moment he had fancied himself at the Ritz.

I was living on board my sloop very much in the same style as I had lived for several years. The table was laid with the Service outfit of china, linen, and cutlery which is issued for the use of captains of ships, and this modest display quite impressed the soldiers, who were leading rather a hand-to-mouth existence, without many luxuries.

Of course, as I explained to them, the conditions under which the Navy live on some of our foreign stations—and particularly on this one—are not very different whether in time of war or of peace. We had been cruising about in our sloop for several years before the War, chasing gun-runners in the Persian Gulf, or off the Somali coast, where the Mullah had been active. During that time the General was possibly living in a palace in India. The only difference is that we in the Navy take our home about with us, while the Army leave theirs behind. Unfortunately, with us, the whole lot may go up together. The General remarked, after I had enlarged upon this theme, that he thought, on the whole, he preferred the Army's conditions of service. The value of a dug-out may have passed through his thoughtful mind !

Occasionally we came across some regiment—particularly among the cavalry, who appeared to have solved in a most satisfactory manner the problem of living in plenty any-where—with a mess which was a better oasis than the desert had ever seen before. An oasis with refreshments of a modern type—which would certainly not have been permitted by the Prophet !—but resembling the older ones in that the refreshment was at full strength, and that there were no newfangled limits to the times at which you might consume it.

There is no need for one to be more uncomfortable than one can help, even at war.

However, to return to our muttons ! We also patrolled the rivers, and in the Tigris to the north of Kurna armed launches usually co-operated with our cavalry patrols on the left bank in the direction of the Turkish positions.

On January 12 the armed launch *Miner* was on this duty. Observing a white enemy launch and Turkish troops in the vicinity of what we termed the " Peardrop Bend "—about a mile above Rotah Creek—she opened fire on them. We in the *Espiègle* went up to support her, but on drawing close to the sunken lighters, to the south of Rotah Creek, could see Turkish cavalry and infantry to the north, as well as some of their steamers a long way off up the river. We were able to creep up within range of the white launch in the " Pear-drop Bend " and sink her, and then we shelled a nearby village in which the Turks appeared to have settled them-selves. The enemy returned our fire with vigour, using field-gun and rifles. The *Espiègle* was hit by rifle bullets, but luckily we had no casualties. A return was made to camp during the afternoon.

At this time there were signs of considerable enemy activity. Reports also reached us of large reinforcements arriving at the Turkish camps at Sachricha and Rotah— to the north of Rotah Creek. From time to time parties of Turkish cavalry and infantry were seen on the open plains above Kurna, and the smoke of their steamers was beheld in the far distance. Our camps at Kurna and Mezera were being strongly fortified, the 18th Brigade, under General Fry, remaining at the former, and the 17th, under General Dobbie, being entrenched at the latter.

The Turks apparently tired of dilly-dallying. They soon approached nearer to us, and occupied some sandhills about six miles north of Mezera. Sir Arthur Barrett, however, determined to drive them back, so as to impress upon our troops, as well as upon our adversaries, the fact that it was not our intention to maintain a merely passive defence of our prepared positions. It was decided that this operation should take place on January 20, and orders were issued accordingly. The advance guard were the 33rd Cavalry (less two squadrons), half a battalion of the 17th Brigade, and a section of No. 17 Company Sappers and Miners. The main body consisted of the remainder of the 17th Brigade, most of the 10th Brigade, R.F.A., No. 30 Mountain Battery, the remaining sections of No. 17 Company Sappers and Miners, with the 2nd Battalion of the Norfolk Regiment in reserve.

The Navy was to co-operate from the Tigris, and also guard the mouth of the Shaib and Euphrates; the river-steamer *Mejidieh*, with two eighteen-pounder field-guns of the 82nd Battery, R.F.A., and half a double company of the 120th Infantry on board her, was also placed at the disposal of the Senior Naval Officer. The remainder of the Force was left in garrison at Kurna and Mezera.

The troops assembled at a rendezvous north of the central redoubt at Mezera, and at dawn marched off towards the enemy position. The *Espiègle*, followed by the *Miner* and the *Mejidieh*, proceeded up the Tigris in concert with them, some Army signal *personnel* having been embarked in the *Espiègle*.

At 7.30 A.M. the ships came into action with the enemy's guns posted on the south side of the village of Rotah, and we anchored the *Espiègle* in a reach of the Tigris to the north-east of another Arab village, Baharan, heading east-north-eastward in such a position that she lay in the river current with all one broadside bearing on the enemy position, against whose guns she became hotly engaged.

At 8.15 the *Mejidieh* anchored about a quarter of a mile south of the *Espiègle*, and, after warping her stern round to bring her guns to bear, opened fire. The *Miner* was attacked by Arabs from Baharan, near which she had anchored. She drove them back, making some prisoners, and then continued to engage Arabs and enemy cavalry on the right bank. Meanwhile the cavalry of our advance guard, after drawing the enemy's fire from his position in the sandhills, moved to the right flank in order to cover the advance, sending a patrol also to watch the villages along the river-bank. The main body then advanced and cleared the enemy from the sandhills, afterwards coming under fire from six Turkish guns and the main Turkish position, some trenches of which were on the south side of Rotah Creek. A large expanse of ground in front of the Turkish position was marshy, treacherous in the extreme, and the men of the leading battalions had to wade forward up to their knees in water. The cavalry likewise were floundering over wet, boggy ground.

The *Espiègle* was at first engaged entirely with the enemy guns, of which, from the ship, five were plainly visible, mounted in pits south of Rotah village—that is, of course, just north of the creek—the *Mejidieh* assisting ; and by 10.45 A.M. we had succeeded in nearly silencing them, having, as we afterwards heard, seriously wounded the Turkish general. The Turkish fire had been good in direction, but badly laid for elevation, and no damage had been done to the ships, although shots and fragments of shell often fell near.

We also shelled the enemy's trenches and parties of Turks who, advancing under cover of a *bund* on the left bank, proceeded to snipe the ships. In this latter connection the field-guns were particularly useful with their accurately burst shrapnel.

At about 10 A.M. a large body of enemy infantry, estimated at between 1000 and 2000, were observed from the *Espiègle* to leave the camp at Sacricha and reinforce the Rotah position. We were able to drop a few shells among them before they scattered and took cover.

It had been intended only to carry out a reconnaissance, and not to cross the Rotah Creek, the farther advance to which, as it would have to be made across the marshy ground, would probably have entailed considerable casualties. Also, our forces were not considered large enough, in the event of more enemy troops coming down the river from Baghdad, to hold a position at Rotah as well as that at Kurna, so it was now decided to return to camp.

The ships thereupon redoubled their fire, shelling the enemy trenches and at the same time dropping back downriver. The Turks, already largely reinforced by Arabs, kept up a heavy fire with guns and rifles until we were out of range.

On the way back to camp, which, incidentally, the troops reached by 2 P.M., they destroyed the village of Halla, and the *Miner* raked the flimsy dwellings of Baharan. Both villages had been occupied by enemy troops.

Our military casualties had amounted to only 58, and we had no naval ones. One Arab report stated that the enemy casualties were between 200 and 300 killed, and many wounded, including their General—Sulaiman Askari Bey—who had recently arrived from Constantinople to take command. It seems rather doubtful if any useful end was attained by this reconnaissance; our withdrawal was, of course, hailed by the Turks as a victory, and made useful for propaganda purposes among the Arabs as an advertisement of Turkish prowess. They redoubled their activity, collecting troops from the neighbourhood of Amara for a raid on Ahwaz, making night attacks on the camps at Kurna and Mezera, as well as commencing a big concentration of Turkish troops and Arabs in the neighbourhood of Nasiriya, for an attempt to retake Basra.

At about 1 A.M. on the 30th of January some 300 Turks

attacked Mezera from the north-east, but were driven off with considerable loss, leaving several prisoners in our hands. It was fairly evident why they had chosen that side for their attack. It was at such a distance from the ships anchored in the Tigris that the Naval guns could not assist in the defence.

The Kurna garrison moved out to the northward on the morning of that day, supported by the armed launches *Miner* and *Lewis Pelly*, and destroyed the walled villages Aoola and Jala, the Mezera garrison co-operating. Both villages had harboured nests of enemy snipers. At this time there was constant sniping at night into the Kurna and Mezera camps, as well as against the ships lying in the river near those places. Attacks were occasionally made on the camps by small forces from Rotah Creek, and on several occasions the hostile Arabs of the vicinity assembled under their tribal banners to the north-west of Kurna, making a fairly good target for the *Espiègle*, the *Miner*, the *Lewis Pelly*, and the Field Artillery. It was reported on the 24th of February that the Turks were placing mines just south of the obstruction at Rotah Creek.

The river rose to an abnormal height about this time, and a large part of the country in the neighbourhood of the Turkish camps north of Kurna was flooded. It soon became evident that the Turks were sending troops from these flooded camps to join their forces near Ahwaz. At Ahwaz the situation had become so critical, owing to the spread of the *jahad* movement instigated by the Turks and Ghadban, the powerful leader of the Beni Lam tribe of Arabs, that on January 30 our Vice-Consul there sent all the Europeans down-river to Mahommerah in the river-steamer *Shushan*.

One of the effects of Turkey coming into the Great War on the side of the Central Powers which was to be expected was that agitation would be started and astutely fanned to arouse religious sentiment against the Christian Powers who were at war with the Caliph. The Germans made great efforts to use this point against us, and professed great sympathy with the Mohammedans. Indeed, it was said at the time that a German report had been spread in some Eastern parts that the Kaiser had embraced, or was going to embrace, the Mohammedan faith. By the end of 1914 German emissaries had arrived in the East, penetrating to Mesopotamia, Syria, and Persia, to preach a *jahad*, or holy war, and an endeavour was made to spread it on the Indian frontier, among the Arabs, and wherever it could do us harm. It could be used to persuade disaffected people to side against us, and was a movement which throve in inverse ratio to our fortunes.

The German representative at Ahwaz, a man named Wonkhaus, who, sheltering under the neutrality of Persia, was known to be in communication with the enemy, elected to stay. As this could not be allowed, he, together with other German agents, were placed under restraint and deported. However, he managed to escape later on from Bushire, and subsequently gave us an immense amount of trouble in Persia.

Towards the end of January I sent the armed launches *Shaitan* and *Comet* to Nasrie—which is the port of, and is just below the rapids at, Ahwaz—to support our body of troops at that place, who were encamped at Aminia, opposite Nasrie, on the right bank of the Karun. The Sheikh of Mahommerah assisted us with 1000 armed Arabs and two Maxims.

An individual act of fanaticism—probably a result of the *jahad*—resulted in the murder on January 1, at Ahwaz, of Mr. S. C. A. Smith, the much-respected gunner of the *Comet*. He was shot in the back by an Arab who had been detailed as his escort by the Deputy-Governor. The summary execution of the murderer had a salutary effect on local opinion thereabouts, but the neighbourhood remained for some while a dangerous one for Europeans.

On February 5 our ally the Sheikh of Mahommerah received a report from his representative at Ahwaz that the Bawiyeh, a tribe of nomadic Arabs of Arabistan, living mostly east of the Karun, had risen against him, and in the forenoon of that day had looted the Oil Company's store at Musane, cut the telephone-line, shot holes in the pipe-line, and set the oil alight at Girana, with the result that oil ceased to reach Abadan on the afternoon of the 6th.

Reinforcements were sent to our forces at Ahwaz under

General Robinson, with two eighteen-pounder R.F.A. guns, and our cavalry patrols had occasional brushes with the Arabs roaming throughout the vicinity. About the 28th of February reports indicated that Ghadban, the Arab chief, had Turkish troops with four guns assisting him, and was camped a few miles away to the north-west.

Meanwhile, on the 21st of February the Sheikh of Mahommerah's force of Muhaisin Arabs attacked and defeated the Bawiyeh tribe on the left bank of the Karun, and occupied Wais, thus clearing the Karun of the enemy as far as Bund-i-Kir. It was found possible now to send parties under escort to mend the pipe-line, while European residents and traders were allowed to return to Ahwaz.

The outlook farther south, however, had not improved. The section of the Chaab Arabs who remained loyal to the Sheikh of Mahommerah were defeated with considerable loss by those members of their tribe that had joined the *jahad*, and, in consequence, retired to camp at Narid, about ten miles up the Karun from Mahommerah, where the *Espiègle* and the *Lawrence* went in turn to support them.

There had been rumour of an intended attack on Mahommerah and Abadan by these rebel Chaab Arabs from Fallahieh, a district about thirty miles north-east of Mahommerah, and for this reason I took the *Espiègle* on a visit to the Khor Musa, getting up as far as Mashur, where it was considered desirable to show the flag.

The Turkish Government had expressed its intention of driving the little British force out of the country, besides recapturing Basra, and we now began to obtain intelligence concerning considerable forces of Turks and Arabs concentrating for this purpose in the locality of Nasiriya, on the Euphrates. The pro-Turkish Arab *sheikh* Ajaimi, with a large force near Grainat, we learned additionally, was associated with them. Troops under General Delamain were therefore sent out to Shaiba, about eight miles to the south-west of Basra, to establish a camp from which to watch the enemy's movements. Our Intelligence Department showed great efficiency in the exactitude with which they kept us informed of the enemy's numbers and the progress of his reinforcements, some of whom came direct from Constantinople. Much useful information could be obtained from Arabs, although without doubt many of these were selling it to both sides. A curious source of information was the Arabs who went to and fro between Turkish territory and ours, ferrying up-river the corpses of devout Shiah Mohammedans to be buried in their holy city of Kerbela, on the Euphrates. This traffic could not be stopped—indeed, it would have been most impolitic to have done so—and the observant Arabs were able to give very useful information as to the numbers and description of enemy troops they passed on the rivers.

This enemy concentration to the west of Basra continued to grow. On the 18th of February reliable Arab sources reported further Turkish reinforcements coming down the Euphrates and the Shatt al Hai, while at Grainat, the head-quarters of Ajaimi, there were now 800 infantry and 700 cavalry ; at Nasiriya there were reported to be 1500 infantry, and more were coming from Feluja.

On the 20th of February the enemy's advanced troops were reported as having probably reached the line Nakhaila-Barjisiya ; but on February 25 our cavalry patrols near Shaiba came into conflict with hostile cavalry—whose advance guard was at Shuebda—and infantry and guns were sent up in support.

On the 4th of February the Viceroy of India, His Excellency Lord Hardinge, arrived in H.M.S. *Northbrook* to pay a visit to Mesopotamia, remaining until the 8th. He conferred with General Barrett and myself at Basra, inspected the troops, and then paid a visit in the *Lawrence* to Kurna. Coming on board the *Espiègle*, whence an extensive view could be obtained, the Viceroy saw a sight that Viceroys seldom see—the tents of the enemy camp miraged in the distance, and the smoke of their ships.

During March the floods caused by the Tigris and Euphrates rivers were exceptionally high, and caused much inconvenience on the Kurna section of the front, where the movement of troops was greatly impeded. The enemy, realizing this, now withdrew considerable numbers of their force from this part, and added them to their columns preparing to attack Basra and Ahwaz.

Besides patrolling the Tigris the armed launches *Miner* and *Lewis Pelly* had frequently to patrol the Euphrates as far as Chabaish, owing to the presence of two Turkish motor patrol-boats based at Nasiriya, who occasionally visited and intimidated the Arabs of these parts. The enemy had a great advantage over us in their knowledge of the tortuous channels in the shallow Hammar Lake, of which, at the time, we had no survey.

An Arab informer had previously told us that twenty-five mines had been brought from Amara to Rotah, where we knew there were four Germans. Attempts were made to blow up our ships at Kurna by floating mines down the river ; one exploded near the *Odin*, which had returned from Bombay, and was lying off the town on the night of the 10th of March.

The *Odin* had another interesting experience when on the morning of the 19th the Turkish gunboat *Marmariss* was seen to be under way in the vicinity of the " Peardrop Bend "—where the Tigris forms a loop about a mile above the Rotah obstruction—and appeared to be coming farther down the river than usual. She weighed, went up-river and engaged her, and, although the *Marmariss* did not come down past the obstruction, she was supported by Turkish guns at Rotah. As the *Odin* advanced up the river a large observation mine was exploded, luckily ahead of her. As Captain Wason had acutely divined, the activity of the *Marmariss* was a ruse to draw the *Odin* over the minefields. This fact was definitely established afterwards when the *Marmariss's* log of that date fell into our hands and was examined by our Intelligence Department.

The enemy continued actively digging earthworks and constructing fortifications in various positions on sandhills and knoll-like eminences to the north of Kurna, but on the nights of the 18th and 19th they fired shells into our camp. The Arabs informed us that the Turks had used two mountain guns mounted on a large *bellum*[1] which they had brought down through a channel in the marshes to the west of Baharan. The *Odin* and the *Miner* both engaged the enemy at Baharan on the 27th, on which occasion the *Miner*

[1] A local canoe.

had one stoker and one native rating slightly wounded by snipers from the bank.

The enemy were also approaching Ahwaz, on the Karun River. From information brought in by spies in the first days of March, supplemented by our reconnaissance, a Turkish force under Khalil Bey, with Arabs under Sheikh Saiyad Namieh, numbering from 5000 to 6000, was located about ten miles north-west of that place. It was reported that the enemy intended to advance on our position there when joined by the Arab Sheikh Ghazban and his Beni Lam tribesmen ; so Brigadier-General Robinson, who was in command at Ahwaz, decided to attack before this reinforcement arrived.

Our troops therefore moved out of camp at 2 A.M. on March 3, and came in touch with the enemy as soon as it was light. Large bodies of Turks, together with irregular Arab cavalry, poured out of their camp, and endeavoured to outflank as well as surround our force. It was soon apparent that the Sheikh and his Beni Lam tribesmen had arrived. Accordingly, far outnumbered, the General ordered a retirement, and it was only after severe fighting at short ranges, and even hand to hand, that, thanks mainly to the splendid work of the Dorset Regiment and the cavalry, our force got back to camp, not, however, without suffering heavy casualties and the loss of an eighteen-pounder gun. Just towards the end of the retirement the enemy's guns, which were apparently directed by trained gunners, came into action.

General Barrett stated in his report on this action that in the circumstances he considered this bold initiative, with the idea of breaking up one portion of the enemy's force before it could be joined by the other, was the best course to take. Unfortunately, the time chosen was just a day too late to effect this object. Consequently our weak force had had to act almost entirely on the defensive, and, in addition, to fight a rear-guard action on disadvantageous terms. On the other hand, the enemy lost very heavily, and undoubtedly the action had effect in breaking the confidence of the Arab tribes and in checking the spread of fanaticism throughout the district.

The *Shaitan* and the *Comet* were able from the river to support the retirement with gunfire, the former remaining to the north, and the *Comet* to the south, of the camp. The *Shaitan's* fire from her twelve-pounder was especially useful ; she burst several shrapnel shells right over the Arab horsemen, undoubtedly relieving what was a tense situation, as the Arabs scattered forthwith, being unused to shellfire. Our force then reached camp in safety. The enemy after this withdrew some miles farther away from Ahwaz.

We were therefore placed in a rather doubtful position up the Karun, but a much more serious situation was developing to the north-west of Basra, where the concentration of the enemy continued. Several minor engagements were fought between the outposts.

With a view to harassing the enemy's communications from the westward from March 3 onwards, we employed a small flotilla in the arm of the Euphrates near Gurmat Ali, which operated in the vicinity of Nakhaila. Military 4-inch guns were mounted on a barge, and this was convoyed by two stern-wheel shallow-draught steamers, the *Shushan* and the *Muzaferri*. The *Shushan* was armed with two three-pounder guns and crews from the *Espiègle*, Lieutenant-Commander A. G. Seymour, R.N., of that ship, being in command. They were also accompanied by a tug and a motor-boat, as well as a detachment of troops, and their efforts met with considerable success. They sank, shelled, and succeeded in setting fire to some of the enemy's *dhows* and *mahelas*,[1] which were conveying stores ; and, despite the extremely shallow water, they crept near enough to shell the enemy's camp on several occasions.

After attacking the enemy's ships and those of their troops stationed near Nakhaila—from which neighbourhood, and near El Lowi, the Turks engaged them with a field-gun —the steamers proceeded on the 22nd of March to Ghubasiya, where the *Shushan* managed to get within twelve hundred yards of the fort, and about six hundred yards of a large number of the enemy's transport *mahelas*. She did considerable damage, burning some of the *mahelas*, before retiring for the night. There were no casualties, though

[1] A kind of local *dhow*, used in river transport.

throughout the *Shushan* was under a persistent rifle-fire from the fort.

On the 23rd of March the whole flotilla returned to the attack. The fort was destroyed by a bombardment from the 4-inch guns, and, under cover of the other vessels, the *Shushan* ran close in and set fire to some more *mahelas*. She had great difficulty in manœuvring in the shallow water, however, eventually running aground, and had to be lightened before it was possible to tow her out. These minor operations were well devised and adroitly carried out, and the flotilla succeeded in damaging considerably the enemy's lines of communication.

On one occasion the Turks sent out two of their motor patrol-boats. These, camouflaged to some extent with branches of trees and bushes, tried to sneak near enough to attack the *Shushan* ; but the disguise was not sufficiently deceptive. A few rounds from the latter's three-pounder sent them chugging back upstream, the concealing foliage hurriedly discarded.

This blockade by the gunboats on the Euphrates came in time to have a considerable effect on the Arabs. It resulted ultimately in changing their line of supply from the easy and cheap method of carriage by native craft on the water to the difficult and painfully slow and uncertain transit by land, across the desert wastes and marshes. The change occasioned a keenly felt shortage of supplies, with resultant disaffection and desertion.

In the neighbourhood of Shaiba, which was our most distant outpost in the desert, some eight miles to the south-west of Basra, our cavalry patrols frequently came in touch with the outposts of the enemy, and on the 3rd and 16th of March were fought actions in which our cavalry, Horse Artillery, and infantry were engaged.

These were both purely military engagements, so hardly fall within the space and scope of this work. They evidenced, however, in striking degree, the efficiency and dash of the enemy irregular Arab cavalry, and showed likewise what a determined effort was being prepared by the Turks to recapture Basra and to eject us from the country. However, it is understood that in the engagement on the 16th of March with our forces at Shaiba the Arab cavalry got out of hand and attacked on their own initiative, contrary to the advice of the Turks and their own *sheikh*, Ajaimi. They had no artillery to support them, and once having approached within easy range of ours, were repulsed with heavy loss. The moral effect of our gunfire was quite considerable, resulting in not a few desertions from the Arab ranks.

Our force in Mesopotamia had by now grown to comparatively large dimensions ; reinforcements were pouring into the country, and the Indian military authorities decided to place the whole on the footing of an Army Corps, under the command of General Sir John Nixon, who arrived at Basra on April 9. The Poona Division remained under the command of Lieutenant-General Barrett, and the 12th Indian Division under Major-General Gorringe.

By the 18th of March the enemy opposing us were estimated to consist of about 20,000, with 36 guns, on the Euphrates line for the attack on Basra ; about 4000, with a few guns, on the Tigris north of Kurna ; while between the Karkheh and the Karun, near Ahwaz, there were about 5000 troops, 30,000 tribesmen—of whom about 25 per cent would have fire-arms—and 6 guns.

Reports were coming in that the enemy were digging entrenchments and showing considerable activity near Birbeck Creek, to the north of Kurna, and it seemed advisable to ascertain whether they were mounting guns in that vicinity. I therefore went up the river in the *Espiègle* on the 3rd of April to reconnoitre, and had gone only a short way up when the enemy opened fire on us from three guns mounted on the sandhills just north of Birbeck Creek and another in the vicinity of Baharan ; they also opened a heavy rifle-fire on the ship from their trenches and from behind mud walls they had erected. We replied, vigorously, silencing one, if not two, of the guns, and shelling the trenches, our military 4-inch guns at Kurna at the same time endeavouring to assist, but finding it rather too long a range. The *Espiègle* was hit twice by shells. First a ricochetting fifteen-pounder common shell hit the water thirty yards short of the ship, on the port side, glanced off the port after-davit, went through and wrecked the charthouse, and was deflected down the wardroom skylight. It was afterwards picked up where it had fallen, not having burst. The second shell which hit her passed through the poop awning, then through the base of the charthouse and the poop-deck, exploding on a base underneath, just above the starboard steering-compass. Fragments splintered the upper deck and made a hole in a steel door in the superstructure, wounding three men. The glass of the steering-compass was smashed and the helmsman bowled over, but the hard-headed sailor escaped unhurt. The ship was also hit by a number of rifle bullets. Several of the Goanese cooks and stewards also were wounded. It appeared strange that their casualties should have been proportionately so severe, until an inquiry being made, it was found that during the firing they had all crowded into the little wardroom pantry. They had probably thought themselves safe in there—for surely no enemy would be so ill-behaved as to attack the *sahibs'* cups and saucers !

As the result of this reconnaissance it was decided to add two 5-inch guns to the defences of Kurna. Reports received afterwards from spies stated that we had left a good many casualties among the enemy, including one of the four Germans who were with them. After this episode the enemy continued to show an intermittent activity, both increasing the range of their guns and floating more mines down the river. Two of these floating mines exploded near the *Odin* on the night of the 10th of April, while another went up on the 14th ; but a fourth seriously damaged the pontoon bridge which spanned the Tigris just above Kurna.

CHAPTER V

THE VICTORY OF SHAIBA AND SUCCESSFUL OPERATIONS ON THE KARUN

O**N his arrival in Mesopotamia, General Sir John Nixon found himself presented with a difficult problem, and the manner in which he retrieved the situation became the subject of universal admiration.**

The Expeditionary Force—or, in other words, our hold on the country—was threatened by the enemy on three sides. The strong forces of Turks and Arabs concentrating to the westward of Basra, whose base was Nasiriya, on the Euphrates, had been strongly reinforced with regular Turkish troops, and had received definite and explicit orders from the Porte to retake Basra ; in the neighbourhood of Ahwaz, on the Karun, our oil interests and pipe-line were likewise threatened by another enemy force ; while Kurna, our own forward base, was being attacked by a mixed force of Turks and Arabs from the north.

The concentration west of Basra was by far the most important of the three, and it was here that the enemy decided to make his main effort.

As has been previously narrated, the enemy outposts and cavalry had already been in several brushes with the outposts of our force at Shaiba. This fortified position defended Basra on its western—that is, the desert—side. The enemy had now massed a large force in that vicinity. Their approach through Nasiriya, Khamisiya, Allowi, and Grainat, however, had been accurately reported by our spies and agents ; and our garrison at Shaiba, therefore, had been considerably strengthened. In the defensive perimeter at this place, which extended over three and a half miles, we had now the

16th and 18th Brigades, the 10th Brigade R.F.A., the 23rd Mountain Battery, the Cavalry Brigade, with " S " Battery R.H.A., the 17th and 22nd Companies Sappers and Miners, and No. 34 Divisional Signal Company.

Owing to this being the flood season, the flat waste of desert between Shaiba and Basra was under anything between one foot and four feet of river water, sufficient to make it impossible for the passage of troops, owing to the creeks in it being too deep for wading and not deep enough for light-draught craft, except the native *bellum*, a flat-bottomed canoe, which is punted by two men, and could carry eight or ten men or their equivalent weight in stores and ammunition. These conditions made the passage of reinforcements, ammunition, and supplies from Basra to Shaiba very difficult.

In short, the familiar Mesopotamian conditions again prevailed here—namely, that while there was too much water for the Army there was not enough for the Navy, who could not approach Shaiba and support the troops due to the shallowness of the water. The ships, however, as before stated, found plenty of useful work elsewhere, at Kurna and Ahwaz, preying on the enemy's lines of communications on what was known as the New Euphrates.

The important operations culminating in the battle of Shaiba now developed apace.

On the 10th of April a party of enemy horsemen were observed reconnoitring close to that place, but they retired before our cavalry could come up with them. The next day it was learned that enemy cavalry had occupied Barjisiya Wood, and that some 4000 infantry were moving into Shwebda ; Major-General Fry, in command of the division, reported that he considered these troops to be the advance guard of the enemy's main force, and that, from the indications he had, he believed a serious engagement was probable in the course of the next few days.

General Nixon, the officer commanding, took immediate steps to consolidate our position. He ordered the 30th Brigade, under General Melliss, and the 30th Mountain Battery to move forward so as to arrive at Shaiba on the morning of the 12th. However, owing to the difficulties of

passage, the reinforcements did not reach Shaiba until
10.30 P.M. that night. General Fry had been attacked in
force at 5 A.M. from the south and west, and later from the
north ; but after a heavy and gruelling contest, the enemy,
who had brought up and placed a number of guns, were
repulsed. During the afternoon—and again as dusk was
falling—furious attacks were launched. But no headway
was made, and they died into intermittent rifle-fire and
machine-gun sniping. Further persistent attacks were
launched at odd intervals throughout the cheerless and
damp night.

Major-General Melliss, V.C., C.B., late on the night of the
12th arrived with reinforcements, and, being senior officer,
took over command. At 7 A.M. he launched a cavalry
counter-attack, supported by Horse Artillery, towards a
position known as the North Mound, in order to clear his
right flank. This attack met with such determined opposition that it had to be withdrawn, after sustaining heavy
casualties, including the serious loss of the gallant Major
Wheeler, and a jemadar of the 7th Lancers, who were killed
in an attempt to capture the enemy's standard.

At 8.30 A.M.—barely an hour and a half afterwards—
General Delamain, with three battalions, supported by
artillery, was ordered to attack and to capture the position
at the North Mound. Advancing determinedly, despite the
whittling hail of bullets which poured into his ranks, he
gained possession of the North Mound before noon, driving
the ousted enemy in full retreat towards the desert to the
north. Meanwhile consistent sniping and desultory attacks
were in progress to the west-south-west as well as south
of the perimeter, and enemy in large numbers were plainly
visible—actively—in these directions.

General Melliss decided to continue the clearing movement against this unbroken enemy, and this was gallantly
carried out by our infantry, supported by artillery fire.
The enemy formation crumpled before the unwavering
advance, many were killed, and a large number surrendered,
with two guns, so that by 2.30 P.M. the vicinity of our camp
was clear of the enemy. It was now decided to break off
the engagement ; our exhausted troops bivouacked for the

night, and, for a change, were not disturbed by hostile sniping or shellfire.

The enemy's casualties were estimated at something like 1000, many dead being left on the field, while over 200 prisoners, two guns, and a standard fell into our hands.

After dawn on the 14th, considerable bodies of enemy were seen to the south-west, from the Kiln post, the desert immediately surrounding the fort being clear of the enemy. Still, the exact whereabouts of the enemy's main force was uncertain. Two days before—on the 12th—a large force had been reported at Old Basra, and all subsequent reports pointed to the Barjisiya Wood being strongly held; but it was becoming evident that the enemy had been severely shaken by the fighting on the 13th.

General Melliss therefore decided to advance again, discover the enemy and engage; so operation orders were issued, the troops moving off at 9.30 A.M. towards the enemy's positions, with lines of cavalry protecting the flanks and the guns. Divisional Headquarters remained in rear of the centre.

South Mound—another enemy position—was quickly occupied, and it then became apparent that the enemy's main force was in position in the vicinity of Barjisiya. Dispositions were made accordingly, although reconnaissance was extremely difficult, owing to that strange desert phenomenon the mirage. Out there in the flat desert, dotted here and there by small mounds of sand and tufts of dwarf-like scrub, distances were dangerously deceptive, and in the steely-grey light of early morning were well-nigh incalculable. It must be remembered, too, that at this time we had no aeroplanes in the country.

The General, however, decided to engage the enemy along his front, while threatening his retirement towards Nakhaila with the 18th Brigade. By 11 A.M. it was known that the enemy occupied a very extensive front of over three miles, extending from the west of the " Watchtower " to the northern end of Barjisiya Wood. The 18th Brigade was, therefore, brought into line with the 16th, and a general advance maintained for about a mile without incident. Our front lines then became heavily engaged by the enemy in position in trenches. These had been well sited, and were practically invisible from our front, the gradual slope making them ideal for defence. In fact, it was the difficult nature of the ground hereabouts that was chiefly responsible for a large proportion of our casualties. Heavy firing soon became general all along the line, our artillery being engaged in close support of the infantry, whose attack was now swiftly developing, the cavalry co-operating vigorously with Horse Artillery on our right flank. We heard afterwards from a prisoner that during this phase of the battle the enemy were greatly disheartened by what they took to be a large reinforcement with guns joining our troops. What *really* had been observed was a long convoy of mule and pony carts, bringing ammunition, which, due to the effect of the " mirage," providentially deceived the Turks.

For a while the fight remained practically stationary, the enemy clinging to his strong position with desperate tenacity. As the day wore on, and there came no sign of either side giving under the high pressure, General Melliss decided on a general advance, with the whole artillery in close support, to attack the enemy position. The troops responded gallantly to this fresh call, and at 4.15 P.M. dashed at the enemy's position with the bayonet. It was short, sharp, desperate, and bloody work while it lasted, but our men were determined. They captured the position, killing many of the enemy, and putting the remainder to flight. After the vigorous assault our men were too exhausted to pursue, but next morning it was seen that the enemy were in full retreat. Subsequently information was received that, harassed and robbed by their former allies, the treacherous Arabs, they fled across the desert in wild confusion, abandoning stores and guns, and scarcely halting until they reached Khamisiya —a distance of ninety miles from the scene of their defeat. Sulaiman Askari, the Turkish commander, is reported to have shot himself at Nakhaila, after assembling his officers and, in true Eastern fashion, denouncing the faithlessness of the Arabs.

The ships waiting patiently on the Euphrates were able to assist in harassing the retreat, and they did considerable damage to numbers of the enemy who were making off to the north in native craft. Four Naval 4·7 guns had just arrived from England, with four Suez Canal horseboats for them to be mounted in. These guns were immediately mounted, and sent to join the small flotilla in the Euphrates, which also had a short engagement on the 24th of April with a Turkish Thornycroft launch armed with a pom-pom, which expended much ammunition harmlessly and then withdrew.

At the same time as the Turks were attacking at Shaiba they had shown considerable activity at both Kurna and Ahwaz. The *Espiègle* and the *Odin*, the armed launches *Miner* and *Lewis Pelly*, at Kurna ; the *Shaitan* and the *Comet* at Ahwaz, had all been able to render important assistance to our forces, the *Comet* being hit and slightly damaged on the 11th by shell from a gun which the enemy had brought down near the river.

Reports were now received that quantities of arms and ammunition, looted from the Turks after their retreat from Shaiba, had fallen into the hands of Arabs on the river. Several villages were searched by parties of troops conveyed in the ships. A certain quantity of both was found ; and on the 26th, Lieutenant Hallett, R.I.M., of the *Espiègle*, with a small party and a Maxim, unearthed and confiscated about 20,000 rounds of Turkish ammunition, a few rifles, and other equipment at a village about two miles above Gurmat Ali, on the right bank of the Shatt al Arab.

The signal defeat of the Turks at Shaiba having altered the entire situation in Mesopotamia, General Nixon now took immediate steps to free his flanks. He dispatched General Gorringe with a force up the Karun River to re-open communications with Ahwaz and to disperse the enemy in that district estimated at about eight battalions of Turkish Regulars, with eight guns, and about 7000 hostile tribesmen. The enemy's object was to cut in behind our position at Basra and to threaten our line of communications with Ahwaz *via* the Karun River. Indeed, news arrived that the *Comet* had again been attacked, this time by a body of Arab horsemen, on the afternoon of the 14th, at Ummet-to-Mer. These, however, were probably a band of freebooters. Her gunfire speedily dispersed them.

Hostile bands of Chaab and Davi Arabs, amounting in all to some 2000, were also reported to have approached Ahwaz from the south-east. General Gorringe was instructed to deal summarily with this situation, and, after expelling the enemy from Arabistan, to take such military measures as might be necessary for the early repair of the oil pipe-line. These operations need not be described in detail, as they were entirely military, the enemy, after our victory at Shaiba, having left the neighbourhood of the Karun River and retired across some most difficult desert and marshy country to the westward. In brief, General Gorringe pursued their retreating forces, and, in face of incredible difficulties—during which he and his troops were involved in great hardship—drove the enemy, as will be seen later, into our arms at Amara. He then put into effect punitive measures against the Arabs.

The Navy could therefore do little further to help progress on the Karun, but was able to continue useful work in harrying the enemy's sea communications during his retreat towards Nasiriya from the battle of Shaiba.

The flotilla was then employed in exploring the waterways from the Hammar Lake towards Chabaish, with a view to an eventual advance on Nasiriya, the occupation of which General Nixon considered to be essential for an effective hold on this part of the country.

On Wednesday, the 28th of April, our armed launch *Lewis Pelly*—of which ship Lieutenant W. V. H. Harris had succeeded Mr. Coleman in command on the 16th—found three improvised mines off El Huir Creek, about five miles west of Kurna. They had been moored in the river, and were of such faulty make that Chief Petty Officer Toye of the *Lewis Pelly* was able to wedge up the striker of one, which had fallen, and they were all weighed without doing any damage.

Some small combined operations were also carried out on the Euphrates during May, where, on the 5th, the *Espiègle* proceeded to the vicinity of the village of Hallaf, with the *Odin* in company, troops and guns being carried in the river-steamers *Salimi*, *Shushan*, and *Massoudieh*; and, with the assistance of Arab tribesmen of the friendly

Sheikh of Medina, this force inflicted considerable damage on the hostile inhabitants of Hallaf. We certainly were an extraordinary-looking flotilla as we went down the Euphrates on this expedition, and one could not help thinking what a sensation our appearance would have caused had we been steaming round the lines at a Spithead review ! When our allies—the Arabs in canoes—joined up we must have looked even more remarkable ; and they were delighted when, returning after a bloodless victory, but with plenty of loot, we greeted them with blasts on our siren.

On the 8th another small operation—or perhaps one might term it " demonstration," for such it really was— was carried out on the Euphrates. The *Espiègle*, the *Clio*, a sister-sloop who had recently reinforced our squadron, the river-steamers, with troops and guns, and twenty-four *bellums*, with crews who had been trained from among the troops of the Kurna garrison, carried out a punitive operation against the Arab villagers of Mazra, a small place about three miles west of Kurna. The ships and troops returned to Kurna in the evening after having destroyed eleven large native *mahelas* and captured five.

On the 9th the river-steamer *Shushan*, with Lieutenant-Commander E. C. Cookson, R.N., of the *Clio*, in command, carried out an examination and reconnaissance of El Huir Creek, in order to ascertain its value for an outflanking movement. The *Shushan* was armed with two three-pounders and three Maxims, and besides her Naval crew she had on board thirty men of the Oxford and Bucks Light Infantry.

Considerable opposition was encountered from Arabs, who kept under the cover of the high reeds at the water's edge and maintained a heavy rifle-fire at close range. Lieutenant-Commander Cookson was severely wounded, and three soldiers received flesh wounds.

The *Clio* had anchored in the Euphrates near the entrance of the creek in order to be able to support the *Shushan*, and when the position of the enemy was located she opened fire on them with a 4-inch gun. This stern treatment dissuaded the enemy from following the *Shushan* any farther. Lieu-tenant-Commander Cookson, who had been badly hit in the right side of the chest early in the action, resumed command after his wound had been temporarily dressed, and, with the help of Mr. Lyte, the civilian captain of the *Shushan*, succeeded in extricating her from a perilous position. Sub-Lieutenant Tudway, of the *Clio*, and Lieutenant Davenport, of the Oxford and Bucks Light Infantry, are mentioned in the report on this operation by Captain Colin Mackenzie, commanding the *Clio*, as doing well in charge of the Maxims, Captain Cochrane, of the Intelligence Department, as being of the greatest assistance on account of his local knowledge, and Mr. Lyte, who acted as pilot, for handling his vessel with coolness under fire.

As I have mentioned previously, our shallow-draught launches were also employed at this period in examining the channels in and at the end of the Hammar Lake. On the 14th of May they had a short but indecisive engagement with two enemy Thornycroft launches, who opened fire on them from behind the shelter of a dam which the enemy had placed across the Akaika Channel, on the west side of the lake. Shots were again exchanged between our Naval patrol and these enemy launches and enemy riflemen in the same vicinity on several occasions, and it was afterwards reported that the captain of one of the launches had been killed.

On account of the obstruction offered by the dam with which the enemy had blocked the channel, however, it was impossible to approach near to them, as they always kept on the upstream side of it, whence they could speedily retreat up-river, out of range. Their constant presence showed that the enemy was keeping a good look-out on the approach by water to Nasiriya, and we also heard that mines had been placed in the Akaika Channel, and steamers sunk between Nasiriya and Suk es Sheyukh, to block the fairway of the Euphrates.

Having ascertained that the Turkish force had fallen back from Arabistan—and having thus accomplished the first of his operations—General Gorringe was directed not to continue the advance towards Amara *via* Diwairij, but to arrange for the protection of the oil pipe-line, placing a garrison at Ahwaz, and, before withdrawing his force, to punish the

Arab tribe who had treacherously murdered Major Anderson of the 33rd Cavalry, Lieutenant Bailward, 7th Lancers, and eight Sowars, on the 29th of April, while watering their horses near an Arab village. The latter General Gorringe did on the 16th of May ; and he reported afterwards that the punishment had been most thoroughly accomplished. Large Arab villages and quantities of grain were destroyed ; a hundred dead found, many wounded ; approximately 1000 sheep and 100 cattle taken. Gorringe added in his report that the operation should have a most beneficial result, and that, after taking reasonable military precautions, no further trouble on that border need be expected A garrison under General Wapshare was therefore placed at Ahwaz, and the remaining troops returned by steamer to Basra.

By the 22nd of May the Anglo-Persian Oil Company's pipe-line was repaired, and, arrangements for safeguarding it having been made with the local tribesmen, pumping recommenced at the oilfields on the 22nd ; leakages in the pipe at first caused a short cessation, but by the 15th of June the oil was again received at the refinery at Abadan.

General Gorringe next carried out a demonstration towards Bisaitin, in the direction of Amara, with a small force, his object being to prevent the Turks from reinforcing their troops at Kurna, and to place himself in a position to co-operate with our impending operations on the Tigris.

At the end of May the officers and men from the armed launch *Lewis Pelly* were transferred to the more convenient shallow-draught tug *Sumana*, in which we mounted a twelve-pounder eight-hundredweight gun, two three-pounders, and Maxims.

The first aeroplanes for the Force now arrived. One of our Maurice-Farman biplanes made successful trial flights in the vicinity of Basra on the 27th, and two of them were used for reconnaissance from Kurna to the northward.

CHAPTER VI

OUR ADVANCE UP THE TIGRIS IN 1915

OUR decisive victory at Shaiba had driven the main body of Turkish forces back in a disorganized condition towards Nasiriya and had safeguarded Basra. The enemy had also been swept back from the Karun and the neighbourhood of the oilfields, to straggle back to Turkish territory through the swamps and marshes. It remained for Sir John Nixon to deal with the difficult situation north of Kurna on the Tigris.

He decided to entrust the conduct of these operations to Major-General (afterwards Sir) C. V. F. Townshend, who had just arrived from India and taken over command of the 6th Indian Division. All available extra forces were likewise placed under his command, with river transport, and Sir John asked me to confer with Townshend and devise a plan of combined operations, with the object of attacking the enemy to the north of Kurna, driving them from their position, pursuing them up-river, and occupying the important town of Amara, about ninety miles farther up the Tigris.

Considerable reference has been made to the enemy activity north of Kurna. They would be based on Amara, as the attacks on Basra had been based on Nasiriya, Amara being the most important town in the northern, as Nasiriya was of the western, part of the Basra *vilayet* ; each was a considerable centre of trade and an important strategical position.

Amara had a mixed population of about 20,000 in 1915, and was the headquarters of a *sanjak*, with garrison, customs-house, harbour-master, etc. The town has a fine river frontage to the Tigris on the left bank, and is bordered to the northward by canals, and to the east and south-eastward by marshes.

So it was decided to occupy Amara in order to occupy effectively the Basra *vilayet*, and also because this occupation would contribute to the safety of the oil pipe-line.

We had come to Mesopotamia to safeguard the head of the Persian Gulf and the oilfields. It had then been found necessary to hold Basra, to protect which we were led to capture Kurna and to occupy Ahwaz. Now, in order to ensure the security of these holdings, the little force was led farther into the hostile country, to Amara and Nasiriya. The will-o'-the-wisp was to lead it still farther.

General Townshend's career had up to this time been brilliant. He had seen, for those days, a considerable amount of fighting, and, among versatile abilities, had made a study of the art of war. His name had come conspicuously to the front as the commander of the garrison of Chitral Fort during that famous siege ; it will again figure in following pages, in the gallant but ill-fated defence of Kut.

Sir John Nixon arranged a meeting between General Townshend and myself one morning at General Headquarters in order that we could plan the co-operation of the naval and military forces in the Kurna–Amara operations.

We had an interesting and satisfactory conference. I found the General very talkative—indeed loquacious—and he constantly referred to Napoleon's campaigns, maxims, and doings. This was a frequent subject of his, and he used to carry about with him books on Napoleon's various campaigns. Indeed, I remember that later, during the retreat from Ctesiphon, when I went to see him in his desert camp I found him seated in his chair at a little camp-table immersed in a well-worn volume. I fancy that the period of his captivity in Turkey passed quickly while he perused them, and his book on these events is full of extracts from and comparisons with them.

We had a very friendly talk, however, and arranged for a further and final meeting at Kurna just before the advance was made. The one thing about Townshend that I did not care about was his rather pompous and boastful style of conversation.

Then came a busy time preparing for the operation, and towards the end of April I took the *Espiègle* up-river to Kurna, and concentrated my other forces there also.

One morning I went into General Townshend's advanced headquarters, and we completed the final plans for the operations.

There was not much housing accommodation at Kurna, and our meeting-place was on the upper floor of the local G.H.Q. Here the staff and I sat on camp-beds round the room, and Townshend at a table on the only chair available. A large map had been hung up on one wall, with lines indicating the proposed movements of the troops. These he explained to us at long length, together with a good deal about what he suspected Napoleon would have done in the circumstances.

After Townshend had finished I talked about the Naval part of the affair, and we fitted our plans together.

It was decided to commence operations on the 31st of May by a combined frontal and turning attack, the combined frontal attack by the Army and Navy on the west bank being the decisive one. A turning attack was to be delivered at the same time on the left or eastern bank in the direction of what was known as One Tree Hill, while demonstrations were carried out on each flank by small vessels up the Shaib and Al Huir Creeks.

The Tigris that year rose to an abnormal height. As in the days of Noah, Mesopotamia underwent another flood. Almost the entire countryside and the marshes round Kurna were covered by a great spreading sheet of shallow water, dotted here and there with the blunt tops of sandhills and the spiky heads of high reeds. On some of these sandhills and higher pieces of land the enemy had placed gun-positions.

The flood-water was in many places very shallow, it is true, but the area was intersected by deep water-cuts, ditches, and canals—which, incidentally, were usually invisible until you fell in. Consequently wading became impossible for marching troops. In fact, as I have said before, there was too little water for the sailors and too much for the soldiers.

These peculiar conditions gave a great advantage to the mixed force of Turks and Arabs who were opposing us. Their local knowledge, superior mobility, their very means of transport, adapted to this country by long experience, and, in addition, their ability to live on scanty and simple rations, and habituation to the intense heat, were great assets to set off against the superior equipment and supplies of our forces.

The intense heat was indeed trying to our troops. One rather forthright Tommy was heard to remark that if this was really the site of the Garden of Eden it wouldn't have needed an angel with a flaming sword to have kept *him* out !

The main enemy position was in the vicinity of Abu Aran, Muzaibila, and Ruta, on both sides of the Tigris, and they also had advanced positions perched on the sandhills in front of Ruta, on One Tree Hill, and north and south of Birbeck Creek. Their strength in the vicinity was estimated at five or six battalions, with eight or ten guns, and some 2000 Arabs, under the command of Halim Bey. Their activity, work on gun positions, and the frequent arrival of reinforcements showed that they were nervous and on the jump, expecting our advance. Indeed, with spying as rife and as easy as it was they must have realized that we were making preparations for a push forward. The enemy had occupied many of their positions since January, gradually strengthening them until Kurna was to all events and purposes invested, when the garrison, as we have seen, was constantly subjected to sniping by night and artillery fire by day.

Due to the peculiar and novel conditions imposed on the troops, a number of infantry had been trained to propel the *bellum*, or local canoe, by paddling in the deep water, and punting or dragging it through the shallows, and a number of these craft had been fitted with armour-plating, for use in the advance. A *bellum* had a crew of one N.C.O. and nine men, and second-line *bellums* followed with ammunition and other supplies, which, according to the arrangement, they drew from their supply *mahela* or *dhow*.

Machine-guns and field-ambulances on rafts, and mountain-guns on double *bellums*, also moved up with the troops in the shallows, while in the river were military heavies and field-guns on barges, field-guns on river steamers, *mahelas* roofed like Noah's Ark, and fitted up as field-hospitals, etc.

There were also *mahelas* and barges for ammunition columns, bridging and repairing material, and such-like. Reserve troops followed in river-steamers, and the men's kits were brought along in paddle-steamers or *mahelas*.

When all advanced, led by the sloops and armed launches in the river, with mine-sweepers ahead, the procession was a most remarkable sight.

I directed Naval affairs from the *Espiègle*, and had under my command the following :

H.M.S. *Clio* (sloop). (Commander C. Mackenzie, R.N.)
H.M.S. *Odin* (sloop). (Commander C. R. Wason, R.N.)
H.M.S. *Lawrence* (sloop). (Acting-Commander R. N. Suter, R.N.)
H.M.S. *Miner* (armed launch). (Lieutenant C. H. Heath-Caldwell, R.N.)
H.M.S. *Shaitan* (armed launch). (Lieutenant M. Singleton, R.N.)
H.M.S. *Sumana* (armed launch). (Lieutenant W. V. H. Harris, R.N.)

and four 4·7-inch guns mounted in horse-boats, with Naval crews.

The military force consisted of :

The 17th Infantry Brigade. (Lieutenant-Colonel S. H. Climo.)
The 16th Infantry Brigade. (Brigadier-General W. S. Delamain.)
Divisional troops, consisting of the 63rd Battery, R.F.A., 1/5 Hampshire Howitzer Battery, 86th and 104th Heavy Batteries, 2nd Battalion Norfolk Regiment, 30th Mountain Battery, 48th Pioneers, No. 22 Company Sappers and Miners, No. 34 Company Divisional Signal Company, Sirmur Sappers, and Bridging Train 1st Sappers and Miners.

In addition to these were the paddle-steamers, tugs, barges, lighters, etc.

For the purpose of facilitating matters the division was divided into numbered groups, with differently coloured flags, and transport vessels and tugs were allotted to each group.

After strenuous exertions in the intense heat everything

was ready, and the advance planned, as I have said, for the 31st of May. General Townshend came on board the *Espiègle* the evening before, and remained with me during the early part of the operations. Some of his staff came with him, and the remainder were divided between the other sloops, and although discomfort was caused by this crowding up of our limited accommodation the arrangement, nevertheless, helped mobility of movement.

In these combined operations it was of great advantage that the General Officer Commanding and the Senior Naval Officer should be able to decide together any point as it arose in the rapidly-changing situation. Also we had wireless telegraphy, and naval and military signallers under our direct control to communicate with the troops on either bank and the heterogeneous collection of vessels. One could not help wishing at times, however, when the military signallers were clattering about, that Tommy Atkins did not wear such heavy boots.

I am sure that both the great success of the operations and the small casualty list they incurred were very largely due to this close co-operation between the two Services.

On the evening of the 30th we had a very cheerful dinner, and the General proved that he could be excellent company when one got him off the subject of Napoleon. On this occasion, too, there was also a good omen, on which the General discoursed at length—namely, that a celebrated ancestor of his had won a victory on the first of June.

At 5 A.M. on the 31st of May, therefore—dawn was nearly breaking—the bombardment of the Turkish position commenced, the Navy co-operating with the 4- and 5-inch B.L. guns and 4-inch howitzers of the Kurna fortress. The Turks soon returned the fire.

The turning attack had started early towards One Tree Hill, and the advance on the right bank commenced before 6 A.M. The *Espiègle* and the *Clio*, having passed through the boat-bridge, and then the boom, proceeded slowly up-river, supporting the troops, and preceded by mine-sweepers, soon became engaged with the Turkish guns on a position we knew by the rather obvious name of Gun Hill.

The *Odin* took up her assigned station in the Shatt al

Arab about a mile below Kurna, in a position to enfilade the gun emplacement on Tower Hill, the *Lawrence* and the *Miner* remaining in the Euphrates, with three of the 4·7-inch guns in horse-boats, firing up Norfolk Creek.

The 22nd Punjabis, under Lieutenant-Colonel Blois-Johnson, left Mezera Camp at 1 A.M. and by 6.30 A.M. had captured One Tree Hill, on the left bank of the Tigris, and were thus enabled to enfilade Norfolk Hill, their machine-guns covering the infantry section of the frontal attack which moved on the west of the Tigris. These troops consisted of the 17th Brigade and Mountain Battery, under cover of whose fire and that from the sloops they advanced in *bellums*, in the face of a heavy fire, and captured Norfolk Hill at the point of the bayonet. This was about 7.25 A.M.

At 8.10 A.M. the further advance of the 17th Brigade, covered by the fire of the naval and military guns—which had by now engaged the enemy guns and trenches at close range—was launched, their objective this time being Tower Hill, and at 8.15 A.M. the *Espiègle* and the *Clio*, with the armed launches *Shaitan* and *Sumana* mine-sweeping ahead, moved farther up the river, and, anchoring off Norfolk Hill, engaged the Turkish guns and trenches near Tower Hill at even closer range. The *Odin*, the *Lawrence*, and the *Miner* were also moved up in support, the launches *Bahrein* (Lieutenant-Commander C. R. Campbell, R.I.M.) and *Lewis Pelly* (Lieutenant Duncan, R.I.M.) being kept in reserve as spare mine-sweepers.

The ships were by this time under a continuous fire from the Turkish artillery, which, as none of us were armoured, could have inflicted very serious damage to us. It was mighty unpleasant to contemplate the effect of an enemy shell bursting in our unprotected shell-rooms or magazines ! For we presented prominent targets as we lay there in the river, which was then running nearly bank high. This, of course, meant that the ships were visible from masthead to water-line, and, in addition, were thrown into sharp relief against the dun-coloured expanse of desert background.

The only way to render the enemy gunfire innocuous was to locate an enemy gun when it opened fire, and immediately endeavour to smother it with our own fire before it could do much harm. But there was always an anxious period when shells zoomed over from some new direction—until we caught the flash of the gun !

Just before nine o'clock the *Espiègle* was hit on the port quarter by a shell. Some damage was sustained, and three men were wounded. The *Odin* also was hit, but luckily without serious hurt.

The Oxford and Bucks Light Infantry were now moving steadily to the attack of Tower Hill, part of them in *bellums*, and part wading. We in the *Espiègle* had moved well up, and from her bridge and forecastle got a good view of the scene, which was illumined by brilliant sunshine. Our shellfire was keeping the enemy down in their trenches, rendering their rifle-fire very ineffective—a great help—and comfort—to our attacking troops. Through our telescopes we could see details of a scene such as, I suppose, had never been seen before from the decks of a man-of-war. We lifted our fire as our troops got close, and could see them swarming up the mound. I particularly watched a big soldier who climbed on to their parapet holding his bayonet as if he were just about to select a nice fat Turk to stick it into. Next appeared a row of enemy with their hands up, and the position was taken.

By now we were under fire from Gun Hill, the enemy's next important position, and while the 103rd Light Infantry advanced towards it we smothered it with our fire, the ships being assisted in this by all the military guns. One by one the enemy guns were silenced, and the position was occupied before noon, our left flank having been heavily engaged in the marshes to the west by the Arabs, who fired slugs and bullets from all manner of ancient blunderbusses and muskets, besides the rifles looted from our camps and battlefields more recently. It had been hot during the night ; the heat grew intense during the morning ; and now it had become even more intense. It was decided not to ask the troops to struggle further under the pitiless sun, and we spent the remainder of the day in consolidating our positions, with a view to continuing the advance the following morning.

We anchored and placed a boom across the river ahead

of us to catch mines floating down, several of which had been seen, and some exploded on the river-bank. A minefield observation-post, with switchboard, had been found on Tower Hill. Other mines were subsequently exploded by our R.E. officers, who also located and destroyed many mine connections.

The Turkish engineer officer in charge of the mines in this locality had fallen into our hands, and our Intelligence Department handed him over to me that night, as he had offered to point out where mines were laid. So he was allotted accommodation aboard the mine-sweeper *Sumana*. I argued that he would be sure to take great pains to give accurate information from her deck, because she went first, ahead of us all.

He proved very useful, incidentally, and gave us information of no little value, particularly when the *Sumana* was searching for and destroying the cables of the enemy minefield just south of the obstruction across the Tigris, near Rotah.

During the foregoing period our flank demonstrations had been as follows :

On the right H.M.S. *Comet* (Lieutenant-in-Command Irving M. Palmer, R.N., having under his orders a 4·7-inch Naval gun in a horse-boat, a launch, and a force of infantry in a paddle-steamer in support) proceeded at daylight on the 31st of May up the Shaib Creek, and bombarded the enemy position on the sandhills and the Rotah position, thus diverting some of their attention from the main attack.

On the left flank the river sternwheeler *Shushan*, with two three-pounders and guns, crews from the *Espiègle*, and a detachment of troops with machine-guns under the command of Sub-Lieutenant R. H. Lilley, R.N., of the *Odin*, and the sternwheeler *Muzaffari*, under the command of Sub-Lieutenant L. Sanderson, R.I.M., with troops and machine-guns on board, proceeded up the Al Huir Creek at daylight on the same day, acting in co-operation with about 2000 friendly Arabs under the Sheikh of Medina, an important friendly *sheikh*.

They encountered great difficulty in navigating the

shallow creek, could make only a little progress, and came under rifle-fire and also the fire of a small Turkish gun which had been placed near the Arab village of Rumla. They had no casualties, however, and rejoined the main body in the afternoon, having undoubtedly contributed towards diverting the marsh Arabs from attacking the left flank of our troops in the main advance.

The night passed quietly, and bombardment of the enemy position at Baharan was commenced again early the following morning, Tuesday, the 1st of June. No reply came from them, however, and we weighed anchor about an hour later, and, preceded by mine-sweepers, led the squadron up the river. This took us directly towards Baharan ; we had all hands at quarters, and guns that could be brought to bear firing on the enemy position, from which we must appear a more and more prominent mark as we made headway against the strong and rapid river current.

Every moment we expected a burst of gun- and rifle-fire at a range that was diminishing as we advanced. But the enemy still remained silent, the rain of shot and shell never came.

We continued in a state of suspense for so long that it began to seem possible that the position had been deserted, and at length an aeroplane dropped a message telling us that this was the case. The enemy were in full retreat up the river to the northward, in every available craft.

We steamed on and anchored near Baharan about half-past ten.

During all this time we were keeping careful look-out for mines which might be swept up or floating downstream. We placed riflemen to shoot at anything suspicious drifting close, and saw several of the Turks' rather inferior, home-made-looking mines washed aground among the reeds and bushes fringing the river-bank. These our marksmen fired at. While this was continuing a large wild pig—there are many of them in those parts—came down the river-bank quite close to us for a drink. He soon shared the fate of the beached mines. Townshend appeared much amused by the incident, and when we lowered the dinghy to fetch the brute, exclaimed : " You don't mean to say that you're going to pick him up ? " " Certainly," I said, " we'll have him for dinner."

The old porker provided an excellent supplement to our campaigning fare.

I went on with Lieutenant Harden, Navigating Officer of the *Espiègle*, in the armed launches, to reconnoitre the obstruction made by the sinking of the lighters just below Rotah Creek and the minefields, and on the way found that the leads of three large observation mines had been discovered and cut. Lieutenant-in-Command Harris of the *Sumana* and his crew were underlaying them.

It is of interest to record here the statement of Captain Khalil, of the Turkish Mining Engineers, who was taken prisoner on the 31st of May. He said that his mining company had arrived at Rotah four months before, from Baghdad, and had placed fixed mines in the river as follows : Four opposite the mouth of Birbeck Creek, four opposite Baharan, three about 1500 metres upstream from Baharan, three about 1500 metres below the Rotah obstruction, and three at Rotah. These mines were round in shape, and contained a very large charge, which, according to Captain Khalil, was 150 kilos of gelatine. They were moored below the surface of the water, and could be exploded only by electricity. Captain Khalil had been assisted by a German major, who, he thought, had been formerly employed in the railway workshop at Baghdad. In addition, this officer stated that there were no less than 150 floating mines in the charge of German officers at Mazeeblah. The large mines were all afterwards raised by our force, and some of them were emptied and utilized as buoys in the river.

While we were near the minefield General Nixon and his staff arrived in his motor-boat from Kurna, from which place he had been viewing events from the observation tower. He joined General Townshend and myself, and together we discussed the situation.

I must confess that the arrangements of the Military High Command in this and other parts of the campaign were—and still are—a puzzle to me. I suppose that General Nixon, having confided this operation to General

Townshend's division, would be—or thought that he would be—committing some military discourtesy if he took over and ran the show himself. The force engaged, however, was very much more than General Townshend's division, and, further, was engaged on an expedition which, if successful—as was most likely—would develop into an advance of many miles, and would result in the capture of important towns and.the acquisition of a great area of Turkish territory. Surely, therefore, it would have been better if he had taken over the direct control of the whole affair !

The physical conditions under which the Ahwaz and Nasiriya operations were carried out made devolution of command necessary, and thus differed from this. It is not, of course, for a moment meant to hint at any criticism of General Nixon's gallantry. If he had been at the front with us we should have got on quicker !

On this occasion he was insistent on the advisability of pushing forward, of taking advantage of our success, and, if possible, of pursuing the enemy, whose smoke we could see fading away as they retreated up-river in the distance. It was General Nixon's energy in urging this course which decided Townshend after a little hesitation.

Before we could get on, however, it was necessary to ascertain whether a passage could be negotiated through the obstruction across the river and the minefields in the vicinity. General Nixon was very keen to be present personally when we made this examination, and I had to point out the dangerous possibilities. There might still be " live " mines about, and it would be a serious handicap to the Expedition if the Army Commander were blown to heaven ! With that naïveness that in the popular eye invariably characterizes members of the Navy I have always supposed that Army Commanders do not go to the other place.

However, General Nixon gave in to me. The A.D.C. then got hold of his motor-boat and took me to investigate. We found that the obstruction—which consisted of large iron lighters that had been sunk across the river—was nearly under water in this time of high flood, and could see what looked like a possible passage, even for the sloops, near the western bank.

Harden then sounded and afterwards buoyed the passage, which appeared to be clear of mines and apparently practicable.

I at once hailed the armed launches *Shaitan* and *Sumana*, telling them to pass through and pursue the enemy at full speed. Getting back onboard the *Espiègle*, we weighed anchor, and, leading the *Clio* and the *Odin* up-river, successfully negotiated the passage through the obstruction shortly after three o'clock, and then took up the chase.

Navigation was extremely difficult, owing to the turns and twists in the river, of which we had only a rough sketch made many years before ; and since that time the river had altered its channel considerably. Owing also to the extensive floods on each side, it was not easy in many places to make out the channel—our only guide was often a line of reeds on the bank just showing above the flood-water, so we could not help bumping into it occasionally. Luckily it was all soft mud and sand, so no damage was done.

It was necessary to keep the ship stemming the river current in its convolutions round the bends, in order to retain control over her movements. Once her stem got on either side of the direction of the current, and its force came on either bow, she could not easily be straightened up by helm or screws before she took the bank. It must be remembered that these were the largest ships which had ever proceeded so far up the Tigris, and the river was rapidly becoming too small for them in every way. It had narrowed from between 270 yards at Kurna to about seventy at Ezra's Tomb, in which vicinity the only way to turn round was by letting the stern ground in the mud, while the stream swung the bow round like a top, the stern acting as a pivot.

The water was gradually shallowing, too, as the Turkish gunboat also found.

The sloops of the *Espiègle* class were ill-equipped for the peculiar type of navigation which I have described. We possessed only a hand-steering wheel, which was under the poop, so that the steersman had to steer by a compass, or, as from his position the view ahead was obstructed, in accordance with directions given by the navigating officer above. Great exertion and constant movement of the wheel was necessary to keep the ship on her course in the rapid current, and relays of men relieved each other, each being soon exhausted in the intense heat. Our chief quarter-master, an oldish man, never recovered from the over-exhaustion of that afternoon.

The Turkish gunboat *Marmariss* and river-craft of every kind were shortly afterwards discerned in flight up-river ahead of us, and just before six o'clock the *Shaitan*, which was leading, opened fire on the enemy at long range, and soon did considerable damage.

From the *Espiègle* we opened our foremost 4-inch guns on the Turkish river-steamer *Mosul* at about a quarter to seven, and not long afterwards changed target to the *Marmariss* when she came into range. The *Clio* and the *Odin* joined action almost immediately, and it was soon evident that considerable damage was being inflicted on the enemy.

It was not long before we sighted the blue dome of the mosque of Ezra's Tomb. Close by it was a solitary palm-tree, which showed up prominently in a landscape displaying little other than arid desert wastes. The tomb marks the place where the prophet Ezra died and was buried. He was on his way back to " Shushan the Palace," which we read of in the Scriptures, from Palestine, where, by order of the King of Assyria, he had been arranging for the repatriation of the Israelites. Doubtless useful bargains in " real estate " had been struck !

In order to facilitate their retreat the Turks now cast loose and discarded the lighters, *mahelas*, and other craft full of troops, guns, stores, and ammunition, which the steamers had been towing, and near Ezra's Tomb, which we passed shortly after seven, we found several lighters that they had abandoned. I detailed the *Odin* to seize them, and as they were found to be loaded with mines, guns, and stores she saved a quantity of valuable booty from the Arabs.

The chase continued in the gathering darkness, and half a mile farther on we came up with the *Shaitan*, which was taking possession of a *mahela* crowded with Turkish troops that had surrendered to her. It had now grown too dark to discern the enemy through the gun telescopes, so we gradually ceased fire. Navigation had also become increasingly intricate and difficult ; it seemed impossible to get along any farther in the dark in this unknown river, so I decided to halt, and await the rising of the moon.

We therefore anchored shortly after nine near some more of the enemy's abandoned lighters, likewise full of troops, guns, and stores. Our searchlight also disclosed the Turkish steamer *Bulbul* partly submerged just ahead of us. She had been sunk by a well-aimed shot from the *Shaitan*, with the result that the large lighter she had been towing, and which carried more troops, artillery, and munitions, fell into our hands. The only occupant of the *Bulbul* when we boarded her was a small terrier, who appeared quite ready and pleased to join the *Espiègle*, where he was rechristened " Bulbul," as befitted the occasion. " Bulbul " lived aboard with us happily for a short time as a pet, but fell into a decline. It was thought that he never got really used to people who washed !

Several Germans who had been onboard the *Bulbul* had managed to escape to the shore, but they were only too glad to give themselves up afterwards—having had all their effects stolen by the Arabs, from whom, stripped nearly naked, they narrowly escaped with their lives.

Then we settled down to a dinner which included some of the celebrated pig, and over it we thoroughly discussed the situation. It was decided to leave the Chief of Staff and most of the Staff behind, in order that they could reassemble the troops as they came up, and arrange for them to follow us as soon as possible. One of my lieutenants had suggested this bright idea to me, as there was hardly any room to move on board the little sloop when all the Divisional Staff thronged aft, and the place was crowded with brass-hatted officers ; some of them climbing up and down the ladders with difficulty—in spurs !

Townshend said he would agree to the suggestion, and seemed positively pleased at the idea of getting away from some of them ; but he made it a condition of the agreement that I should be the one to tell the Chief of Staff. This piece of diplomacy, however, was duly accomplished.

Then we had a little rest, and at 2 A.M. (Wednesday, the 2nd of June), the moon having risen, we weighed anchor and went slowly on in the dim, steely light, the *Espiègle* leading, with the *Clio* following ; then came the *Comet* which had rejoined during the night, and also the *Miner*, the *Shaitan*, and the *Sumana*. The little fleet made headway only with difficulty, as the river was gradually becoming shallower and still more narrow, its surface broken by patches of shadow and wavering runnels of moonlight.

A conflagration, which was evidently caused by a burning vessel, had been observed a few miles farther up-river during the night, and frequently loud explosions had been heard. As we steamed slowly and with difficulty through the shallow water we gradually approached near enough to make her out. As the breaking day brightened we saw that it was the *Marmariss*, apparently stationary. Rapid fire was immediately opened on her, but, receiving no reply, I signalled " Cease fire," and went with an armed party to take possession.

By this time (4.15 A.M. on the 2nd of June) the *Espiègle*, scraping along the river bottom, was practically at a standstill near Garbi, in latitude 31° 23·5′ north, longitude 47° 27′ east, about six miles above Ezra's Tomb, with the *Clio* a few cables astern—that is, by a long way the farthest that ships of their size have ever ascended the Tigris.

The *Marmariss* was aground and burning fiercely, her hull showing signs of having been hit in many places by 4-inch shells. Her captain, it was plain, had realized that she could not escape, owing to the shallows at the Devil's Elbow, a little farther on, so had run into the bank and set her on fire. Most of her officers and men had got ashore and escaped during the night.

A lighter and a *mahela*, loaded with arms and ammunition, were found near her, with a few wounded men and stragglers. Her mainmast, burned through, toppled over while we were near her. Later our speculations as to her fate were confirmed by one of her officers, who told us that she had been hit several times during the evening and that the fire had been started by our exploding shell.

Leaving the blazing wreck, we next made out the Turkish

river-steamer *Mosul* a little farther up-river. A few shells soon persuaded her to stop and surrender. I went on in the *Shaitan*, General Townshend accompanying me, and we took possession of her. We learned that she had been hit badly the night before. She was full of Turkish officers, men, and stores. Several *mahelas* were also seized near her, crowded with retreating troops.

It was a very hot morning, I remember, and we had a wearying time of it. I recollect how gratefully I accepted the invitation of the captain of the *Shaitan* to take a cup of tea. This was brought us by the old Turkish engineer officer who had laid the mines. Now a prisoner of war aboard the *Shaitan*, he had settled himself down very comfortably, and was most solicitous as to our welfare. *Kismet!*

Enemy craft taken in this vicinity were the *Marmariss*, the *Mosul*, and two steel lighters ; we also captured quantities of rifles and ammunition, 1049 Turkish gold coins, some silver found in a *mahela*, and two fifteen-pounder field-guns.

From what we had seen and experienced there appeared to be no doubt that the enemy forces were thoroughly demoralized, so after consultation with Townshend I decided to push on in the lighter-draught vessels to endeavour to keep the Turks on the run, and find out the condition of affairs at Amara.

Before going on in the *Comet* we moved the *Espiègle* and the *Clio* a mile or so down-river, into deeper water, as they were practically aground. The river, now abnormally high with the changed tide, had commenced to fall, and I did not want them to become immovable, and have to be left to decorate Mesopotamia in company with the *Marmariss*. We moved downstream stern first, as there was not enough room in which to turn round.

Leaving Commander Mackenzie, the senior officer, in charge, I went on up-river at noon in the *Comet*, accompanied by General Townshend. The other small vessels followed, and Sir Percy Cox, principal political officer, and Staff came in his steam-launch.

Early in the afternoon of the same day (2nd of June) we arrived at the small town of Qualat Salih. White flags of surrender were flying, and the principal Arab citizens came

H

onboard to tender submission. Qualat Salih, to give it its due, is quite a well-built little town for those parts, with a few decently verandaed houses facing the busy street on the river. This river front was now alive with Arabs, and an extraordinary assortment of people they were. The principal citizens who came onboard were of the superior type of town Arab, evidently men of substance and responsibility. Their surrender was accepted, and they were told that the British were their friends as long as they showed themselves deserving of that honour. Townshend then instructed them to collect supplies for 15,000 troops who would shortly arrive. This demand was made, of course, with a view to the news spreading, and as a set-off to our really scanty numbers.

The Arabs had just left when there was a commotion on the quay, and two Turkish soldiers in khaki rushed along it, hailing the ship. The interpreter reported that they were asking to come onboard, but the little ship was so crammed already that we not unnaturally did not want to take on any more. Besides, we had been collecting such crowds of prisoners that an odd brace like this hardly seemed to matter. So I had them told that they could run away. At this they began their antics afresh, shouting indignantly that they were prisoners of war, and, as such, apparently considered that they were entitled to everything free—rather like going on the dole. Finally, I gathered that the poor devils would certainly be murdered by the Arabs if we left them, so they were allowed to come onboard if they found their own passage.

We anchored for the night a few miles north of Qualat Salih, where the small flotilla concentrated, and went on again at 6 A.M. the next morning, Thursday, the 3rd, towards Amara, with the *Shaitan*, the *Sumana*, the *Lewis Pelly*, three horse-boats, each carrying a 4·7-inch gun, and the steam-launch " L2." Sir Percy Cox in his steam-launch followed.

No enemy were seen, and the Arabs on the banks displayed white flags as we steamed along. We stopped at a place called Abu Sidra for a short time, and there tried in vain to procure some information regarding the retreating Turks from the natives.

Finally we moved on, and when about thirteen miles to the south of Amara I sent the *Shaitan* and the " L2 " launch scouting ahead, with orders to reconnoitre towards that place. Captain Peel of the General Staff went in the *Shaitan.*

We had looked upon our advance up the river as a reconnaissance, and when General Townshend and I that morning discussed the question of how far we should proceed, and where stop to await the arrival of the troops, I suggested that the best place to bring the river-steamers up to would be a position just beyond gun-range of the Amara batteries. In this he acquiesced.

We had only a very rough sketch map of the river onboard, however, and it became rather difficult to say exactly how far we had gone, so, although the General insisted on stopping at one place to look round, we persuaded him to agree to move farther on when no signs of any enemy were seen. He kept saying that we were very much " *En l'air,*" and seemed rather doubtful as to what Napoleon—who had never apparently been in a similar position—would have done in the circumstances. I was, as he remarks in his book,[1] anxious to go on—he adds something about sailors being rash—but at the time it seemed to me, and to Lieutenant Harden also, whom I consulted, that the *Shaitan*, which was scouting a long way ahead, was a safeguard against any sudden attack. Besides, we had a clear view over the wide plain of desert rolling back from each bank of the river. Anyway, we were in a fairly risky situation already, but could always turn and retreat down-river faster than any troops could follow—and it must be borne in mind that we had destroyed their Naval force.

Finally, however, he agreed to go on ; and we accordingly proceeded, creeping round one corner of the river after another. This went on, no guns opening fire on us, until we were forced to conclude that the *Shaitan*, which had proceeded a long way ahead of our necessarily more cautious selves, must be entering Amara.

The *Shaitan*, the heroine of the day, was a little

[1] Major-General Sir Charles V. F. Townshend, K.C.B., D.S.O., *My Campaign in Mesopotamia*, p. 70.

flat-bottomed tug-boat designed for river service on the
Tigris. She had been taken over by the Navy for the
operations, armed with a twelve-pounder Q.F. gun in her
bows and a smaller gun aft, and given a Naval crew of a
lieutenant (Mark Singleton) and eight sailors.

The *Shaitan* reached a point about three miles south of
Amara at 2 P.M., having sighted no enemy or gun position
until, when entering the reach of the river just below the
town, which is on the left, or eastern, bank, enemy troops in
large numbers were observed crossing a bridge of boats
from the middle of the town to the right bank, and getting
into a barge which was secured to a steamer there. The
bridge was then opened, and the steamer was on the point
of steaming through when a shot was fired from the
Shaitan's twelve-pounder. Without more ado the enemy
scuttled out of the barge and made off up the right bank.
The *Shaitan* steamed on, and as she passed through the
bridge of boats found the town full of troops. About half
a battalion of Turks were debouching through the streets
on to the river front. On seeing her they bolted back, and
when she reached the turn where the Tigris bends to the
westward there were many more Turks retiring on both
banks—some within a stone's throw—and she was practically surrounded. However, they did not fire, presumably
being afraid of drawing her gunfire, so she proceeded about
a half a mile farther, and called on another party of about a
hundred Turkish soldiers with six officers to surrender, and,
taking the officers, rifles, and ammunition on board, compelled them to march along the river-bank abreast of her.
She then returned towards Amara, and did the same with
some 150 more Turkish soldiers, who emerged from the
trees and threw down their arms. Then she steamed slowly
back to Amara, the prisoners walking unattended along the
bank until near to the bridge of boats, where they sat down
close by a coffee-shop, to await disposal.

As the *Comet* was still about a mile away, only just entering
Amara, the *Shaitan*, at the expenditure of two or three
shells, had captured some 250 Turkish troops, with eleven
officers, and contributed largely to causing about 2000
enemy troops to evacuate Amara.

The official history of the campaign pays a fine tribute to the exploit by saying in its description of the taking of Amara that greater daring than that shown by the *Shaitan* can hardly be imagined. There is little doubt that the amazing success of the day's operations was largely due to this intrepid advance and to the cool audacity of Lieutenant Singleton commanding the *Shaitan*, which had only a crew of eight bluejackets. The feat becomes breath-taking when one realizes that a few resolute Turks among the numbers swarming along either bank could have accounted for the crew of the little armed tug, or even sank her with rifle fire, at point-blank range ! For this fine piece of work Singleton was afterwards awarded the D.S.O., and the coxswain, Chief Petty Officer A. J. Roberts, R.F.R., and Gunlayer Leading Seaman Rowe each received the Distinguished Service Medal.

All this time I was following cautiously up the river, leading the remainder of the flotilla, and as the *Shaitan* had not dropped back for support, as she had been instructed to do if she came across serious opposition, and as no enemy guns had opened fire on the flotilla, we went warily on, and at about 2 P.M. found ourselves entering Amara without having fired a shot. Crowds of people were thronging the river front, but none of them appeared to be actively hostile. Several steam craft—lighters, etc.—abandoned by the enemy were lying alongside in different places, and here and there a timid white flag hung limp in the heat.

We had arrived at quite a decent-looking town, which, situated on the eastern bank of the Tigris, to which it shows a long row of regular, well-built houses, is of symmetrical appearance and possesses a fine frontage to the river. Amara looks across the river towards groves of feathery crested palm-trees and scattered dots of houses along the western bank—the whole effect, under a blue sky, in brilliant sunshine, being very picturesque. We, however, had very little time in which to admire the scene's picturesqueness !

Having anchored the flotilla, distributing the 4·7-inch guns so as to command, as far as was possible, each approach to the town, I commenced to arrange the collection of the abandoned shipping and dispose of the numbers of prisoners who were crowding in.

We were in a really remarkable situation, miles ahead of our troops, with only about fifty white officers and men on board, while the flotilla itself consisted of only the little armed paddle-yacht *Comet*, two small improvised tugs, three 4·7-inch guns mounted in horse-boats, and two small launches. The Turks had, of course, not the faintest idea of the distance we were ahead of our army.

The enemy troops were by now thoroughly demoralized by their continued defeats, and, furthermore, were harassed by the fear of falling into the hands of the treacherous Arabs. The number retreating from Kurna was now being increased by those retiring from Ahwaz, as the result of General Gorringe's operations. Indeed, as we found out afterwards, the whole force under Mahommed Daghastani Pasha, which had retired across the Karkheh River upon General Gorringe's approach, was surprised by us when we entered Amara, where parts of its advance guard were captured. Two thousand, as I have said, were dispersed by the *Shaitan*, and the remainder had to seek safety in dispersion, after abandoning two of their guns. It was probably in no small measure due to General Gorringe's demonstration from Bisaitan from the 18th to the 29th of May that the enemy's retreat up the Tigris was so precipitate after our successful action of the 31st, and that thus we were enabled to enter Amara practically unopposed.

I sent a party ashore, had the Union Jack hoisted over the customs-house, which was the nearest prominent building belonging to the Turkish Government, and posted sentries over a few of the Turkish official establishments, but could not spare many men from our tiny force.

Then we received a message that the Turkish Governor and the General Commanding wished to come onboard in order to surrender. The *Comet's* jolly-boat, manned by her only three sailors, was sent for them, and soon an imposing procession of officers came along the quay, many of them glittering in full-dress uniform—although I must say that most of their gold lace and braid hadn't much glitter left in it.

They were received with formality at the gangway. General Townshend was most affable, talked French volubly, and gave the most stringent orders to the Civil Governor to arrange at once for the collection of supplies for 15,000 men. I stood with him while we received a large and varied collection of swords and pistols.

The crowd of Turkish officers nearly filled the small quarterdeck of the *Comet*, and it was obvious from their attitude towards us that they had not the vaguest idea how few of us there really were.

I had seen to it that all my officers and men had revolvers on them, and in order to keep our prisoners occupied coffee was served. Not without some internal trepidation we hoped for the best.

Among the Turks was one Naval officer who had escaped from the ill-fated *Marmariss*. He spoke English well, and eagerly told us that before the War he had been on the Staff of the British admiral in charge of our mission at Constantinople. This was rather a foolish admission on his part. Had he kept quiet he might have stirred up trouble, and, with a little astuteness, have turned the tables on us. When told what he had said I had him taken below to the wardroom, with strict orders not to go on deck, so that he would not be able to communicate anything that he had heard us say to the others, and thus give the show away.

We were so short of men that the only available sentry to guard him was a private of Marines who was lying on a camp-bed recovering from an attack of fever. The bed was placed near the top of the ladder, and the man brightened up tremendously when given a revolver and told that should the Turk try to come up the ladder he was to tell him to stop, and to shoot him if he persisted.

I sent Lieutenant-in-Command I. M. Palmer of the *Comet* ashore with all the men that could be spared from the flotilla to keep order on the town front ; these consisted of two seamen, one Marine, and a corporal and twelve men of the West Kents and 1/4th Hampshires, who were temporarily serving as Marines on board the *Comet*, in place of men who had been invalided. At the barracks, where Palmer went with a seaman, a Marine, and an interpreter, he found a battalion of the Constantinople fire brigade regiment—about 400 Turkish soldiers with their officers, all fully armed—drawn up in the square ready to surrender, and, concealing his surprise, he gave orders to ground arms, and they were forthwith marched out of the barracks. About that time a body of fifty Turkish soldiers marched up to the Turkish Naval barracks and surrendered to three of our soldiers who had been posted there. A large body of Turkish troops, estimated at about 2000, were sighted coming towards Amara from the north-eastward during the afternoon, evidently retreating from Arabistan. The *Shaitan* fired a few shells at them from the northern end of the town, and made prisoners of about fifty of their advance guard, the remainder making off in confusion.

Such large numbers of Turkish troops were by this time coming in as prisoners that it was becoming a question of how to dispose of them. We were busy disarming them as rapidly as possible, at the same time throwing into the river a large number of rifles for which we had no room on board the little ships.

So I sent Sub-Lieutenant Lilley of the *Odin*, who had come up with me in charge of the 4·7-inch guns, with two men to get hold of a small tug which the Turks had abandoned, with steam up, with a large lighter alongside her, and told him to stow as many of the Turkish prisoners in the lighter as possible, and then to anchor the lighter in the middle of the river in a position commanded by our guns. It seemed as safe a place as any in which to put them, as it was unlikely that many of them could swim. Lilley managed to load the lighter with nearly 80 officers and 800 men, many of whom he and his two men had to disarm.

We had already sent messages down the river for our troops to be pushed forward as fast as possible, and at about 4 P.M. I sent Gunner McKay, R.N., down the river in a launch with dispatches from Townshend and myself, and further urgent requests for reinforcement.

Placing the small Naval force in position for the night along the river facing the town, we sent ashore a proclamation to the effect that the inhabitants were to remain indoors after dark, and that we would shoot anyone seen in the streets. I also arranged for the lamps along the front to be lighted. The Turkish town lamplighter agreed to carry out his duty as usual, but only on condition that he was paid in advance.

We posted the few sentries we could spare on shore, and all the officers on board took turns in keeping watch that night. I kept the Turkish Naval lieutenant from the *Marmariss* aboard the *Comet* with us, nominally to arrange to do *liaison* work between us and our prisoners, but, of course, actually because he knew English so well that he must have gathered from our conversation how few we were.

We also found that an old Turkish Colonel of Engineers had got left behind, and had not gone to the barge. So we invited him to dinner, and he became a very entertaining guest, as it turned out that he had been one of those in charge of laying the Turkish mines. He said that their failure was largely due to the fact that he had not been able to devote sufficient time to them, as he was given so much regimental duty. He became quite angry as he recited all this, telling it in French to General Townshend, who translated it to the rest of us at the dinner-table amid applause, especially when, under the influence of good liquor, the old man lugubriously lamented the hard luck he had had in not blowing us all up !

It was an anxious night, however, and as soon as daylight dawned the Arabs commenced to be troublesome, and we had to use the Maxims to quieten them. During the night we had seen a steamer's searchlight in the distance, coming up the river ; and we were all very glad when one of the river transports arrived at 10 A.M. on Friday, the 4th of June, with a battalion of the 2nd Norfolk Regiment aboard. As she ran alongside the men were rushed ashore, and soon quieted the town.

The Norfolks had arrived not a moment too soon, for the Arabs had discovered the true state of affairs, and each minute of that morning that passed the situation of our small force became more and more critical. However, the effect of the troops being loosened in the town was to bring about something more like lasting order, and the days that followed were spent in taking over and exploring the vicinity.

I sent Harden down the river with Lilley and a few men, in charge of the barge-load of prisoners, and some time that same night, in the dark, they took the wrong turning. They were just going down one of the large branch canals by mistake when a Turkish officer came up and tapped one of our fellows on the back and pointed out to him the right way. The fact was they were so short of food that they were keen to get to Basra and enjoy, as soon as possible, the comforts which they knew—as, indeed, every Turk seemed to know— are the lot of British prisoners of war.

On the 5th of June I went in the *Shaitan* on a reconnaissance some forty-two miles up-river, but, seeing nothing of the enemy, left the *Comet* and the *Shaitan* with our forces at Amara, and returned to Basra with the remainder of the flotilla, to prepare for a projected expedition up the Euphrates for the capture of Nasiriya.

Our little force at Amara, including the General, his Staff and officers, had amounted to a total of about 88 officers and men, of whom about 40 per cent. were native ratings, stokers, etc.

It is amusing to record that after their experience on board the *Comet* the soldiers of the West Kent and Hampshire regiments who had been temporarily serving on board her asked to be allowed to see me, and that when mustered on the quarterdeck their senior put forward the request that they might be permitted to change over from the Army to the Navy. Perhaps they had been impressed by our methods, but suspect that they preferred yachting on the river to foot-slogging in the desert. They had never had the chance of being seasick—or seen a submarine.

The foregoing successes had been attained with but slight loss on the British side. During the whole of the operations from the 31st of May to the 4th of June, 1915, our forces captured 140 officers, including the Commander Saif Ullah and Halim Bey and the Civil Governor Aziz Bey, and about 2000 men, sank the gunboat *Marmariss* and the tug *Bulbul*, and captured two steamers, the *Mosul* and the *Kuzima*, two tugs, the *Summarra* and the *Sebeh*, two motor-boats, the *Mosca* and another, and some ten iron barges and six *mahelas*.

Also we captured twelve field-guns, five naval guns, 1,153,500 rounds of small-arm ammunition, 2718 rifles, and a large quantity of other ammunition, ordnance stores, etc.

Throughout the entire period of the operation the heat had been intense, and we all suffered severely from a combined plague of heat, mosquitoes, and flies, especially when lying in the neighbourhood of Ezra's Tomb, among the marshes.

General Nixon was very kind and flattering to us in his dispatches home, and paid a handsome tribute to the part played by the Navy and to the close co-operation between the services. This latter he pointed out as a marked feature of the operations—as it certainly was—and the Navy enjoyed every bit of it.

So this chapter closes with the British in possession of Amara, and reconnoitring to the northward of that place on the Tigris, danger averted from the vicinity of Ahwaz, the oil pipe-line repaired, the Karun River a safe line of communication, and the enemy forces on the Euphrates not yet recovered from their defeat at Shaiba.

Early in June 1915 the Naval officers and men from the sloops, who had taken part in the advance to Amara, returned to their ships near Ezra's Tomb, and the sloops left for Basra on Tuesday, 8th June. Great difficulty was experienced in navigating the shallow river, as the water was now falling, and it was also so narrow that the *Espiègle* and the *Clio*, which were the farthest up-river, had to back down stern first for some miles before it was broad enough for them to swing round. After arrival at Basra the *Clio* was sent on to Bombay for repairs to her port propeller, which she had injured in the advance north of Kurna; the *Lawrence* had already been sent to Bushire, in the Persian Gulf, as German agents were known to be stirring up the Persians to attack that place.

The foregoing successful operations had cleared the Turks from Arabistan, and their effect on the Arabs was such that the safety of our oil pipe-line was practically assured, and through the repaired pipe oil again reached the refinery at Abadan on the 14th of June. The flow was not interrupted again, and an extra and larger pipe was soon laid from the fields to the refinery ; so that during the remainder of the War an enormous amount of oil fuel was shipped in tankers for the use of the Fleet in home waters, and a large quantity was also used by the vessels in Mesopotamia.

It was now deemed advisable, in order to obtain an effective control over the western portion of the Basra *vilayet* and over the powerful Arab tribes in the vicinity, to capture Nasiriya, the most important town in that province on the Euphrates.

Preparations at Basra were therefore advanced as rapidly as possible for that purpose, and I was requested by Sir John Nixon to confer and to arrange Naval co-operation with General (now Sir) G. F. Gorringe, who was to command the military force for the expedition. As the operations were to take place in very shallow waters, it was decided that the Naval flotilla with the expedition should consist of the small sternwheelers the *Shushan*, the *Massoudieh*, and the *Muzaffri*, which we manned and armed, retaining, in addition, their ordinary crews of Arabs and Chaldeans.

Excessive temperatures were experienced during June, and there were many cases of heatstroke in the hot, still weather. The *Shamal*, or cool north-west wind, sprang up, however, towards the end of the month, and somewhat relieved the oppressiveness, but even then there was a great deal of sickness and many deaths among the troops. The Navy also experienced cases of heatstroke, and had the misfortune to lose a few men who could ill be spared.

In order to safeguard the health of the white crews it had been decided that the sloops were to take advantage of any lull in the operations and proceed, in turn, to Ceylon during the hot weather, where, during the refit of the ships at Colombo, their crews could be sent to recruit their health at the Royal Naval Camp in the hills at Diyatalawa. It was also arranged that the crews of the armed launches should be taken in turn to Ceylon in the sloops. I arranged to commence these movements on the completion of the pending Nasiriya operations and on the return of the *Clio* from Bombay.

The question of the further provision of shallow-draught

gunboats had been fully gone into by the Admiralty, and an effort was being made to send out two sternwheel gunboats from Egypt, but they sank during bad weather in the Red Sea. It was finally decided to send out plates and material, and put together small gunboats on slips at Abadan, on the Shatt al Arab, at the Anglo-Persian Oil Company's works. The construction was placed in the hands of Messrs. Yarrow. The materials for the first four gunboats left England during August, in the *Lorenzo*, and Messrs. Yarrow also sent out as local manager, Mr. William Grant, one of their most experienced overseers, who had been employed by them on these rivers before, and thus had the advantage of knowledge concerning local conditions. These gunboats, of which materials for twelve were at first ordered—afterwards four more were commissioned—are usually described in Admiralty papers as being of the " small China gunboat " type, and this name effectually concealed their real destination from the inquisitive. They were constructed four at a time, and will be described in more detail later.

It was also arranged to send out four vessels of " the large China gunboat " type; and the *Mantis*, which left in November 1915, but was followed later by the *Gnat*, the *Moth*, and the *Tarantula*, were all towed out. Another contemplated addition to the flotilla consisted of a Turkish motor patrol-boat which had been sunk in action by the *Espiègle* in November 1914. She was found to be lying in a position where she could be salved, so the Anglo-Persian Oil Company's representatives at Mahommerah successfully effected this and refitted her for service. She was renamed the *Flycatcher*, and commissioned with a Naval crew for service in the river towards the end of 1915. I found her very useful as a dispatch boat, and used her often in my trips up and down the river between the front and the base, and while inspecting the gunboats on the way there and back.

The name *Flycatcher* given her by the Admiralty revealed the fact that there was plenty of wit still to be found in that august institution, even in those war-worn days.

I found after a time that my going up the river gave rise to rumours that either some advance or " push " was afoot, and my return to the base was held to betoken a probable temporary cessation of active hostilities. However, I soon corrected this impression by occasionally sending the *Flycatcher* up and down without me, though flying my pennant, thus mystifying watchers as to my movements.

On account of the considerable increase of numbers in the Naval rivercraft it was found necessary to establish a Naval depot for their manning, storing, and refit. It was obvious that the little *Espiègle* had neither the accommodation nor staff to cope with the accounts, storage, refitting, medical superintendence, and the like, for the rapidly increasing flotilla, and there was not at the time suitable accommodation ashore. The *Alert*, sloop, was therefore fitted at Bombay for this purpose. She was provided with a nucleus crew of officers and men, commissioned by Commander Walter J. W. Steward, R.N. (called up from retirement at Nelson, New Zealand), and arrived and berthed at Abadan in October.

Meanwhile our troops continued to consolidate their position at Amara, where the leading detachment of General Gorringe's force from the Karun joined hands with them on the 15th of June.

The enemy, whose flight up the Tigris and past Amara had, as we ascertained from officer prisoners, been an absolute rout, retired in the direction of Kut, together with Mahomed Pasha Daghistani's force, which was falling back from the Karun front. Aeroplane reconnaissance from Amara on the 14th of June observed camps and trenches on both sides of the Tigris at Daqq-al-Hajjaj, eight miles downstream from Kut. Aeroplanes also bombed another camp about six miles farther upstream, the troops in the vicinity being estimated at about 3000.

By the 23rd of June further reports indicated a concentration of the enemy's forces at Kut, with an estimated force of 8500 infantry and 23 guns ; also it was reported that they had placed a regiment in advance at Sheikh Saad, were placing an obstruction of barges in the Tigris near Kut, and were patrolling downstream of that place with patrol-boats and armed launches. As an outcome of this information General Townshend sent a small force, consisting of a battalion, a troop of cavalry, and two guns, to occupy an advanced post at Kumait, about twenty-nine miles up the Tigris, or twenty-four by the land route from Amara. The armed launches *Shaitan* and *Comet* acted with them, patrolling upstream from there.

On the Karun line the Sheikh of Mahommerah's force of 3000 of the Muhaisin (Arab) tribe gained a victory over the rebellious Chaab tribesmen in operations commencing with an advance on June the 3rd, both the towns of Falla-hieh and Buzieh being captured, and the Chaabs severely defeated at both places. As a result of this success of our allies the relations between the turbulent tribe and the Sheikh of Mahommerah were again placed on a satisfactory footing, and the situation in Arabistan returned to its normal —which, by the way, isn't any *too* quiet !

The erection of a wireless telegraph station was also commenced during this month at the oilfields at Maidan-i-Naftun.

VICE-ADMIRAL WILFRID NUNN, C.B., C.S.I., C.M.G., D.S.O.

FIRST LANDING OF MAIN BODY OF EXPEDITIONARY FORCE
IN SHATT AL ARAB, NOVEMBER 8TH, 1914
Shows transports and troops landing in boats.

A TURKISH PATROL BOAT SUNK BY US IN EARLY DAYS OF THE
WAR IS HERE SHOWN WHEN AFTERWARDS SALVED AND
COMMISSIONED AS H.M.S. *FLYCATCHER*

HAMBURG–AMERIKA STEAMER *EKBATANA*, SUNK BY TURKS ACROSS
SHATT AL ARAB IN ORDER TO TRY AND BLOCK THE FAIRWAY

H.M.S. *ESPIÈGLE*—TWIN-SCREW SLOOP

CUSTOM HOUSE AT BASRA FOUND ON FIRE WHEN WE ARRIVED
ON 21ST NOVEMBER, 1914
Our sailors shown on guard as Military had not yet reached Basra.

ASHAR CREEK, BASRA
Our troops shown, having just marched in at the occupation. British Flag
(in centre) has just been hoisted.

CAPTURED ENEMY TROOPS AT KURNA, DECEMBER 1914
Shell-damaged buildings in background.

MYSELF (LOOKING UP) AND MILITARY OFFICERS EXAMINING A
CAPTURED GUN IN A TRENCH AT KURNA
Our Interpreter " Salem " on the left (mentioned in text).   Surrendered enemy
arms piled behind.   *Espiègle* in background anchored in the Tigris.

OUR ARAB ALLIES MOVING TO ATTACK A HOSTILE VILLAGE IN
MAY 1915, SUPPORTED BY OUR SHIPS

OUR ALLIES RETURN VICTORIOUS WITH MUCH LOOT!

BIRD'S-EYE VIEW OF KURNA FROM ARTILLERY OBSERVATION
TOWER
Boat-bridge in foreground. H.M. Sloop *Odin* anchored in river.

SHOWS ARAB ALLIES AND SOME TROOPS TRAINED TO PROPEL
" BELLUMS " ON A SMALL EXPEDITION UP THE EUPHRATES
IN MAY 1915
The flooded condition of the country can be seen.

CLOSE-UP VIEW OF OUR ARAB ALLIES WITH SACRED FLAG

THE NAVAL FLOTILLA DURING ADVANCE UP TIGRIS TO NORTHWARD FROM KURNA,
MAY 31ST, 1915

VIEWS OF TURKISH GUNBOAT *MARMARISS*
Taken on June 2nd, after the action.

THE TOWN OF AMARA ON THE TIGRIS

H.M. STERN-WHEELER *SHUSHAN*
She flew my pennant as Senior Naval Officer during the Nasiriya operations

VIEW OF EXPLOSION, JULY 1915, WHEN A PASSAGE FOR SHIPS
WAS BLOWN THROUGH THE BUND PLACED BY ENEMY
ACROSS AKAIKA CHANNEL

VIEW OF JUNCTION OF AKAIKA CHANNEL WITH THE RIVER
EUPHRATES

VIEW OF PART OF NASIRIYA, SHOWING TURKISH BARRACKS FROM WHENCE *SHUSHAN* WAS FIRED ON WHEN SEYMOUR WAS WOUNDED

A VIEW OF PART OF THE TOWN OF SAMAWA, ON THE EUPHRATES
It was surrendered to us onboard the *Shushan* as mentioned in text.

H.M.S. *Mantis*   Three "Fly" class gunboats

ON THE TIGRIS WITH FORCE ATTEMPTING TO RELIEVE KUT
IN APRIL 1916

H.M.S. *FIREFLY* IN ACTION AT THE BATTLE OF CTESIPHON ON
22ND NOVEMBER, 1915

A "FLY" CLASS RIVER GUNBOAT STEAMING UP THE TIGRIS

H.M.S. *JULNAR* STEAMING AWAY UP THE TIGRIS ON APRIL 24TH, 1916,
ON HER FATEFUL AND HISTORIC VOYAGE
Probably an unique photo of this historic incident.

JULNAR LOADED WITH PROVISIONS, ETC., FOR HER GALLANT
ATTEMPT TO RELIEVE KUT

H.M.S. *FIREFLY* SHORTLY AFTER WE RECAPTURED HER

British White Ensign can be seen flying above Turkish ensign.

VIEW OF KUT IN RUINS AFTER THE SIEGE AND RECAPTURE
Mosque with cupola knocked off can be seen in background.

TOWNSHEND'S GUNS, AS WE FOUND THEM IN THE ARSENAL AT
BAGHDAD ON OUR OCCUPATION IN MARCH 1917

BOOK III

FROM THE CAPTURE OF NASIRIYA TO THE INVESTMENT OF KUT

CHAPTER VII

THE CAPTURE OF NASIRIYA

THE preparations for the advance up the Euphrates were completed towards the end of June, and on the evening of the 26th the force detailed for these operations concentrated on the Euphrates, about twenty-eight miles to the west of Kurna, and about two miles to the east of the village of Chabaish. The *Espiègle*, the *Odin*, and the *Miner* were unable to proceed beyond this point on account of the shallow water, but furnished men, guns, and stores for the small craft, and remained near Chabaish as a support and line of communication for the Expedition.

These small craft were the three small sternwheel river-steamers *Shushan*, *Massoudieh*, and *Muzaffri*, which, as noted before, had been prepared and armed for the expedition, the Naval crews being put onboard at Chabaish.

The *Shushan* was to fly my pendant as Senior Naval Officer, and was given a twelve-pounder eight-hundred-weight gun, a three-pounder gun, and a Maxim from the *Espiègle*. She was also allotted Lieutenant-Commander A. G. Seymour, a party of seamen, and a Marine from the *Espiègle*, in addition to her own captain, Lieutenant F. W. Lyte, D.S.C., R.N.R. (who was to act as second-in-command and pilot), and native crew.

With the object of making life more comfortable during our stay in the little sternwheeler I took with me my blue-jacket coxswain and Goanese cook. The coxswain enjoyed enormously this getting away from man-of-war routine, and was prominent whenever any scrapping was going on —but not so the cook !

The Goanese are a peaceful native race, under Portuguese

rule, and only leave their homes in Goa to become stewards, cooks, and servants, and to perform similar work in ships and hotels. They are a careful, quiet, well-behaved people, and when they have saved enough generally retire, to live peacefully at Goa, which must be chock-full of cooks. But they are also very timid, and this trip became too exciting for my good lad. He never returned from his next leave to Goa ! First I was told that his wife was very ill, then the children, then his mother—a plague seemed to be engulfing the family. He never rejoined, and I realised that he had seen enough fighting, and felt that his constitution did not require any more—at any rate, not of the kind he witnessed in Mesopotamia.

The *Muzaffri* was placed under the command of Lieuten-ant H. F. Curry of the *Odin*, with a crew and Maxim gun from that ship ; the *Massoudieh*, commanded by Lieutenant C. H. Heath-Caldwell, and manned by a crew from the armed launch *Miner*, was given a three-pounder and Maxim.

The armed tug *Sumana*, under Lieutenant W. V. H. Harris, also accompanied the expedition, beside two 4·7-inch Naval guns, which were mounted in horse-boats. The stern-wheelers were curious old craft, but, owing to their very light draught, were the only available vessels suitable in those shallow waters, especially as the high-water season was over, and the levels of both the river and the lakes were beginning to fall. A certain amount of protective iron plating had been put round them, but it was necessary to be sparing with it, in order not to increase their draught to any considerable extent.

Our military force consisted of part of the 12th Indian Division, commanded by Major-General G. F. Gorringe—viz., the 30th Indian Infantry Brigade (which was much reduced by sickness), under Major-General C. J. Melliss, V.C., C.B., the 63rd Battery R.F.A., the 30th Mountain Battery, two double companies 48th Pioneers, headquarters and one section 12th Signal Company, wireless station, the 12th Company Sappers and Miners, and divisional troops, etc.

The troops were accommodated in the river-steamers *Blosse Lynch*, *Mejidieh*, and *Malimir*, each of which had two eighteen-pounder R.F.A. guns mounted on her foredeck. They were also accompanied by the tugs *Shuhrur* and *Shirin*, as well as by the transport tugs *T*1 and *T*4, all of these towing *mahelas* or lighters on each side of them, full of stores, ammunition, etc. The mountain guns were placed on *bellums*, and a number of these were taken for the use of the troops in the flooded parts of the desert.

The instructions given to General Gorringe were to open the waterway from the Hammar Lake to the Euphrates, to secure effective occupation of the towns Nasiriya and Suk es Sheyukh, the object of the operations being to obtain an effective control over the western portion of the Basra *vilayet* and over the powerful Arab tribes in the neighbourhood.

Nasiriya, on the Euphrates, about ninety miles by river above Kurna, and twenty-seven from Suk es Sheyukh, was an important town and outpost of Turkish authority in an unsettled part of the country ; it was the headquarters of the Turkish *sanjak* of Muntafiq, in the *vilayet* of Basra, the officer commanding the garrison discharging also the duties of Civil Governor of the *sanjak*, in which the powerful Muntafiq tribe of Arabs especially gave trouble. The town had a mixed population of about 10,000. It was the centre of considerable trade, contained some good masonry houses, a number of broad, well-lighted streets, and large blocks of Turkish Government buildings, comprising barracks, hospitals, etc.

Suk es Sheyukh was another important town, with a floating population estimated at 12,000, situated on the Lower Euphrates at the western end of the marsh and lake country, at about sixty-three miles from Kurna. It was an important centre of trade—small manufactures, boat-building, etc.—of the Arabs in the vicinity. This fact was indicated by its name, which means " Market of the Sheikh." Under the Turkish *régime* the headquarters of a *kasa* in the *sanjak* of Nasiriya, on a branch of the Turkish telegraph system, it had no garrison, but detachments of troops were quartered at various posts in the neighbourhood.

General Nixon considered the water-route *via* Kurna and the Hammar Lake preferable to the land-route, which

would have involved an arduous march across 110 miles
of desert in the hottest season of the year. The Hammar
Lake, however, is ordinarily very shallow ; but as we have
already noted, this was the season of the falling waters.
Ships drawing only five feet could negotiate the passage at
the end of June, while a maximum draught of not more than
three feet could pass in July. In the lowest reaches the water
in the lake was barely eighteen inches deep ! From the
western end of the Hammar Lake the Gurmat Safha, or
Hakika, as well as several other channels lead into the
Euphrates. It was known, as previously stated, from reports
and air and Naval reconnaissances, that the Gurmat Safha
—the only feasible channel, as it happened—was blocked
by a solidly constructed dam about half a mile from its
entrance to the lake.

On Sunday, the 27th of June, the *Shushan* and the
Massoudieh weighed and left the anchorage at 4 A.M., proceeding to the westward across the Hammar Lake, followed
by the remainder of the flotilla, the steamers and barges
carrying the force. The ships had considerable difficulty
in keeping to the tortuous and almost unmarked channel
through the muddy waters of the lake, and frequently
grounded. Approaching the Hakika Channel out of the
lake on the western side early in the afternoon, we were
greeted as we neared it by two Turkish patrol-boats, who
opened fire with pom-poms from farther up the river,
above the dam. This fire the gunboats returned. At 2.45
P.M. General Gorringe joined me on board the *Shushan*,
and we steamed into the Akaika Channel, the enemy craft
retreating up-river before us. Steamboats swept ahead of
the flotilla, but no mines were found, and the gunboats
anchored in the channel just below the dam, or *bund*,[1]
under which local name it was generally referred to.

I went up with the General and staff in his motor-boat to
inspect the *bund*. We landed on it, and found it a very
solid affair, rising well above water, and about thirty feet
thick at the top. We had just decided that blasting operations would have to be carried out, blasting on a scale that
would please any Sapper, and the General's eyes—he came

---

[1] A *bund* is an artificial bank to prevent the river overflowing.

from that famous corps—were glistening with pleasure, for
he was already thinking out what was the largest quantity of
explosive that could be demanded from Basra, when there
was a sudden *pom-pom-pom-pom-pom-pom*. In a few
seconds' space the *bund* round us was pockmarked by a very
unpleasant hailstorm. One of the Turkish patrol-boats
had poked her nose round the corner and opened on us
with rapid fire. The General remarked that we had better
get off, and walked slowly back to the boat—not anything
like as fast as I should have liked. We found the native
boat's crew almost mad with terror, and it seemed to take a
long time getting away from that unhealthy spot. Our
flotilla was keeping a good look-out, however. The Turkish
fire was quickly returned, and the enemy driven away
under a cloud of shell. We employed the same method of
frightening them when on several subsequent occasions they
tried to disturb working parties in the same way.

The task of making a passage through the *bund* large
enough to allow of passage by our flotilla proved to be one of
considerable difficulty, as it was found that large *mahelas*
had been sunk across the channel to form its core, and these
gave it a very solid foundation. The adjacent villages were
soon occupied, however, and demolition of the dam by
explosives commenced under the close supervision of the
General, who was there at all hours of the night and day.
He was also very fond of coming alongside at the earliest
hint of daylight, and asking the look-out to call me and
inquire whether I should like to go with him to see the latest
developments at the *bund* ; or perhaps he had a particularly
large and impressive explosion on hand, which, as he said,
I really should not miss. On such occasions I often thought
of that well-known ditty, *It's nice to be up in the morning*,
heartily agreeing with the author : it would certainly have
been " nicer to stay in bed " !

At length, on the afternoon of June 29th, a small channel,
down which a cataract of water poured, had been made
through, and the *Shushan* steamed to its entrance. A wire
was then led from her bows, and manned by two regiments
above the falls. The men hauled for a while with the ship
steaming full speed, but she made no appreciable headway.

It was a combined operation : the General on the *bund* shouting through a megaphone orders to the soldiers who manned the towing-wire, while I did my best to encourage our engine-room staff, who were natives, and to whom our interpreter forcibly translated my remarks.

Just then some Indian soldiers, who, from a canoe just above the cataract, had been watching the proceedings, got too close, were sucked into the strong current, and, in spite of every effort to paddle clear, found themselves being sucked into and hurried at an increasing pace down the rapids. Then the canoe hit a partly submerged snag. They were spilled out, and came shrieking downstream. They were really not in much danger, as it happened, because our little steamboat was just below the falls.

While the soldiers drifted yelling down the swift current, and the staff shouted for boats from the bank, the stream seemed suddenly to lessen in strength, and the *Shushan*, steaming at full speed all the while, made some little headway. The favourable moment had apparently arrived, so, picking up a megaphone, I hailed the troops manning the towing-wire to put their backs into it. Under this influence she moved slowly forward, gradually passed up the channel, and anchored above it in the river at the same time that the Indian soldiers were being fished dripping out of the pool below.

The *Massoudieh* and two horse-boats with 4·7 guns shortly followed, and with these craft, and accompanied by a Staff Officer, we then proceeded up-river on a reconnaissance, and located the enemy's entrenched position at the junction of the Gurmat Safha or Akaika Channel and the Euphrates. We found that the enemy had placed two guns on the right bank of the Euphrates to command the line of our advance up the Gurmat Safha Channel. This reconnaissance was a both interesting and exciting experience. Having anchored the ships out of sight from the Turkish entrenchments, a party of us landed and crept along behind the mud walls until, peeping over, we could get a good view of their gun position, only some six hundred yards away. Colonel Brown, G.S.O.I., gleaned enough detail from that brief survey to make a most

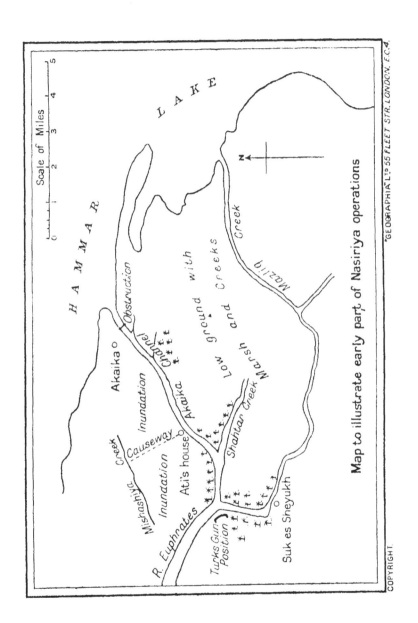

Map to illustrate early part of Nasiriya operations

useful sketch. There were hostile Arabs about, and I much admired his coolness and accurate observation in these dangerous circumstances. For myself, I felt much relieved when we crawled back out of sight of the battery, which we successfully accomplished without a shot being fired. A further reconnaissance was carried out on the 2nd of July, about four miles up the Gurmat Safha from the dam, as far as a conspicuous mud tower on the left bank, known as " Ati's House," which was afterwards used as General Headquarters during the fighting in the vicinity. Fairly good observation was obtainable from it. However, below this position the country was found to be marshy for the most part, but above it both banks appeared dry and covered thickly with date-gardens, which were much intersected with irrigation channels and mud walls ; and, of course, the channel of the river being tortuous, the view was much restricted by the serpentine plantations of date-palms and trees.

A large creek, called the Shahtar, runs into the Gurmat Safha on the right bank about two thousand yards above " Ati's House," where it, together with a minefield—which we were informed by spies had been placed in the vicinity— were commanded by the two enemy guns before mentioned on the right bank of the Euphrates, opposite the entrance of the Gurmat Safha.

All the flotilla having with difficulty been hauled through the gap in the obstructions, the advance commenced at 4 A.M. on the 4th of July. Escorted by the gunboats, and the advance-party under Lieutenant-Colonel Smithett consisting of the 76th Punjabis, one double company 48th Pioneers, and a section of the 30th Mountain Battery, the Expedition proceeded up-river, seized " Ati's House " and a position on the bank opposite. A channel had been dug for the *bellums* from the river to the open water north and west of " Ati's House." A reconnaissance was also sent along the *bund* running north from " Ati's House," but on advancing through the date-groves the party met with such strong opposition that it was at first unable to make good the crossings over Mishashiya Creek. Meanwhile the remainder of the force had arrived in the vicinity of " Ati's House," and then the 2/7 Gurkhas crossed to the opposite (south) bank, with orders to move up to the Shahtar Creek. They were, however, opposed by Arabs, and were soon in difficulties in the date-plantations intersected by water-channels and walls, but they reached the near bank of the Shahtar in the evening, only to find the enemy occupying the farther bank. They were thus held up during the night.

They were later reinforced by the 1/4 Hampshires, and gradually making progress, in the early hours of the 5th of July the combined force seized the point at the junction of Shahtar Creek with the Akaika Channel. This proved to be an excellent observation-point for fire directed at the enemy gun position, which had been giving the gunboats and shipping a hot time.

At 4.15 A.M. on the 5th—about twenty-four hours after the advance had begun—it was continued on the left, or northern, bank by General Melliss's column, consisting of the 76th Punjabis, the 24th Punjabis, and the 30th Mountain Battery, with *bellums ;* the orders being for the General to proceed along the north bank of the Akaika and to establish himself on the left bank of the Euphrates well up-river of the gun position, where it was hoped that he might get across, cut off the enemy's retreat, and also that of the Turkish shipping.

Our forward movement on the opposite bank having, however, been checked by the enemy fire—the Hampshires and Gurkhas had not yet crossed the Shahtar Creek—the 76th Punjabis soon found themselves under heavy fire from the south side of the river, as well as on their right front, and were unable to proceed. Meanwhile the 24th Punjabis and a section of Mountain Battery had moved into the inundation north-west of " Ati's House " and pushed forward on the right of the 76th, all heavily engaged by the fire from behind mud walls on their right front.

The *Sumana* and the *Shushan* had in the interim moved up in support, and they also came under heavy gun- and rifle-fire, the *Sumana* being twice hit by shell, and put out of action by one which hit her main steampipe. Her captain, Lieutenant W. V. H. Harris, and two men were wounded. There was a story current on board her that while the hands were at dinner in the after deckhouse one shell went right down the middle of the table !

By now the 24th Punjabis and the section of Mountain Battery were pushing their way forward. Supported by the 76th and gunfire, they advanced, reaching the left bank of the Euphrates above the junction with the Gurmat Safha just before noon, coming also under heavy fire from the Turkish Thornycroft patrol-boat, which afterwards retired up-river.

They were now able to open a heavy fire on the enemy gun position, while the 76th gradually moved up and joined in on their flank. Their fire and the fire of the British artillery soon overpowered the Turks, who ran up several white flags. They surrendered about 1.20 P.M. Our troops then crossed the Euphrates in *bellums*, occupied the battery, and captured the two guns. Meanwhile on the south bank of the Akaika our force which had been held up by the Shahtar Creek managed to cross at 2 P.M., being greatly assisted by the *Shushan*, which moved forward and directed a heavy fire on the enemy that had opposed the crossing. The latter fell back, discovered to their dismay that their gun position was in our hands, and promptly surrendered.

At four o'clock we moved on in the *Shushan* and the *Massoudieh*, sweeping for mines as we proceeded. Information regarding their positions had been obtained from a Turkish officer who had been captured in the battery. By nine o'clock the channel to the Euphrates was swept clear, and we had found only one mine. All ships now moved into the Euphrates and anchored near the entrance of the Gurmat Safha.

The strength of the enemy during these operations was estimated at some 300 Turks, 2000 Arabs, two guns, and two launches with pom-poms, they having been reinforced during the action by two guns and 700 regulars from Nasiriya. The enemy losses, however, must have been considerable, and our captures included ninety-one prisoners and two guns, besides large quantities of ammunition and equipment. Our total military casualties up to date were 109 killed and wounded ; we had also had one Naval officer and two men wounded.

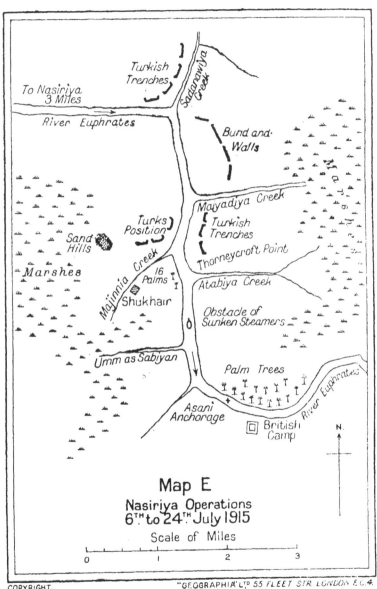

Turkish
Trenches

Sadanawiya Creek

To Nasiriya
3 Miles

River Euphrates

Bund and
Walls

Maiyadiya Creek

Turks
Position

Turkish
Trenches

Majinnia Creek

Thorneycroft Point

Sand
Hills

16
Palms

Atabiya Creek

Marshes

Shukhair

Obstacle of
Sunken Steamers

Umm as Sabiyan

Palm Trees

River Euphrates

Asani
Anchorage

British
Camp

N.

Map E
Nasiriya Operations
6TH to 24TH July 1915

Scale of Miles

0   1   2   3

Early next day—Tuesday, July the 6th—I took the *Shushan* and the *Massoudieh*, towing the 4·7-inch guns, down the Euphrates to Suk es Sheyukh, accompanied by Sir Percy Cox, the Senior Political Officer, in his launch. The Euphrates at this point runs through some of the most fertile parts of Mesopotamia, with cultivated land, squat, dark towers of mud and picturesque villages on both banks, which were generally fringed with date-palms waving their feathery tops in the mild river breeze.

The *Shushan* led, and the *Massoudieh*, with a barge carrying a 4·7 gun in it lashed on each side of her, looked like a curious sort of miniature battleship. There was no need, however, to use the guns, as the white flags of surrender were flying over the town, so we went alongside the bank and were greeted by the principal Arab inhabitants, who eagerly intimated their desire to surrender. There had been such a run on the ships' Union Jacks, for hoisting over captured towns and villages, that on this occasion we could not find a spare one for Suk es Sheyukh. Someone, however, produced an old Indian political flag out of the launch, and the subtle intricacies of flag-lore being un-appreciated in these parts, we hoisted it at the flagstaff of the little town's Customs House in the presence of Sir Percy Cox, myself, and several other officers, while a guard of bluejackets, clothed in the most respectable garments that we could muster, presented arms. Beyond the barrier of their bayonets was assembled a motley crowd of Arabs, with their *sheikhs*. It was a picturesque, albeit somewhat ironical scene : the Arabs watching with awed gaze the makeshift Indian flag soaring high over their mud-walled homesteads !

We afterwards returned to the entrance to the Akaika, and then went on up the Euphrates to reconnoitre, locating the enemy, who promptly opened fire from a position near Majinina, about four miles below Nasiriya. They had sunk the steamers *Frat*, *Risafa*, and a Thornycroft launch about three thousand yards downstream of this position ; but, owing to our speedy advance, the sinking operations had not been properly performed, and we later found we could manœuvre past the obstacles. The remainder of the flotilla was not long in coming up, and then the position was examined more circumspectly. Considerable numbers of enemy were seen working on their line of entrenchments. A Thornycroft launch was also observed at the bend in the river near the enemy position. However, the *Shushan* and the *Massoudieh*, moving forward, engaged with her, drawing also the fire of an enemy field-gun. But the moral effect of our recent drive forward was discernible when the Turkish craft, outfired, sneaked off.

At this point I might break the narrative to say that during this period we were for days in sight of that great square desert sandhill which covers the site of the ancient Chaldean city of Ur, where recently important excavations have been carried out. Not many of our party, however, knew much about the Chaldeans or their city, but when the sailors heard that its name was Ur, they readily resurrected that somewhat hackneyed slang witticism, " There's air." The observation, however, was not as obvious as it might seem. There was air but not the kind one generally associates with the " wide, open spaces " !

The flotilla and troops remained in the Asani bend, and on the 7th of July a further examination was made of the enemy's position. This was found to consist in the main of strong earthworks on both banks of the river, with the flanks resting on treacherous marshes, having in front, on the right bank, the broad Majinina Creek.

General Gorringe decided to seize and to occupy an advanced position on the right bank, about two thousand yards from the enemy's entrenchments. This manœuvre was successfully made on the night of 7th–8th along the south bank of the Sabiyan Creek, and on the succeeding days bombardments of the enemy's position were carried out by both the Naval and Army guns. The enemy position was found to be so strong, however—it was held by 2000 troops, with eight guns, besides numbers of Arabs—that it was found necessary to obtain reinforcements for our force from Basra before launching a general attack on it. General Gorringe consequently decided to send for the reinforcements, and our only light-draught steamers had to bring the troops from Basra across the falling waters of the

Hammar Lake, although they were urgently required on the Tigris.

The *Sumana* also had to be sent to Basra, for repairs to damage received in action, and all the ships had great difficulty in traversing the lake. The *Odin* and the *Clio*, lying at Chabaish, the exit of the passage to Basra, on its eastern side, performed invaluable work in assisting these craft, on which so much depended, while themselves having many men down on the sick-list with fever.

The passage across the receding waters of the lake was becoming a more and more difficult task, but the supplies for and the reinforcement of the Euphrates expedition, whose situation was, incidentally, providing considerable cause for anxiety, called for the utmost exertion, in order that the greatest possible celerity might be attained.

Owing to protracted delays while making this passage, ships sometimes ran very short of rations. One small gunboat reached Chabaish with stores running very low, and signalled to that effect as she neared the *Odin*. It was imperative, however, that she should get on to Basra, which was not a great way farther, without delay, so the usually kind-hearted Wason proved adamant, and sent her straight on, even after receiving the plaintive signal: "Submitted, sir, that we are starving." The grave state of affairs indicated by the signal was, however, belied by the rosy face of her captain, peering over the bridge rails, and the grins of the stout sailors on deck as she slipped by on her way !

On the night of the 8th–9th the Gurkhas moved forward on the left bank, supported by the 76th Punjabis, and occupied a position nearer the enemy, while a section of the 30th Mountain Battery was moved forward on the right bank. Further reconnaissance had disclosed more clearly the extent of the enemy's position in the neighbourhood of the Maiyadiya Creek.

The enemy's guns, of which on the 11th they disclosed six, were frequently active, and we now began our first experience of indirect firing. As the 4·7-inch guns on the horse boats lay so low in the river this was the only way in which they could be utilized—namely, by firing over the date-palms. The Army, as always, came to our assistance with such indispensable *etceteras* as telephone wire. After a little practice—some of it, I must confess, rather exciting for our friends as well as foes !—we began to get the hang of this new style of warfare, and Lieutenant-Commander Seymour distinguished himself as a useful forward observer. However, at 8 P.M. on July 11th our position on the left bank was attacked, the enemy coming up to within fifteen yards of our advance-line trenches before they were repulsed.

Our reinforcements, consisting of half a battalion Royal West Kents, the 67th and part of the 90th Punjabis, the 44th Merwara Infantry, and one section of the Hampshires' Howitzer Battery now arrived, and were assigned to our left-bank positions, the 30th Brigade moving across to the right bank.

Supplies, etc. were towed up near to our forward positions by night, being usually subjected to a heavy fire. In these operations Lieutenant H. F. Curry, R.N., who was temporarily placed in command of the tug *Shirin* for this duty, did some very good service. Frequent gunboat patrols down to Suk es Sheyukh were also carried out as concentrations of hostile Arabs were reported.

On the 14th the 76th Punjabis and the 48th Pioneers seized Shakhair and Sixteen Palms Post, on the right bank. But the 24th Punjabis, who attacked the sandhills to the westward at the same time, wading through water from eighteen inches to four feet deep, met with very heavy fire, and had to retire with heavy loss, among whom all but two of their British officers were killed.

It now became apparent that the enemy was continually receiving reinforcements of men and guns ; while, in addition to our casualties, we had, owing to the extreme heat, a great deal of sickness, besides fever, and the regiments were far below strength. More reinforcements were therefore asked for. These arrived on the 19th and 20th of July, and included the 18th Infantry Brigade, the remaining half-battalion of the West Kents, one section of the Heavy Battery (5-inch guns) and one section 1/5th Hampshire 5-inch Howitzer Battery, other details, and two more aeroplanes. The enemy was again reinforced about this time,

K

and large bodies of hostile Arabs, who appeared and camped to the north-eastward, ready to descend upon us in case of failure or retreat, were an ominous sign to the British force.

General Gorringe was in a most unenviable position : in a hostile country, far from his base, with little chance of reinforcement, and the longer victory was delayed the more the Hammar Lake fell, the approaching of the low-river season meanwhile imperilling his slender lines of communication. An early advance on Nasiriya became therefore imperative, and every possible preparation was accordingly made.

The 4·7-inch guns, besides others, were all now carefully registered on selected parts of the enemy position, and by the evening of the 23rd this had been done, with telephonic communication between guns and forward observers as far as possible completed, although the wires were being frequently severed by enemy fire. The *Sumana*, I might add, had also rejoined us by this time, after being expeditiously repaired at Basra.

It was decided to attack the enemy's position in the early morning of Saturday, the 24th of July, and I arranged for all possible Naval co-operation with the General Officer Commanding. The night before the battle I spent with General Gorringe at the advanced headquarters' bivouac, in order to be in close touch with events, and able to take advantage in good time of any chance which might turn up of a pursuit of the Turks, in the event of their retreat. I found this a useful expedient, and several times stayed at G.H.Q. the night before a battle. On that particular occasion, however, we had a very disturbed night, as we had camped under the lee of a mud wall not far from our lines ; and, besides the firing, that was spluttering the whole time, the enemy enlivened things at one stage by attacking our advanced trenches. When I woke up I remember it sounded alarmingly as if they might break through !

The date-palms near us were constantly hit by flying bullets ; big branches were ripped off and hurled to the ground. There happened to be a large hole in the wall at one place, and I thought it best to put my camp-bed well to one side of this. Altogether one was not sorry when the time

came to get up and prepare for the bombardment—scheduled
to commence at 4.30 A.M.—of the enemy positions on both
banks. Seymour was in the advanced observing position,
so after seeing that he was all right I went back to the
gunboats and moved them up as much as possible, while
keeping under the shelter of the palms as much as
possible.

At 5 A.M. the 12th Brigade, gallantly led by the Royal
West Kents, attacked the enemy position on the left bank.
The enemy guns on both banks soon developed a heavy fire.
They gave us a considerable amount of trouble, as they
were in concealed positions, and difficult to locate ; but
by 6.40 A.M. our forces had swept forward and carried the
enemy trenches near " Thornycroft Point," in spite of a
most determined resistance. In the trenches there was some
grim hand-to-hand fighting ; large numbers of Turks were
shot at close range and bayoneted where they stood.

As soon as the attack on the left bank was found to be
progressing favourably that planned for the 30th Brigade
was developed on the right bank. It was not known what
sort of obstacle the Majinina Creek would be to this advance,
so it had been arranged for the *Sumana* to tow up an
armoured barge, with parties of pioneers and sappers and
miners, accompanied by a covering party in it, with bridging
material. The plan was to run the barge aground across the
mouth of the creek, thus forming a crossing and base from
which bridging could be carried out during the advance.
This difficult and most dangerous enterprise was undertaken
successfully by Lieutenant W. V. H. Harris, commanding
Sumana, under very heavy fire. The bridging party had to
approach so close to the enemy position that both the
Sumana and barge were swept with bullets ; the barge
was holed by enemy shell, and the *Sumana's* steam-pipe
again fractured.

The severity of the rifle-fire under which she came may
be judged from the fact that eighty-seven bullet-marks were
afterwards counted between her bows and funnel. The
military in the barge suffered heavily, but this craft was
successfully placed. Blocking the mouth of the creek, it
had the unexpected effect of lowering the level of the water,

so that it could be forded by General Melliss's 30th Brigade,
which were by this time advancing. Shortly before 10 A.M.
the assaulting column crossed the Majinina Creek ; the
Hampshires and 7th Gurkhas then carried the trenches in
front of them in a most gallant manner, supported on their
left by the 76th Punjabis, and on their right by the gunboats
Shushan and *Massoudieh*, and the *Muzaffri*, with a Maxim
battery on board. These had moved forward, forcing the
enemy, who had made a stubborn resistance, and were also
suffering heavily from our artillery fire, to abandon the
whole of the Majinina position. Five guns fell into our
hands, besides prisoners and a quantity of ammunition.
The *Shushan* and the *Muzaffri* at once steamed on up-river,
the latter landing the military Maxim gun battery at the
enemy's catpured position on the right bank north of
Majinina Creek. This piece of work was carried out by
Lieutenant H. F. Curry, R.N., with great gallantry under
rifle and artillery fire, the *Muzaffri* being holed by shell, the
Shushan likewise being all the time hotly engaged.

Picture all this going on in a temperature of well over
110 degrees Fahrenheit in the shade, and then try to
imagine something of what an inferno it was !

The enemy, falling back from one prepared defence line
to another, still offered considerable opposition, but the
ships and the 4·7-inch guns continued to be heavily engaged
during the forenoon, assisting the 30th Brigade on the right
and the 12th on the left bank in gradually pressing the
enemy back. The main difficulty on these occasions, I
always found, consisted in keeping in touch with the general
situation and in good communication with the Military ;
and I fancy that when once on the move, and away from a
prearranged telephone system, Generals must find the same
difficulties.

By 1 P.M., however, the 12th Brigade were engaging the
enemy at the Sadanawiya Creek, and two hours later,
there being signs of the enemy retiring from this position,
the gunboats were again pushed forward. General Gorringe
came upstream at this stage ; and we discussed the situation. The steamer *Mejidieh*, on which two guns of the
63rd Field Battery, with some troops, were now em-

barked, with G.H.Q. onboard, followed, and did good service with the accurate shrapnel-fire of her R.F.A. guns. The *Shushan* next moved up until abreast of the 30th Brigade, who were on the right bank, but more or less held up by enemy guns at their Sadanawiya position.

We at once engaged these, bringing every gun we had to bear on it as we came opposite, and enfilading it at point-blank range, were able to inflict a heavy punishment on the enemy position. I well remember one of our sailors sitting, quite uncovered, on the forward deck, playing a Maxim down their trenches.

This attack from their front by the 12th Brigade, and from across the river by the 30th, as well as the decimating fire from the Naval 4·7 guns, soon proved too much for the Turks. They swarmed out of their position and retired in disorder northwards. The Sadanawiya position was straight away occupied, and, with the 30th Division opposite, our troops halted, absolutely exhausted. The General informed me of the new situation, and asked me to reconnoitre towards Nasiriya. So we in the *Shushan* moved on in that direction.

We were now near the town, and as we approached it a small craft intrepidly engaged us with a Maxim, but soon went scampering away up the river. Shortly after this we sighted a Thornycroft patrol-boat, which left the town jetty and fled at full speed upstream, opening a rapid fire from her pom-pom and Maxim, to which we replied from the *Shushan* with our Maxim and twelve-pounder. The twelve-pounder was only temporarily mounted in our ancient sternwheel steamer which had originally been built, I understand, to assist in the relief of General Gordon at Khartoum ; and, after so much firing, the mounting was now recoiling violently at every discharge. It had strained the deck on the port side in the forenoon, and had to be shifted over to the starboard side, which was little better, having nearly laid out the gunlayer by throwing him against a stanchion. This made good shooting very difficult. But Lieutenant-Commander A. G. Seymour rushed down to the gun, and handling and aiming it himself, managed to hit the patrol-boat with his third shot, upon which her crew ran her ashore. After another lyddite shell struck her she was soon in flames.

There was no support very near us, but the enemy fleet, being apparently destroyed, we thought that we might as well go on and investigate the state of affairs in Nasiriya. So on we went. Reaching the outskirts of the town, we saw that some Arabs were displaying white flags. Our interpreter, shouting through a megaphone, told them that we would receive the surrender of the town, and they waved us to go further on to the jetty.

On we steamed, and suddenly there opened up before us the large square expanse across which the main Turkish barracks faces the jetty on the river-front. There, on the roof of the barracks, were Turkish infantry, lots of them, with more crowding up, and they promptly opened fire on us at point-blank range. They had apparently not heard the latest news from the front—they had not been informed that we had won !

It was a most awkward situation ; there was no chance to explain. The funnel and protection plates round the ship's side rang and clanged as the bullets smote them. We all dropped down behind cover, and the interpreter dived straight down the ladder on to the lower deck.

I sang out for some one to put the helm over. Lyte, lying down, managed to do so, and thankful were we as she spun round and we got away down-river without serious mishap. The upper works and funnel were drilled through and through with bullet-holes. Lieutenant-Commander Seymour and a stoker were wounded, a bullet having grazed the back of Seymour's neck—a very narrow escape for him. These were the only casualties. We stopped a little lower down and fired a few rounds, one of which went right through the barracks ; and then, finding that the General did not intend to advance farther that night, I anchored a little way below the town, which, it was evident, the Turks were evacuating. It had been a long, exciting, and satisfactory day ; and while finishing our somewhat sketchy dinner we heard a loud explosion as our old enemy the patrol boat blew up.

Next morning I was up early, as at about six o'clock the

look-out reported a *mashuf* full of Arabs coming off to the ship. They proved to be the headmen and *sheikhs* of the town, and asked to see me ; so, having been made to take off their shoes, I had them brought before me. They were fearful lest we should exact reprisals for having been fired on the previous evening, after the white flag had been displayed, and explained that it was all the fault of the Turks, who had now all gone. Very humbly they asked us to come and take over the town. I replied that we were not in the country to fight the Arabs, but to expel the Turks, that I would accept their explanation of the incident of our being fired on ; and that they must see that order was kept in the town until I had communicated with our General and the troops had marched in. Much relieved, they promised to do this, and I went ashore. I soon found General Melliss and explained the situation, persuading him to bring on some of his Gurkhas to Nasiriya. We managed to pack about fifty of them on board the *Shushan* and the *Massoudieh*, and then steamed up to the town and went alongside the wharf opposite the Turkish barracks which had given us such a warm reception the evening before.

General Melliss came ashore with me, and we hoisted the British flag over the barracks, while a small guard presented arms.

Later on General Gorringe arrived, and the town of Nasiriya was fully taken over, the enemy being found to be in disorderly flight to the northward in the direction of Shattra, on the Shatt al Hai. The day became extremely hot, and a sandstorm added to the general discomfort. Everyone was overtired after the excitement and long hours of the eventful previous day ; and to increase our discomforts we had no fresh food, ice, or any of those things which are necessary to make summer bearable in that country. In addition, our big earthenware water-cooler, a thing which all ships on those rivers carry, had been smashed by a rifle bullet—so we had to use the warm, muddy Euphrates water.

The Euphrates at this point, I might add, was shallow, muddy, quite warm, and brackish-tasting, and full of tortoises and snakes to boot. Little wonder that most of us soon had internal troubles ! Before many days passed I was on an unpleasant diet of condensed milk and sparklet soda.

The troops, now suffering greatly from the heat, marched in during the day, and I remember during the intense heat of the afternoon watching the long-drawn-out tail of exhausted soldiers staggering through the driving sandstorm as they crossed the square opposite the ship.

Suddenly a more than normally dusty specimen, seemingly unable to totter much farther, stopped, and descried our gunboat through the drifting haze. He scanned her for a few moments, and then, recognizing what it was, yelled out " Boat ahoy ! " as loud as a parched throat would permit. This customary hail of ours to passing boats was invariably a great joke among the soldiers, who first thought we were singing out, " You go to hell ! "

Soon there were loud greetings from the sailors, a shout of " Come and park yourself 'ere ! " and with other friends he was soon being restored with draughts of Navy rum from the treasured jar which had mercifully escaped the bullets.

The enemy's strength in the battle was now found to have consisted of 4200 men, with 15 guns and 2 machine-guns on the 23rd of July, while ours at that date had been brought up to about 6300 officers and men, with 22 guns and Maxims, besides the Naval force. We had, however, to leave a large number of sick in camp, the fittest of whom had been armed with rifles, in case of attack by the Arabs, who, as I had said, had been hovering near in large numbers, waiting to see which way the battle would go.

On the 24th our casualties were 104 killed, of whom 5 were British officers, and 429 wounded ; 951 enemy officers and men were captured, with 17 guns, 5 machine-guns, and an immense quantity of rifles, ammunition, and stores. Their casualties were very heavy.

On Monday the 26th of July I proceeded up-river in the *Shushan*, with the *Massoudieh* in company, to reconnoitre, but had to send the latter back after proceeding a few miles, owing to running short of coal, and went on unsupported. Finding all quiet, we pushed on and reached the vicinity of Samawa on the next day, Tuesday. We communicated with Arabs on the bank through our interpreter, Salem, whom I have already referred to. He was a most excellent fellow, of considerable intelligence, and of great value to us on such an occasion as this. When not required onboard for interpreting he often wandered ashore and undertook espionage work for us—indeed, I have known him go into a Turkish battery unnoticed among other natives, and bring us back invaluable details concerning such important items as the gun placements. It was useful to have a semi-official spy attached to the ship. All onboard were delighted when he was awarded the Distinguished Service Medal for his valuable services during this campaign.

On the particular occasion of which I am writing, however, he busied himself questioning the natives we passed on the river-banks. He pointed out one of them to us. The man had asked Salem if we were Turks !

I was writing in my cabin when I heard him talking rather more loudly to another one. Then I heard one of the sailors ask, " What's the black blighter putting across ? " " He want to know what we doing here," said Salem. " Tell the old boy we've finished off all the blinkin' Turks at Nasiriya, an' we're just crusin' round lookin' fer some more," said the sailor, who had evidently taken our recent success to heart.

Stopping a few miles below Samawa, we got hold of and sent into the town an Arab with a friendly message to the *sheikh*. Very soon we received the reply that the small Turkish garrison had fled, and were invited to enter. This we did, and anchored where the river passes through the centre of the town, just to the east of the bridge of boats.

Viewed from this spot, the picturesque town, with yellow picturesque-shaped buildings, and mosques crowding the hillside, and reflecting the sun's almost tropic brilliance, might have been a scene taken straight from *The Arabian Nights*.

Samawa is of some importance as a centre of trade on the Euphrates. It is situated seventy-one miles above Nasiriya, and near the point where the Hindiya and Hilla barrages reunite. With a population of about 10,000, it was on the Turkish telegraph-line, and the headquarters of a Turkish *kaza* in the *sanjak* of Diwaniyeh. The Turks maintained there a small garrison and police force, who had fled on hearing of our victory at Nasiriya. On our approach it was evident that great excitement thrilled the town. As we steamed up to the bridge of boats we were the centre of interest for thousands of Arabs crowded along the waterside and on the roofs of houses. The only ones not interested apparently were those who were still busy looting the Turkish barracks. The *sheikh*, Syyd Taffar, together with the notables of the town, came onboard and asked that the British should occupy the place. I accordingly told him that I would at once communicate with the General, whom it seemed advisable to say was close behind us. I also signed a document giving the *sheikh* permission to look after the Turkish Government buildings until our return, and have often wondered since what he did with it.

We left about 2 P.M., and got back to Nasiriya late that night, where I at once saw General Gorringe. Our information was wired to headquarters at Basra and communicated to the Indian Government. No advance farther than Nasiriya, was, however, carried out at this time.

Every one in the force were much gratified by receiving on the 28th of July a message of congratulation from His Majesty the King.

We in the Navy were also much flattered by the reference to our efforts made by Sir John Nixon in his dispatches, wherein he expressed deep appreciation of the valuable and wholehearted co-operation of the officers and men of the Royal Navy under my command, and added that it was in great measure due to our work that these amphibious operations were brought to so successful a conclusion.

On Wednesday the 28th of July I returned with most of the Naval officers and men from the sternwheelers to our sloops at Chabaish, leaving only a small Naval detachment behind. We had the greatest difficulty in getting back across the shallow Hammar Lake ; still more in navigating the *Espiègle* and the *Odin* down the falling river to Basra, where we arrived on the 30th of July. The *Sumana* was also brought back from Nasiriya a week or so later, as she was required for further operations on the Tigris.

At this time a message came from the Admiralty to say

that the Persian Gulf and Mesopotamia Divisions were henceforth to be separated, Commodore Drury St. A. Wake, R.N., taking command of the Persian Gulf, and myself of the Mesopotamia Division, whose southern boundary was to be Fao, at the entrance of the Shatt al Arab.

A message from the Admiralty had also insisted that all Naval officers and ratings employed in the river should take turns to recuperate their health at the Naval hill-camp at Diyatalawa, in Ceylon, so I proceeded there in the *Espiègle*, leaving Captain Colin Mackenzie behind in the *Clio* to carry out the duties of Senior Naval Officer.

The sea-voyage, the change of scene, and life in the hill-camp undoubtedly worked wonders with our health, and probably saved many lives. It made one feel proud of Admiralty methods, and impressed the Army, that such care was taken of our welfare.

We had an awful trip south in the strength of the monsoon, the little sloop tumbling about, and being washed down fore and aft. One lugubrious Marine was overheard to opine that we were surely bound for Davy Jones's locker. However, at last we staggered into Bombay, and then crawled down to Ceylon, needing a refit as much as any sloop ever did, I should think. So the ship had her refit at Colombo, and the sailors their spell in camp, 5000 feet up in the Ceylon hill-country.

In due course ship and company returned with energy renewed to the campaign on the rivers.

The next few pages deal with affairs in Mesopotamia and operations carried out during my absence. They intend to show the sequence of events leading up to the battle of Ctesiphon, at the commencement of which I rejoined the flotilla.

CHAPTER VIII

OUR FIRST CAPTURE OF KUT

BRITISH control had thus been established on the western side of the Basra *vilayet*, but the district lying north and west of the line Amara–Nasiriya still remained outside our control. Strong Turkish forces under Nur-ud-Din Bey were reported to be concentrating at Kut, and he had attempted to cause a diversion by pushing strong detachments to within thirty miles of Amara, while our attention and most of our troops were concentrated on the Euphrates.

The advance to Nasiriya had been advocated and agreed to on both political and military grounds ; a proposal to advance to Kut al Amara had also been made. After considerable discussion between the authorities in India, at home, and on the spot—which we need not detail here—it was finally decided to make the advance.

It was put forward that to hold the ends of the Shatt al Hai would be desirable for strategical reasons. Although it was afterwards found that the Shatt al Hai was navigable only part of the year, this suggestion carried weight. It was also advocated on account of its effect on the Arabs, and as affording a good base for a possible later advance on Baghdad, a project—influenced also at this time by the vicinity of Russian forces south of Lake Van—which certainly loomed in the background.

It being decided that the occupation of Kut should be the next objective of the Expedition, the transfer of troops towards Amara was commenced immediately after Nasiriya was occupied.

Kut al Amara (usually known simply as Kut, and pronounced " Kut," when it should be " Koot ") was a town of some five or six thousand inhabitants on the left bank of the Tigris, about 204 miles below Baghdad by river, and 112 by road. Of importance, as it was at the junction of the communications by river of the Tigris and Shatt al Hai, and of the road communications between the towns on their banks, it was in Turkish times the headquarters of a *kaza* in the Baghdad *sanjak ;* had a small garrison, police, harbour-master, and customs house ; and was a centre of considerable grain traffic. The little town, which stands in a loop of the Tigris, fringed with gardens and date-palms, has a few fairly well-built houses and a quay on the river.

As we have noted elsewhere, General Townshend had pushed forward a small force, supported by the *Comet* and the *Shaitan*, from Amara, and had occupied Kumait, twenty-nine miles above that town, on the 30th of June. On July the 8th the *Shaitan* and a paddle-steamer recon-noitred about thirty-eight miles farther up the Tigris, where, near Filafilah, they encountered an enemy steamer armed with guns, and a Thornycroft launch with pom-poms, which, after an exchange of shots, retreated under cover of guns in prepared positions on the banks of the river.

It was afterwards learned that the Turks had occupied this Filafilah position on the day before. Their strength was about 200 infantry, with guns and cavalry ; and there was also a similar force about sixteen miles farther up-river at Ali Gharbi, which was expecting reinforcements.

Periodical gunboat patrols were continued, and the two steamers were again observed in this vicinity on the 12th of July, and promptly drew the fire of four guns. Reports also came in that the enemy at Filafilah had been reinforced again, as well as at the village of Sheikh Saad, and at Ess Sinn ; it was therefore found advisable to withdraw our small force from Kumait, which was later occupied by hostile Arabs. A river column of river-steamers, having troops on board, together with the *Comet* and the *Shaitan*, was instituted, and on the 22nd arrived there under rifle-fire. Our column replied, shelling the fort. On hearing the news of our victory of the 24th, and of the occupation of Nasiriya, however, the enemy fell back on the Tigris, and by the end of the month were generally retiring towards Kut.

On August the 1st a detachment from the 6th Indian Division at Amara, under General Delamain, advanced up the Tigris in river-steamers, accompanied by armed launches. Ali Gharbi was occupied without opposition, and under cover of this detachment the concentration of our troops was later carried out.

Ali Gharbi is a small town of three hundred or four hundred houses on the right bank of the Tigris, about seventy-eight miles by river from Amara ; it was the headquarters of a *nahiye* in the *kaza* of Amara in Turkish times, and they had here a customs house and Zaptieh[1] post. The river at this part is from 300 to 350 yards wide, and the banks slightly increase in height above it.

The concentration was a slow process, owing to the difficulties and delays encountered by the shipping in crossing the Hammar Lake and in navigating the rivers in this low-water season. There were, of course, at this time no railways in the country to relieve the pressure. It was, therefore, not until September the 11th that the 6th Division, under General Townshend, was concentrated at Ali Gharbi. Thence the advance was continued, most of the troops marching along the river-bank, with the Naval flotilla and shipping near them, struggling through the shallow river. Sannaiyat was reached by the 16th, the enemy's outposts falling back without offering any opposition.

Intense heat prevailed during this period, with temperatures varying from 110° F. to 116° F. in the shade. The column halted at Sannaiyat until the 25th, having to pause to send back shipping to bring up guns and supplies. The men must have been thankful for the respite. During this delay the column was joined by additional reinforcements. Four seaplanes (under Squadron-Commander Gordon, R.M.), which had been employed in the operations against the *Königsberg*, in East Africa, arrived at Basra on September the 5th, and were got to the front most expeditiously, within a week.

Townshend's military force now consisted of nearly 11,000 men, with 28 guns and 40 machine-guns. General Nixon had come up-river, but only to be on the spot in case

[1] Turkish police

questions of policy arose, and he did not interfere with Townshend's arrangements.

Skirmishes now frequently took place between our cavalry and the enemy outposts ; constant naval and air reconnaissances were carried out, considerable information being gained regarding the enemy's forces, which were commanded by Nur-ud-Din Bey, and found to be occupying a formidable prepared position astride the Tigris some seven miles north-east of, and covering, Kut—eight miles from General Townshend's force at Sannaiyat. Their entrenchments continued for several miles on each flank, with the river blocked by a boom composed of barges and wire cables, commanded at close range from both banks by guns and fire-trenches. In front of the entrenchments and redoubts were barbed-wire entanglements, pits, and land-mines ; and behind were miles of communication trenches.

The 35th Division of the Turkish Army held the right, or southern, the 38th the left bank. They had four battalions of army troops in reserve, near a bridge of boats about five miles above the main position, and it was learned subsequently that they had 38 guns. Their mounted troops, comprising two regiments of cavalry and 400 camelry, under the command of Subri Bey, a dashing cavalry leader, were most of them absent during the battle, carrying out a daring and destructive raid against our communications near Sheikh Saad. In addition, there was a number of Arab horsemen operating on the Turkish left flank, to the northward. On September 26th General Townshend advanced to Nukhailat, some three and a half to four miles from the Turkish position. He decided to make his main attack on the northern bank, but, as a feint, disposed his troops beforehand, so as to give the enemy the impression that he intended to make his attack on both banks. In this he was entirely successful.

He divided his force into two columns. Column A, the principal force, was to demonstrate against the enemy's southern defences, on the right bank, then, moving across the river by boat-bridge, make its decisive attack on the northern flank. While this was going on Column B was to advance on the left bank, against the enemy's centre, and pin him to his trenches. It was arranged that the Naval flotilla was to co-operate with the force by moving up the river and protecting the flank of Column B.

The Naval vessels in this manœuvre consisted of the *Comet* (Lieutenant-in-Command W. V. H. Harris, D.S.O.), the *Shaitan* (Lieutenant-in-Command Mark Singleton, D.S.O.), the *Sumana* (Sub-Lieutenant-in-Command L. C. P. Tudway), four 4·7-inch guns in horse-boats, under Lieutenant M. A. B. Johnston, R.A., and Gunner J. Mackay, R.N., and also two small steam-launches, R.N.1 and R.N.2, for towing purposes.

This flotilla was under the orders of Lieutenant-Commander Cookson, who was at the time Senior Naval Officer ; for Captain Colin Mackenzie, who had relieved me of that duty during my absence in Ceylon, had been invalided to hospital with malaria.

On arrival at Nukhailat the boat-bridge was thrown across the river, and on the morning of the 27th of September, Column B, under General Fry, advanced, covered by the artillery and Naval guns, and established themselves some two thousand yards from the centre of the enemy's horse-shoe position. Meanwhile Column A, under General Delamain, made demonstrations on the right bank during the 27th, withdrew under cover of night, according to plan, and crossed to the left bank. They were deployed by 5 A.M. on the 28th, attacking at a point some eight thousand yards east of the northern section of the hostile position, and by 2 P.M. the whole position north of the Suwada Marsh was in their hands. The 16th and 17th Brigades reformed at 4 P.M. on the north-west corner of the Suwada Marsh.

In the centre, Column B had closed on the enemy at 6 A.M., but received orders not to make a decisive attack until the turning attack by Column A had developed further. At 11 A.M. the enemy south of the river stirred themselves, and pushed forward a column to enfilade them ; but the Naval flotilla, which during the night had brought forward the Naval 4·7-inch guns, besides military 4-inch and 5-inch guns mounted in barges, now advanced, shelled the enemy, and speedily drove them back to their entrenchments.

At 5.45 A.M. the 4·7-inch guns also opened fire on the

enemy's right-bank position, were received with an accurate shellfire, and at 11 A.M. the gunboats moved up to closer range, abreast of Saffa Mound, also coming under shellfire and intermittent rifle-fire, the *Comet* being hit by a shell on the funnel.

Column B again worked forward in the afternoon, under cover of the very effective support of its guns, and those of the gunboats, which, as General Nixon stated in his report, practically silenced the Turkish guns.

Column A had by this time reformed, and about 5 P.M. commenced advancing to assist Column B by attacking the enemy in the rear, but half an hour later, when some three thousand yards west of his objective, General Delamain found that strong hostile reinforcements were advancing from the southward. These turned out to be the Turkish general reserves. He immediately changed his objective, and, forming front to the south, attacked them with his whole force. As the official report states, our infantry had shown sings of weariness and exhaustion after their long and trying exertions in the extreme heat ; but the prospect of getting at the enemy with the bayonet gave them new life. They delivered a most gallant attack, routing the Turks, and capturing four guns. The Turks, after a stubborn fight, made good their escape in the darkness, and Delamain's force, now completely exhausted, bivouacked for the night.

About 6 P.M. General Townshend sent a seaplane to acquaint the flotilla of General Delamain's success, also requesting the Senior Naval Officer to proceed up to, examine, and if possible, destroy the obstruction across the river. He was convinced that the Turks would retreat, and wished thus to enable the pursuit to be pressed home by water as well as by land. After dark therefore, at about 6.30, the three gunboats, followed by launch R.N.1, moved stealthily up-river for this purpose, showing no lights.

When near the obstruction a very heavy rifle- and machine-gun-fire was opened on them from trenches lining both banks of the river. The obstruction was found to consist of two iron lighters, with a *mahela* in the centre. An attempt to sink the *mahela* by ramming it proving unsuccessful, gallant Lieutenant-Commander Cookson, who was

L

onboard the *Comet*, ordered her to be placed alongside. Under the menace of almost certain death, he himself jumped into the *mahela* and with an axe attempted to cut the wire hawsers securing it to the two iron lighters. He immediately came under heavy rifle-fire, was hit with bullets in several places, and was finally helped back onboard the *Comet*, where he died within ten minutes. To quote the wording of General Townshend's dispatch : " He found that he could not send a man over the ship's side to cut away the obstruction because it meant certain death, so he took an axe, and went himself."

Cookson was a great loss to us. His dash and bravery had shone conspicuously even amid the high level of those qualities which obtained in the Naval forces that I had the honour to command. He was awarded a posthumous V.C. for this devoted self-sacrifice. Twelve men, including four of the Royal West Kent Regiment, who were serving onboard, and two Goanese, were hit at about the same time. As it was clear that nothing further could be done under such a heavy fire—at ranges from 75 to 100 yards—Lieutenant Harris, the commanding officer of the *Comet*, decided to withdraw. He signalled to the remainder accordingly, and they dropped back and anchored in Nukhailat reach for the night.

Lieutenant Mark Singleton of the *Shaitan* now became Senior Naval Officer, and on the following morning—that is, the 29th of September—the gunboats again proceeded up the river, the *Shaitan*, which led, was fired on once, howbeit ineffectually, by an old muzzle-loading gun dug into the bank abreast of the obstruction, and manned by two Turks, who were subsequently captured.

These were the only enemy seen near the river, the main body having fled during the night. Aeroplane reconnaissance ascertained that they were in full retreat towards Baghdad.

The gunboats finally got through the obstruction, arrived off Kut about 10 A.M., and continued in chase of the enemy's steamers, which were fleeing up-river. However, owing chiefly to the extremely difficult nature of the navigation, due to the lower river-level, it was not until the following morning, the 30th, that two of them—the armed tug *Pioneer* and the new steamer *Basra*—were sighted. By this time the *Sumana* had broken both rudders by grounding, while the *Shaitan* had been hit by a shell from the Turkish rearguard, and was stuck in the shallows near Kut; so the *Comet* pressed on alone and engaged the steamers, being joined by the *Shaitan* when she got afloat again.

It was not long before the *Basra* showed signs of having been badly hit. Dropping two *mahelas* full of ammunition, which she was towing, she fled up-river out of range with the *Shaitan* and the *Comet* struggling through the shallow water in desperate and eager pursuit. About noon, however, fire was suddenly opened on our two ships from astern, by two enemy mountain guns, which were afterwards found to belong to an enemy mounted detachment that had been sent down below our force to carry out a daring and destructive raid on our lines of communication. At the time of their firing on the two gunboats they were returning to rejoin their main body. The *Shaitan* had just stuck again, and for a while the gunboats were in a very precarious position, with considerable chance of being cut off from our forces, who were far behind; but fortunately the *Shaitan* was got on the move again just in time, and they eventually arrived back safely at Kut.

In the successful battle of Kut the Turks had lost about 4000 men, including 1153 prisoners, who had fallen into our hands, together with 14 guns and a large quantity of ammunition and stores. Only the low state of the Tigris, hampering our movements, and the skill of their withdrawal saved them from a far greater loss. The British casualties had been 1233, of whom 94 were killed—this small number being, as General Nixon expressed in his report, due to Townshend's masterly scheme of turning the Turkish left wing and his ruse on the southern bank of the river.

CHAPTER IX

THE BATTLE OF CTESIPHON

WITH our arrival at Kut al Amara, the headlong retreat of the Turkish forces, and our occupation of Kut al Amara was brought up again the question of an advance to Baghdad.

The possibility of the capture of Baghdad had, as we have noted before, always been in the background of our considerations and plans ; and, although put off on former occasions, it now came prominently to the fore. It also appeared desirable that, if we were going on, we should take advantage of the confusion of the Turkish retreat and push ahead as soon as possible.

Between the Home Government and War Office, the Viceroy and heads of the Indian Army, and the generals on the spot the question was again discussed. Multitudes of private telegrams, personal telegrams, official telegrams, and clear-line telegrams—in fact, every sort and kind of telegram—were exchanged, and a multitude of appreciations called for from Staffs—General Staffs and War Staffs.

Finally it was decided that the reinforcements needed to hold Baghdad after capture could be sent. General Nixon was confident that he could beat the remnant of Nur-ud-Din's army, the only remaining enemy then known to be between him and Baghdad.

The possibility of failure at the Dardanelles had been a potent factor in this decision, thus taken partly in order to restore our prestige in the East. We had, as we have seen, in the first place gone to Mesopotamia in order to protect our oil supply and influence the tribes ; and it was then decided to hold the port of Basra, at the head of the Persian Gulf. But one thing leads to another—we had then taken

Kurna to protect Basra, and later Nasiriya for the same reason, and next Amara, to make the oil and our position still more secure. It had then been decided that the line Kut al Amara–Nasiriya was a better line for defence and also for influencing the Arabs.

Now our difficulties at the Dardanelles were leading us on to a premature attempt on Baghdad. Our force had so far invaded successfully an enemy's country. It was the only invasion of considerable enemy territory at the commencement of the Great War. Some enemy colonies had been taken, but in France and Belgium we were ourselves helping our allies against invaders.

Here, in Mesopotamia, we were invading enemy territory. All had been made possible by command of the sea, which had made practicable our skilfully planned surprise arrival in the country. This, also, made it possible to obtain supplies, and to stay here. Command of the river arteries of communication had given us the advantages of interior lines, and had made it possible also for us to shift troops rapidly from place to place, deliver sudden and smashing blows, and reap advantages of swift and harrying pursuit. We had stretched the line of our communications to the utmost that our small equipment of shallow-draught steamers could manage in supplying the troops. Now we proposed to stretch it farther, and that, too, at the worst season for navigation in those shallow rivers. What wonder that the line would stretch no more, but snapped ? In the broiling sands of the desert, with tired infantry, bogged guns, and foundered horses, we were to compete with the dusty marching Turk and his nomad Arabs.

This question of provision of light-draught steamers and railways, should an advance to Baghdad be contemplated, had been raised at the joint meeting of the Naval and Military chiefs and Staffs on our first arrival at Basra, at which I had been present ; and, I suppose, was referred to India, but shelved owing to our uncertain policy at that time.

Also it should be remembered that the force had been operating continually all summer ; that in the Indian regiments there was a serious shortage of their familiar, irreplaceable British officers ; and that we were meeting more, better disciplined and equipped, German-staffed Turkish forces.

To return to the narrative, however. On the 1st of October the *Sumana* was sent to Basra for repairs, but the *Shaitan* and the *Comet* continued up-river, convoying four river-steamers carrying General Townshend and a brigade. After four days' passage, a large part of which was spent aground, they reached Aziziya, about ninety miles above Kut, and thirty below Ctesiphon. There an advanced post was formed, for the enemy had already reached his prepared position at Ctesiphon, covering the road to Baghdad, whence reinforcements joined him.

During the six weeks following the arrival of our advanced troops on October 5th at Aziziya, reinforcements, supplies, and transport animals were brought up, preparatory to a further advance up the Tigris. The *Comet* in the interim had time to reach Basra and undergo the repairs necessary to her improvised gun-mountings, which had been a severe strain on her lightly constructed hull and decks.

Reconnaissance by aircraft and cavalry soon disclosed the fact that the enemy had pushed out advanced detachments to Kutuniya and Zor, about seven and fourteen miles respectively above Aziziya, and frequent skirmishes occurred between their outposts and ours, affording evidence that our farther advance would be vigorously resisted. The attitude of the Arabs also changed to one of open hostility ; attacking outlying posts, raiding, and sniping the shipping, many of these attacks, of course, being instigated or helped by the Turks.

The permission to advance on Baghdad reached Townshend on October the 26th with news that reinforcements would be sent to him. On the night of the 27th and 28th he made a successful raid on the Turkish detachment at Kutuniya, and then returned to Aziziya. This had an excellent effect on our men, who, though suffering a good deal from sickness, and worn with the long summer campaign, were confident of beating the Turks and of capturing Baghdad. Meanwhile reports spoke ominously of coming Turkish reinforcements ; but, owing to our shortage of aeroplanes, the long-distance reconnaissances necessary in the circumstances could not be undertaken at the critical time.

On the 11th of November our advanced forces, accompanied by the *Sumana*, occupied Kutuniya, where the entire force arrived by the 18th. Continuing this advance movement up the left bank on next day, Zor was occupied, and then Lajj on the 20th. Only slight opposition was met with. Here—in Lajj—Townshend made his final preparation for attacking the Turks at Ctesiphon. He decided to advance only on the left bank, and turn the Turkish left; thus, as we shall see, circumscribing very much the gunboats' value later.

News was pouring in now of the approach of Turkish reinforcements under Von der Goltz and Halil Bey, but no proof of any large numbers within striking distance was received. Major Reilly, our intrepid airman, when flying over Ctesiphon had descried the true numbers and state of the enemy forces, but unfortunately he was shot down and captured, and we were left without this priceless information.

The Turkish combatant strength at Ctesiphon on the 21st of November consisted of about 18,000 rifles, 52 guns, 19 machine-guns, and 400 cavalry, besides several thousand Arabs.

The enemy position lay astride the Tigris, covering the approach to Baghdad, from which city it is situated some eighteen miles to the south-eastward. The defences, which formed two main positions, and one beyond the Diyala river, had been under construction for some months; fairly accurate knowledge of the position had been obtained by the efforts of the Royal Flying Corps and officers of the R.N.A.S. There were a first and second line of entrenchments on each bank, and in rear of the second line of the left bank was a bridge of boats. Farther to the rear again the Diyala river, near its junction with the Tigris, was bridged at two points, and entrenchments commanded the crossings.

The first line of the Turks had been most thoroughly prepared on each bank, but principally on the northern, where it extended for about six miles to the north-eastward, following a line of low, dun-coloured mounds, with redoubts and trenches protected for the most part by barbed-wire entanglements. In this vicinity is the great Arch of Ctesiphon ; and two narrow ridges, about forty or fifty feet high, called " High Wall " are outstanding landmarks. The latter were in about the centre of the first Turkish line.

The Arch of Ctesiphon is the only edifice remaining sufficiently entire to show what a splendid city once stood hereabout. It is built of brick, and is part of the great central hall, the only remaining section of the great palace of Chosroes. It provides a landmark for miles around. The ancient city of Ctesiphon, which surrounded it, rose into importance when the city of Seleucia, on the opposite bank, declined, and it was for long the capital of the Parthian kings, and then of the Sassanids. It fell into the hands of the Roman Emperor Severus about A.D. 232.

In 637 it was seized by the Arabs, and after this date the city rapidly declined. The modern name of the place is Sulman Pak—after the barber of Mohammed, who is said to be buried nearby. Ctesiphon is thus a neighbourhood where armies have fought since the dawn of history, and it is interesting to consider what great historic figures had passed this way before the coming of the men in khaki, with their aeroplanes and wireless.

General Townshend's force amounted to 14,000 combatants, with 35 guns and 5 aeroplanes. The Naval force consisted of H.M.S. *Firefly* (Lieutenant-in-Command Christopher J. F. Eddis, R.M.), the *Comet* (Lieutenant-in-Command G. E. Harden, R.N.), the *Shaitan* (Lieutenant-in-Command Aubrey C. Thursfield, R.N.), the *Sumana* (Sub-Lieutenant-in-Command Lionel C. P. Tudway, R.N.), and in addition there were present the four Naval 4·7-inch guns, as usually, mounted in horse-boats, with the *Shushan* (Lieutenant-in-Command F. W. Lyte, D.S.C., R.N.R.) and the *Massoudieh* (Lieutenant F. C. Henry, Indian Army, in command) to tow them. The *Shushan* and the *Massoudieh* each mounted a pom-pom and Maxim.

I arrived at the front on the morning of the 22nd, having only recently returned from Ceylon in the *Espiègle*, and encountered great delay, like every one else, in getting up the river in small craft. Frequently we were aground for hours at a time. I had thus had no opportunity to discuss affairs with General Townshend, and, in especial, his plan of not advancing on the right bank of the river.

I got there, however, just before the battle commenced, and directed the Naval part of the operation from the *Comet* or the *Firefly*, as occasion demanded. The *Firefly* was the first of the new " small China gunboats," which were sent out in pieces from England and put together at Abadan by Messrs. Yarrow. She carried a 4-inch Mark VII gun, a six-pounder, Maxims, and was equipped with wireless.

General Townshend, after a night march from Lajj on the 21st–22nd, attacked the enemy position on the left bank at the centre, and on the north-east flank about 8 A.M. A severe fight lasted throughout the day, resulting in the capture of the enemy's first-line position and of more than 1300 prisoners. All the British forces remained on the left (north-east) bank throughout the operations, the plan of attack being briefly as follows :

The British force was divided into four bodies—viz., Columns A, B, and C, and a flying column. Column C was to make the first attack at dawn on the 22nd, against the enemy's centre—near what was later called the Water Redoubt—to establish themselves within long rifle-range of the enemy, making a great display, so as to pin him down, causing him to bring up reserves to his menaced position. The column was to remain there until Column A moved forward, when, having got into the enemy's position, Column C was to sweep south and assist the Naval flotilla.

After the battle had well commenced Column B, on the right, was to advance upon the enemy left and rear and menace his retreat, and the flying column (consisting mostly of cavalry and base artillery) was to co-operate in this manœuvre, making a considerable *détour* on Column B's outer flank against the enemy's rear, threatening his line of retreat.

Column A (the strongest column), under General Delamain, would be ordered forward as soon as the enemy felt the turning attack of Column B. Column A would then attack the strong redoubts marked " V.P." on its officers'

maps, to the left of the enemy position. (" V.P." stood for
" vital point " in General Townshend's orders.) With
its advance the whole force would move forward to the
attack, all possible guns firing on " V.P."

The Naval flotilla was to operate from the river as circumstances permitted. Its first objective was to be a
redoubt at which, our aeroplanes reported, the Turks were
busy digging, near Bustan. The next point of attack was
the enemy trenches, in support of Column C. The flotilla
was also to watch carefully for any hostile infantry advance
along the right bank directed towards our boat-bridge at
Lajj. As regards pursuit, a free hand was left to the Senior
Naval Officer.

Thus it will be seen that at the commencement of the
battle only the enemy force on the left bank of the river,
and only the northern half of their position on that bank,
was to be seriously attacked. It was hoped that we should
roll up this flank of the enemy's position. In this event our
cavalry were to cut off the enemy's retreat up the river,
somewhere in the neighbourhood of the Diyala river. This
would have left the enemy only one bridge of boats by which
to escape, and this, in turn, might be destroyed later by
artillery fire, or a bomb from an aeroplane. So much for
our arrangements.

As previously decided, the gunboats moved from our
advanced base at Lajj on the evening of November the
21st, followed by the naval 4·7-inch and two military 5-inch
guns, which were mounted in barges. They took up a
position overnight for bombarding the redoubt near Bustan
at daylight. On the way the *Firefly* and the *Shaitan*, which
were leading, ran into an ambush of snipers—who had been
lying in wait for them on the bank—and had rather a lively
ten minutes before they cleared that particular hornet's
nest, the *Firefly* sustaining one casualty. At daylight next
morning (November 22nd), for about an hour, the Naval
flotilla bombarded the position on the river-bank near
Bustan, where the redoubt was reported to be, though no
sign was seen of any redoubt, nor could one be found when
the ships moved on afterwards.

Preliminary military movements proceeded according to

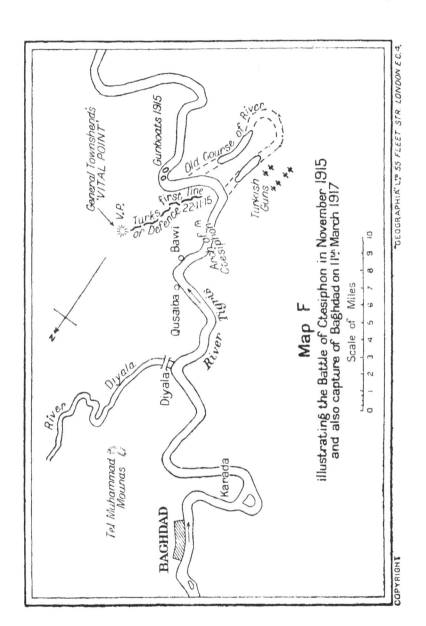

Map F

illustrating the Battle of Ctesiphon in November 1915
and also capture of Baghdad on 11th March 1917

Scale of Miles

plan, but it was not long before the enemy had knowledge of them. After a few hours' rest the British troops rose in the cold dawn of the 22nd, and, handicapped considerably by a shrouding mist, Column C advanced. Just before 7 A.M. the battle commenced, the guns of the Naval flotilla opening fire.

The gunboats tried in vain all day to advance, and also on the days that followed, but the enemy guns—some of heavy calibre—placed on the right bank, commanded the reach which runs south-south-west after passing Bustan. Throughout the ensuing three days' battle the Naval 4·7-inch guns and Army 5-inch guns remained approximately in the same position, bombarding various points in the enemy's lines according to conditions and circumstances. As the river-banks at this point were about fifteen feet high, these guns were invisible to the enemy. The country everywhere about was dead flat, and consequently they had to use indirect fire, which was a considerable handicap. The four gunboats meanwhile cruised in the reach, south of Bustan, but on the 23rd and 24th managed at intervals to get round the bend into the next reach. This bend, how-ever, was rather an unhealthy place, for the Turks had apparently got all the ranges near here marked off, with forward observers out, and they made some very good shooting. Since General Townshend's plan of battle was to attack only on the left bank, and did not allow of any of our troops advancing on the right bank, these enemy guns on the right bank were able to hold up the advance of the flotilla during the whole period.

During the forenoon of November 22nd the Turkish river craft were seen to move down, evidently embarking the Turkish infantry from the right bank prior to taking them farther up-river. The enemy had no doubt soon deduced the fact that the British attack was to be entirely on the left bank, as had been the case at Kut. Besides, on this bank was the shortest road to Baghdad. The gunboats, which had great difficulty in making any satisfactory shooting over the high river-banks, engaged the enemy's ships, which retreated up-river. The operations continued on the 23rd, 24th, and 25th of November, during most of

which time the flotilla was under a heavy fire from the
Turkish guns, especially those before mentioned on the right
bank, which were well dug in, and most difficult to locate
from the river, while, of course, the gunboats' masts and
funnels provided good marks for the enemy gunners. The
Comet was hit at her port quarter on the waterline on
November 22nd, but luckily it was found possible to execute
repairs there and then, and a nasty leak was stopped.
Otherwise she would have been forced to withdraw from the
action.

On shore the turning movement of the enemy's left
began about 8.30 A.M. and shortly afterwards the general
advance of the whole force was launched. In spite of strong
opposition, however, and although brought to a standstill
for a while by the barbed-wire entanglements, our force
captured the " V.P. " position shortly after 10 A.M. But
our loss was heavy ; and, furthermore, the turning attack
to the northward was checked. Further advance from
" V.P." however, showed that the enemy were defending
their second line, it very soon became clear that the enemy
was stronger in numbers and *morale* than had been antici-
pated, and that, in short, the battle was by no means over.

Our troops penetrated to the enemy's second line,
capturing eight guns, and establishing themselves in their
trenches, but once in their new position they were subjected
to fresh counter-attacks, as the enemy were reinforced. The
captured guns changed hands several times amid some
fierce and grim fighting. Finally these guns had to be
abandoned, as before nightfall it was found necessary to
withdraw our force from the positions they had gained
nearby, and in that segment of the enemy second line
neighbouring the " V.P. " position.

General Townshend had decided that he could not do
more that day. He would concentrate and reorganize there.
As the exhausted troops came in, and the heavy tale of
casualties was told, it became patent, however, that the
offensive could not be resumed next day. Our casualties
had been very heavy, some 4500 killed, wounded, and
missing, out of 14,000 combatants. The Turks, too, had
suffered great losses.

On the 23rd our troops were still under heavy shellfire. Owing to continued heavy losses it was considered inadvisable to renew the offensive ; while a dust-storm blowing up further delayed reorganization. So the troops remained in the positions they had captured, and every effort was made to evacuate the large number of wounded to the transport steamers lying at Lajj.

General Townshend then decided to hold a position near the " High Wall " of Ctesiphon, where he could water from the river. Accordingly he moved part of the force there on the 23rd. But owing to heavy counter-attacks by the Turks on the night of the 23rd, this movement was not completed until the 24th, a day which passed more quietly.

On this day I had sent Lieutenant Hugh Lincoln, R.N.R., ashore to obtain information from the General Officer Commanding, communication by wireless and otherwise between the troops and the ships having been scanty. He managed to get back to me on the 25th, with valuable information.

As the battery on the right bank had not opened fire on the 25th, I proceeded during the forenoon a little farther up-river in the *Sumana*, the handiest ship I had, landed, and was able to find and confer with General Townshend, who was then with most of the troops near the high wall in the vicinity of the Arch of Ctesiphon. The Turkish guns, however, opened a heavy fire again about midday, and the ships that had moved up the reach had to drop back. It seems likely that these guns had been abandoned by the Turks, but that upon the arrival of their reinforcements, and after discovering, too, that our forces had fallen back, they again manned them. Anyway, they kept up a heavy fire on both ships and troops throughout the rest of the day, the ships and guns replying vigorously. Later on the 25th our air reconnaissance reported a fresh movement of large columns, estimated at three enemy divisions, coming from the direction of the Diyala river. General Townshend considering his force too weak to engage in another battle against such odds, decided to fall back under cover of darkness on the river transport at Lajj. As he stated in his report, " My duty seemed clear to extricate and preserve my division by a steady retirement until near enough to our own reinforcements to be able to make a stand."

Thus ended the battle of Ctesiphon, during which our troops had fought with the utmost gallantry, though sustaining appalling losses. Of the 317 British officers 130 had been killed and wounded ; the 255 Indian officers were reduced in number by 111 ; and there had been 4200 casualties among the rank and file, out of about 14,000 men. The Turkish losses also had been very heavy, a Turkish account placing them at 9500, including desertions.

The evacuation of our wounded to Lajj proved to be a difficult task. The medical *personnel* was insufficient, stores were inadequate, and means of transport insufficient. The resource, energy, and physical powers of our medical officers were taxed to the utmost. The Mesopotamian Commission afterwards gave them very great credit for their achievements in the face of considerable difficulties.

CHAPTER X

THE RETREAT FROM CTESIPHON

GENERAL TOWNSHEND marched at about eight o'clock at night on November 25th, preceded by his transport, and reached Lajj during the night. He had notified us by wireless, which I received about 2 A.M. on the 26th, and I sent the 4·7- and 5-inch guns on, following with the *Comet* and the *Firefly* as a rearguard. We encountered no enemy, and reached Lajj during the forenoon.

Meanwhile the Turks, hearing of our retreat, were hastily reoccupying their Ctesiphon position, and Nur-ud-Din despatched cavalry, camel corps, and Arab levies in pursuit of the British forces. It is of interest to note that Halil Bey, commanding the XVIIIth Corps, arrived from Baghdad on the 25th—his first appearance at the front in Mesopotamia, where he was to be so prominent a figure later.

The same day both the Air Service and Cavalry reported the advance of large columns of enemy, estimated at 12,000, with guns and a cavalry brigade. In this position, so far from bases of supply, with a vulnerable line of communications along the winding and shallow river, General Townshend was in an unfavourable position for defence ; and it was necessary to withdraw farther downstream, to a more secure locality, until conditions might enable a resumption of the offensive. So he continued his retreat in the afternoon, the enemy being only some 6000 yards distant when our columns moved off.

A considerable quantity of stores had to be abandoned, but, leaving tents standing to deceive the enemy, he marched through the night *via* Zor and Kutuniya to

Aziziya. Here he halted for the 28th and 29th, in order, as far as was possible, to evacuate the wounded and to accumulate stores. This was done by the river-steamer *Mejidieh*, with barges, which left for Kut on November the 29th.

It is well again to consider some of the conditions under which the force was operating. The latter was nearly 500 miles up-river from its base, the port of Basra, at the highest point in the Shatt al Arab which sea-going ships can reach. As there were no railways, supplies had to be sent up from the base by river, in shallow-draught steamers, the number of which was very limited, and the majority of which could not at this time get above Kut. Above this place there are many shallow places, limiting river navigation to only about three feet ten inches draught at this the period of lowest river-levels.

These vessels, mostly paddlers and small tugs, would each tow two large steel lighters, one on each side of them, a method which made them most unwieldy. The journey was therefore slow, and it seldom took less than nine or ten days to reach Lajj from Basra ; but frequently considerably longer, depending on the amount of time the ship spent aground in the shallow reaches, where it was often possible to get along only by laying out an anchor and heaving or kedging the ship over the shallow part.

It should be noted also that, besides supplies for the troops, all fodder for horses and mules, firewood, etc. had to be transported by river. There was at that time no such thing as " living on the land " ; the land, through the destruction of the ancient irrigation, had become a desert.

From what I have explained above it will be realized that the army was necessarily accompanied by a miscellaneous, but most unwieldy, collection of barges, lighters, and other river craft. As long as the force was advancing, of course, it did not matter much if one or more of these stuck on a mudbank for twenty-four hours ; but when it came to a retirement it was another matter altogether.

Owing to the tortuous course of the river, we had much farther to go than the Army, who marched direct along the Baghdad road, which runs fairly direct, touching the bends of the river only at certain points. It will be readily seen

M

that this also meant that we were practically out of touch with, and very often some distance away from, the troops. Our very isolation there on the deserted river made us easy marks for sniping Arabs and hostile forces.

It was an unenviable situation ; much of the time being stuck in the river, or trying to move some other craft that was stuck, with the knowledge that a hostile pursuing army was coming along and might arrive on the river-bank with field or mountain guns at any time—or be lined up and awaiting us round the next corner !

Very slow progress was made with the transport barges after leaving Lajj ; they were constantly grounding. The gunboats, which remained behind to set fire to such stores as had to be abandoned, and then acted as rearguard, had great difficulty in towing the barges.

On the 27th of November the gunboats were engaged all day in towing off transport barges which had grounded in the shallows, and about noon the *Comet* and the *Shushan* found that launch " L.3 " had taken a wrong channel, grounded near Zor, and then been abandoned by her crew. The *Shushan*, covered by the *Comet*, managed to extricate her, both ships being sniped by Arab cavalry during the operation.

General Townshend reached Aziziya on the 28th, and the same night the two pursuing Turkish Army Corps were in the vicinity of Zor. That evening both the *Comet* and the *Shaitan* again grounded, some eight miles above Aziziya, having got the transport barges clear away. We remained aground all night under fire from a number of snipers on the banks. During the dark hours it was discovered that the *Shaitan* had sprung a leak. Before it could be stopped the low gunwales of the little tug were submerged, and she was resting on the bottom, in shallow water. She had probably overstrained her light hull during the efforts of the preceding days.

Every endeavour was made to lighten her ; her guns, ammunition, and the rest of her movable equipment being transhipped into a barge, while the *Comet*, the *Firefly*, and the *Shushan* manœuvred to drive off the Arabs, who were lying under cover of the banks, constantly sniping ships and working party at close range. This state of affairs lasted most of the day, until, in response to my wireless request, the General sent out in the afternoon to our assistance the Cavalry Brigade, which had been joined by the 14th Hussars at Aziziya. The troopers charged the Arabs and some Turkish cavalry, getting well into them, and accounting for about 150 : the remainder fled, and for a while the situation was relieved.

After this I went on in the *Comet* to Aziziya, arriving there about 6 P.M., to arrange with General Townshend for an attempt to salve the *Shaitan* the next day ; but while I was at General Headquarters a wireless message arrived from the *Firefly*, stating that the Turks had just opened fire with guns from the left bank on the ships guarding the wrecked *Shaitan*. As it was now evident that the enemy's advance guard had arrived, the submerged vessel had necessarily, howbeit reluctantly, to be abandoned. The enemy's main body was next reported to be at Zor, and General Townshend decided to retreat on Kut, orders being issued for the force to march at 9 A.M. next day (30th) for Umm at Tubul. I asked General Townshend that any craft which could be spared might be sent right through to Kut, without halting each night with the land force. It was arranged that the Naval 4·7-inch and Military 5-inch guns in barges, together with the *Shushan* and the *Massoudieh*, should proceed in this way. These craft got safely to Kut, well clear of the vicissitudes which we, who remained with the troops, were to encounter. I pointed out to the General at the same time the difficulties that the river-transport craft had to cope with, owing to it being the season of low river, and showed him how, because of the wide, sweeping bends in the river, the distance which we had to travel was much greater than that covered by the road between Baghdad and Kut, along which the army was marching.

Next day, November 30th, the remainder of the tugs and barges left at about the same time as the force, the gunboats following and reaching Umm at Tubul, which is south-east-ward of Aziziya, about 2 P.M. It was learned that the army was to halt there for the night. After only a short march of about eight miles the troops arrived and set up camp.

Meanwhile General Townshend had received a message to the effect that the steamer in which the Army Commander, Sir John Nixon, was going down-river, convoyed by the new gunboat *Butterfly*, had been attacked below Kut, near Sheikh Saad, by Arabs. In response to urgent messages he sent on General Melliss's 30th Brigade to reopen the line of communication.

Going ashore to talk matters over with General Townshend that afternoon, I found him seated at a table covered with books on the campaigns of Napoleon, which, as usual, he was studying. I had a long talk with him, and commented on the short distance that had been marched that day, pointing out that the river craft had wasted several useful hours of daylight through anchoring so early, and that it would have been much more advisable for them to have employed this spare time in negotiating the shallow and tortuous Shidhaif Reach, a little farther on, in which we were sure to have trouble with the heavy-laden barges. To have proceeded thus far would have entailed only a little longer march for the troops.

This fact, as I pointed out before, of the river craft having to travel a much greater distance than the troops introduced a considerable element of danger for the gunboats, which were at this time acting as a rearguard ; and, owing to the turns and twists of the river, instead of being in line with the rearguard of the army, they were frequently struggling along many miles behind. If a gunboat then stuck on a mudbank it had to work out its own salvation in a hostile country, as the Arabs invariably turned pugnaciously on the retreating force—not to mention the Turkish cavalry and advance guard, who were following closely.

General Townshend first replied that the troops were very much exhausted, but afterwards took up my suggestion to lengthen slightly the march projected for the next day. Orders had already been issued to march to the vicinity of the north-east end of the Umm-Zanaim Reach, but I pointed out that if the march could be extended to the top of the next farther loop of the river (Nahr Kellack) it would, while entailing only a short extra march for the troops, provide the flotilla with a considerable length of the river to negotiate, and so valuable daylight would not be wasted. The General readily assented to this ; the Chief-of-Staff, Colonel V. W. Evans, C.B., was called up, and the orders were altered accordingly.

It is well to note here that Sir John Nixon, in his dispatch on this subject, appeared to be under a misapprehension. He at first made it appear that the troops and ships were surrounded on the morning of December 1st by the pursuing Turkish Army owing to the troops having been delayed by the ships ; but, as I have striven to point out, this was not the case. The ships were up to the camp early in the afternoon, and could presumably have gone a good way farther before dark, since at the time none of the barges was straggling. As stated above, I had represented this personally to General Townshend after arrival in camp that afternoon, and the march for the next day was lengthened in consequence. On my representations to Sir John later he communicated with the Chief-of-General-Staff, at Simla, who had the *Official Gazette* altered in accordance with my desire (supplement to the *London Gazette* of March 22nd, 1918). A similar misapprehension occurs in General Townshend's report and book ; but it is probably owing to the fact that he and I met again only for a few minutes at Kut, before the siege, that this discrepancy occurs, for we had little time in which to compare notes upon all that had happened.

Orders were therefore given for the retirement on Kut to be continued on the following morning (December 1st).

The British camp at Umm at Tubul was roughly a square in shape, the river its southern side, with the flotilla and barges in the vicinity. I placed the *Firefly* at the south-western corner, as a look-out on the western side ; the *Comet* remaining near the centre, in closer touch with head-quarters.

An anxious and disturbed night was passed at the camp. It was attacked after dark—between 8 and 9 P.M.—and the Turks fired some light shells. The *Firefly* switched on a searchlight and returned the fire but, being twice hit, she switched off. Luckily, shortly afterwards the Turks ceased firing.

The Turkish main force had moved from Kutuniya some time about midday, and, after pausing awhile at Aziziya, left that place about sunset, in pursuit of the British. Their reports state that they saw our lights about 7 P.M., and, being fired on, they replied ; that later for a few minutes, a British searchlight was turned on, but on their opening fire with field-guns the lights were extinguished.

Nur-ud-Din came to the conclusion that the British with whom he had caught up were a weak rearguard, who probably retired in the darkness. He thereupon halted for the night, giving orders for continuing the pursuit at 9 A.M. He then sent the 44th Regiment forward to occupy the presumed empty British camp. The 44th Regiment lost itself in the darkness, but, reaching the river-bank south-west of the British camp, also halted. I have heard it suggested that the departure of General Melliss's column had been reported by Arab spies, and mistaken for our main body, so this would account for the foregoing events.

I was called to headquarters by messenger twice during that night. Townshend told me that he had heard gun-wheels in the distance ; this sound, and the glare of camp-fires seen later on, convinced him that the reinforced Turkish Army had arrived in the near vicinity. He therefore decided to continue the retreat at daylight, as it would be difficult to move either troops or ships before. He issued orders that he would deliver frontal and enveloping attacks with his cavalry on the outer flank ; the transport was to move off as soon as there was light enough to see by. The barges were to get under way at daylight and I arranged to co-operate.

When I saw him again—as far as I remember it was at about two in the morning—he told me that he had sent off an urgent message by cavalry volunteers to recall Melliss's force, and I arranged to send a motor-boat down the river. This was entrusted to Sub-Lieutenant Wood, R.N.R.[1] The soldiers got through with their message all right, but in the pitch darkness the motor-boat was unable to find General Melliss's column, which possibly was some miles from the river at the time. The motor-boat therefore

[1] Sub-Lieutenant Wood afterwards received the D.S.C. for this service.

returned to the flotilla. She had been heavily sniped both going and returning by Arabs on the river-banks, one man in the boat being killed in this gallant attempt, while Sub-Lieutenant Wood himself and the other man were wounded.

I had had a wakeful night, and having at last made all arrangements, was lying down when, at earliest daylight, a signalman rushed to my cabin and reported, " Please, sir, there's a big army of Turks camped quite close on our starboard bow." Sure enough daylight presented a most remarkable sight to the flotilla. A very large body of the enemy had come up during the night, and were plainly visible in masses round two tents. These they had pitched only some 3500 yards to the north-westward of the position where the *Firefly* and the *Comet* were anchored, near the south-west corner of our camp, which the Turks had also nearly surrounded. General Townshend had by now practically taken up his positions. The infantry brigades, in trenches and a dry water-channel, more or less in line, faced the westward, with the cavalry brigade moving up into position on the extreme right.

Both sides at once opened fire ; our gunboats, Horse and Field Artillery, probably finding the best target they had ever encountered, as the Turks were in massed formation, and the range anything between two and three thousand yards.

We could see that our fire was doing great execution, for the enemy's advance was checked, amid great disorder. The effect on the Turkish troops and camp was paralysing as we now know. Their whole XIIIth Army Corps fled in panic.

A Turkish historian states that our fire totally disorganized the XVIIIth Army Corps (whose commander was killed), as well as the 45th Division, and kept them for hours out of the battle. He says, further, that from his observation and experiences he can confidently assert without exaggeration that, had not our cavalry been held back by the Turkish 7th Regiment, which deployed in time, they could have ridden over and captured the whole three Divisions. General Townshend, seeing signs of confusion among the Turks, and observing their retreat, determined to take the opportunity for breaking off the action, and continue his retirement to Kut.

But while they had performed great execution the gunboats themselves had been under heavy gunfire since the fight began. As the Turks advanced the latter concentrated a heavy artillery fire on the *Firefly* and the *Comet ;* the third gunboat—the little armed tug *Sumana*—was at this time farther downstream, struggling with two large lighters in an endeavour to save as much of the river transport as possible. Enemy shells were dropping on all sides of the ships, but as a large proportion of the river transport had now got clear away, I ordered (at about 7 A.M.) the signal to be hoisted to drop back down the river. Hardly had I given the order when the *Firefly* was crippled by a direct hit on the steam-drum of her boiler, which rendered her helpless. Her captain, Lieutenant-Commander Eddis, was severely wounded, and one stoker was killed.

We in the *Comet* at once moved up to the *Firefly*, and got her in tow, but the old *Comet* had not got independent paddles, and was therefore most difficult to turn in the narrow river. In fact, with the *Firefly* in tow she was quite unmanageable. She touched on the north bank of the river and swung round with the current, but was wedged more firmly aground by a bump from the disabled *Firefly*, which was then with difficulty got clear. She went drifting down the river. I then signalled the *Sumana* to drop the barges she was towing and come to the two ships' assistance. She did so, making several attempts to tow the *Comet* off, but without success, in spite of all our efforts with the engines, and although, in addition to lighten her, we threw bulky things overboard.

The enemy's fire was increasing intensely all this while. As our troops retreated to the eastward, large bodies of the Turks entered our camp, and as they had by now brought up some field-guns to within short range, they were firing with great rapidity, making accurate shooting. It became evident that the two ships could not be saved. The *Comet*, repeatedly hit, was soon on fire. Since, if we remained, it could be only a matter of minutes before the *Sumana* was disabled also, and as the ships were now practically surrounded by enemy troops, I decided that the *Comet* and the *Firefly* must be abandoned.

I therefore ordered the *Sumana* to come alongside, our officers and men to get onboard her after throwing overboard the breech-locks of the guns and disabling the engines. Lieutenant "Harden and Seaman Ernest Guy, R.N.R., most gallantly pulled over in a small boat under heavy fire to the *Firefly*, which had grounded near, and they brought back her officers and men.[1]

The *Comet* and the *Firefly* were now badly damaged, the former blazing fiercely, so we climbed onboard the *Sumana*, leaving behind all our property except the clothes we were wearing, and Harden, who thought of everything, brought me our two confidential books to take with us. We were all the time under considerable gun- and rifle-fire, the hail of bullets penetrating our protective plating and rattling against the funnel. As I got on to the *Sumana's* bridge the coxswain collapsed with a bullet through him; Tudway took the wheel, and, ordering the engines astern, we backed away down the river.

From the bridge we could see over the river-bank, where, through the haze of dust and smoke, we could discern the long grey lines of the Turkish advance guard. The nearest were only about fifty yards away, and, with bayonets fixed, were already advancing through our camp. I imagine that the shells from their own batteries, bursting and falling near us, had kept them behind the bank, so that the near ranks did not perceive us until we were well on the move down-river.

We now know that we owed our undoing mostly to the Turkish 44th Regiment, who, with two mountain guns, had, as I have mentioned before, lost their way in the night and reached the Tigris river-bank westward of us. Their commander is said to have been astonished by the situation disclosed at daylight, but unfortunately for us, the gunboats presented an easy and conspicuous target at close range, and he promptly took advantage of the fact.

I remember that while steaming down the river, we all

---

[1] Lieutenant Harden received the D.S.O. and Guy the D.S.M. for this gallant act.

sat down to a good breakfast on the bridge-deck of the
Sumana. We were more than ready for it, and mighty
thankful to be there to eat it !

We had to abandon one or two lighters at Shumran, but
the majority had got well away before. The tug *Shuhrur*,
with two large lighters in tow, was, however, found to be
aground at the difficult river-crossing near Shidaif, a few
miles farther down.

The *Sumana* managed to negotiate this crossing with
difficulty, as the little ship was dangerously overloaded.
Precautions had to be taken to prevent her listing or heeling
over the slightest amount, for water would have come over
the raised gunwales, and she must have sunk. Her draught
was also, of course, materially increased.

We anchored below the crossing in order to render
assistance to the stranded craft. It was found that one of
the lighters contained the whole of the divisional ammunition, for both heavy and quick-firing guns, as well as for
small arms, on which the retreat to, and the later holding
of, Kut largely depended. The outer one was the ammunition lighter, and as every military reason pointed to the
absolute necessity of saving her, we made the attempt. As
our efforts were eventually successful, she and the *Shuhrur*
were dispatched down-river. A little farther on our Field
Artillery was able to replenish from the lighter, and later
it safely reached Kut. Attempts were then made to move
the other lighter, but without success, so a steam-launch—
the " L.3 "—under Lieutenant Goad (R.I.M. transport
officer), and a motor-boat, which were present, were sent
to take off as many people as possible. The steam-launch,
however, after getting alongside and taking off a load, ran
aground in the shallows, where the *Sumana* was unable to
render assistance. The motor-boat too broke down, and
drifted into the shallows, where she could not be reached.
It was quite possible that her engine had been disabled by
a stray bullet, for the Turkish infantry had by this time
arrived on the scene, and were firing round after round from
the bank. Neither of the craft was got off. The *Sumana*
had eventually to leave and drop down-river, or she also
would have been cut off. As it was she was several

miles behind our troops, who were retreating steadily on Kut.

It may be noted here that the wounded left behind on this occasion were, a few days afterwards, sent into our camp under a flag of truce, as the Turks frankly stated that they were unable to attend to them, owing to their own heavy casualties.

The *Sumana* struggled on down-river, having constant difficulty in many places, and being often subjected to heavy rifle-fire from the enemy cavalry and the Arabs on the banks. The delay caused by the frequent grounding and steaming round the big loops in the river compelled the ships to fall far behind the troops. From this it will be appreciated what an anxious passage it was for those on-board the *Sumana*. As she struggled round each corner it might be only to find the enemy, with guns in position, at the head of the next bend of the river.

Thanks to the skilful manner in which she was handled by her captain, Sub-Lieutenant Tudway, the *Sumana* arrived near Bghailah at 10.30 P.M., in the neighbourhood of which place she had come up with and transferred wounded as well as surplus ratings to the river-steamer *Salimi*. Going on again at daylight (December 2nd), at about 8 A.M., troops were made out some distance ahead. There were some anxious minutes passed until it was confirmed that they were those of our own rearguard, and that the enemy had not managed to march across and place himself with guns at the head of the next loop, which the little ship would have to round. From that time onward no more difficulty was experienced, and we reached Kut early in the afternoon.

General Townshend's retirement had been carried out with steadiness and precision under heavy gunfire. He was soon joined by General Melliss's column, which had marched rapidly to his assistance. The Turks, however, gradually gave up the pursuit, their cavalry following until about 11 A.M. Townshend had decided to shake off the enemy by making a long march. Consequently the head of the exhausted force reached Shadi about 9 P.M., the rear-guard some time later. At this time of year in these desert countries, with their great ranges of daily temperature, the cold at night is intense. And to add to the discomfort of the troops, they had no food with them.

General Townshend resumed his march at daybreak on on the 2nd, and fortunately no enemy were seen except some hostile Arabs. The Turks, themselves more or less exhausted, had advanced only a slight distance beyond Umm at Tubul. The leading column of Townshend's force reached a bivouac three miles short of Kut during the evening, but the rearguard, bringing up stragglers, was much later. Next day, the 3rd, they marched into Kut. They had been fighting and marching constantly, without sufficient food or water or sleep, for twelve days, concluding the performance by this forty-four mile march under pressure from superior forces. A splendid record, in all conscience!

General Townshend was not aware that the gunboats were in difficulties until during the rearguard action, when the smoke from the burning ships could be seen for miles around. However, he could have done nothing to assist us, for his men were greatly outnumbered, and his position for hours on end remained critical.

The brave 6th Division had lost 5000 killed, wounded, and missing, out of a total of 14,000 combatants with which General Townshend advanced from Aziziya and after the battle of Ctesiphon had retreated between eighty and ninety miles with superior enemy forces on its heels all the way. Nevertheless, Townshend had managed to get clear away with the 1200 Turkish prisoners he had captured at Ctesiphon. The Turks' losses had likewise been very heavy, indeed, and we afterwards heard that of their 2000 casualties at Umm at Tubul a great part had been caused by the gunboats, whose firing into masses of them at close range had performed tremendous execution.

CHAPTER XI

THE INVESTMENT OF KUT

GENERAL TOWNSHEND determined to make a stand at Kut, in order to hold up the Turkish offensive counter-stroke, and to enable British reinforcements to concentrate on the line Amara-Ali Gharbi, so preparations were forthwith commenced for the defence. He asked me to convoy all shipping down-river, as the vessels would be required to bring up the relief force. He also sent the cavalry down-river to join the relief force, as they would be of no use in Kut when the place was invested. The two remaining effective aircraft were also sent to Ali Gharbi.

No one at this time entertained any idea that there would be difficulty—or, for that matter, much delay—in getting reinforcements to Kut. When I saw General Townshend before leaving to take the convoy down-river, our idea was that we should rejoin in about a month; indeed, it was on account of this confidence in the ultimate outcome that the garrison was not for some time put on reduced rations.

The only Naval detachment left in Kut comprised the little *Sumana* and the 4·7-inch guns mounted in horse-boats. The latter could more or less remain hidden under the river banks. I proceeded downstream in charge of the shipping on December 4th. The cavalry followed us, leaving Kut on the 6th, and, as it happened, were only just in time, for on the same day the enemy closed in on the northern front, and by the next day, the 7th, the investment was complete. At Ali Gharbi, which is about seventy-five miles lower down the Tigris, our cavalry were soon reinforced with infantry and guns from Basra, and also the newly completed gunboats *Butterfly* and *Cranefly*. Behind this advanced detachment a force under the command of Major-General F. J. Aylmer, V.C., at once commenced collecting for the relief of Kut.

The entrenched camp at Kut was contained in a U-shaped loop of the Tigris, the town standing at the south-west corner of the peninsula so formed, which is about a mile in width. When some time before this it had been decided to organize on the Kut peninsula the advanced base depot for the Baghdad expedition, a defensive barrier had been started across the northern end of the peninsula. It consisted of a line of four blockhouses, with a mud fort at the northern corner, and connected together by a barbed-wire fence. The fort was about 3200 yards from the town. When Townshend's force reached the town on the 3rd of December the barrier was the position's only defence.

The town of Kut, which recently had been roused from ages of somnolence, and was destined shortly to be a centre of interest for the entire civilized world, was a typical specimen of the usual small dirty Arab town. It contained few more than six hundred houses, some of which were of brick, one or two small shops here and there, besides *cafés*, a mosque, and a small bazaar—but no drains ! Colonel Hehir—the Senior Medical Officer of the force—told the Mesopotamia Commission that it was the most insanitary place which the British force had occupied in Mesopotamia. Take it from me, this meant a lot ! Even more than met the nose !

A detached post was established at a small village, known as Liquorice Factory, or Wool-press Village, on the right bank of the river, opposite Kut, with which communication was kept up by the *Sumana* and the launches. East of the town was a bridge of boats, covered by a bridgehead detachment on the right bank.

After the departure of the ships and cavalry General Townshend's force in Kut numbered 11,607 troops and about 3530 followers, with 43 guns, including Naval ones. Every effort was made to improve the defences as speedily as possible. Redoubts replaced the blockhouses, and the usual trench system was prepared under constantly increasing enemy rifle-fire. On December the 8th the enemy carried out a heavy bombardment from three sides, and

Nur-ud-Din Pasha called upon General Townshend to surrender. This demand being refused, bombardment again ensued, and the enemy moved troops along the right bank across the Hai, and to the east of Kut.

On December the 9th the British detachment on the right bank, covering the bridge, was forced to retire before a heavy attack. As the enemy now occupied the right bank at the bridge-head, it was decided to demolish the bridge. This was accomplished during the night of December 9th–10th by a party gallantly led by Lieutenant A. B. Matthews, R.E., and Lieutenant R. T. Sweet, 2/7th Gurkha Rifles.

Bombardment continued, and several determined attacks were beaten off, during which the enemy losses mounted considerably. The Turks now dug themselves in, and operations devolved into those of more or less orthodox siege warfare. Successful sorties were made on the night of December 14th–15th from the British detached post at Wool-press Village, on the right bank, and on the night of December 17th–18th from our fort at the north-east corner of the defences.

A few days later, Christmas Eve, after concentrating a heavy fire on this fort, the Turks attacked, and after some grimly desperate fighting managed to effect an entrance, but were afterwards driven out, leaving 200 dead behind them. Our troops had little time in which to reflect upon the season's message of " Peace on earth, good-will towards men," for the Turkish attacks were renewed within the space of a few hours, and on the night of December 24th–25th a specially fierce struggle took place, when the enemy again effected a lodgement, only to be ejected again by the morning. On this occasion the Oxfords, the 103rd Mahrattas and the Volunteer battery particularly distinguished themselves. The assault was finally defeated. These attacks, it was reported, had cost the enemy about 2000 casualties.

Boxing Day passed more or less quietly, though not without occasional alarums. On December 28th, however, there was a movement of enemy troops, which continued for several days, from the Turkish main camp (six miles above Kut) to Sheikh Saad, which by now had been occupied by enemy mounted troops for some time. This manœuvre was made apparently with the intended purpose of opposing our force concentrating for the relief of the beleaguered town.

The main *rôle* the *Sumana* filled at this time was guardian to the garrison of Wool-press Village. She lay alongside the bank near the town, and not far from her the Naval 4·7-inch guns, in their horse-boats, were controlled by an Artillery officer from an adjacent observation tower. They were constantly under heavy gun- and rifle-fire, but Lieutenant Tudway, commanding the *Sumana*, on about the 12th, secured a large barge outside his ship, and this acted as a useful shield to her hull. A few days later the enemy brought a gun down to the bank opposite, and opened heavy fire, damaging the *Sumana's* upper works, but fortunately the gun was silenced by our fire. Some days later the Turks tried this manœuvre again, but once more the *Sumana's* twelve-pounder and the shore guns proved too much for them. After this gruelling experience the *Sumana* moved farther downstream, to a less exposed position.

British and Indian reinforcements were now arriving daily in the country, proceeding almost immediately up the Tigris to our point of concentration at Ali Gharbi. Every preparation was being made for the advance, the gunboats *Butterfly*, *Cranefly*, and *Dragonfly* being with them, the *Dragonfly* having been rapidly completed and hurried to the front at short notice. On December the 21st the *Butterfly* and the *Dragonfly* bombarded and destroyed some enemy trenches near Sheikh Saad, the ships themselves coming under a stinging rifle-fire, but sustaining no casualties.

On the Euphrates, in the vicinity of Nasiriya, we employed at this time small armed sternwheelers for patrolling the river. These craft were manned by crews from the *Espiègle* and the *Odin*. By the end of the year the situation there was comparatively quiet.

H.M.S. *Gadfly* (Lieutenant-in-Command I. M. Palmer, D.S.C.), the fifth " small China gunboat," arrived at Basra from Abadan on the 29th of December, and, after dealing with matters at the base, I went up-river in her, leaving Basra on the 30th to direct the Naval part of the operations for the relief of Kut. We arrived at Amara on New Year's

Day, leaving there at noon on that day to join our force concentrating at Ali Gharbi.

By this time strenuous efforts were being made at Basra to forward all the incoming reinforcements to the front, by the river transport, which was showing itself sadly inadequate for the greatly increased numbers of troops, with their necessary supplies and ammunition. Troops were also marching in echelons to the front.

On the way to the front in the *Gadfly* we used to pass many of them, and found it convenient to stop and " bank in " for the night near these marching camps, where we were safe from attack by hostile Arabs. The troops from India, many of whom had never seen a gunboat or Naval uniform before, were always interested in us and our movements. I remember a hospitable regiment insisting on Palmer and me joining them at dinner. They said they had never before had a chance of entertaining guests while on the march.

Hopes were at this time entertained that a Russian expeditionary force which was operating to the northward, and which had occupied Hamadan on the 14th of December, would draw away some of the Turkish forces from Kut and its vicinity. This force had arrived in North Persia about the end of October, having disembarked at Enzeli, on the Caspian, and had at this time a strength of about 10,000 rifles and 30 guns, with motor lorries and cars. Their intention was to advance on Kermanshah, and so threaten Baghdad from the north-east.

The Turks began at this time, however, to receive reinforcements in such large numbers that no deviation of their forces from our front such as would have been of material advantage to us took place.

The German Field-Marshal von der Goltz was known to have arrived in Baghdad about the 10th of December, and visited the vicinity of Kut, where Khalil Pasha was in command of the Turkish forces at the end of the year.

The general situation in Mesopotamia, therefore, at the close of the year 1915, was as follows :

The 6th Indian Division was besieged at Kut by strong Turkish forces, who were also constructing entrenched

N

positions between the town and Sheikh Saad, which place they had occupied in order to oppose the advance of our forces for General Townshend's relief.

A British relieving force, given the name of the "Tigris Army Corps," was being concentrated under General Sir F. J. Aylmer at Ali Gharbi, about thirty miles below Sheikh Saad ; reinforcements from Great Britain and India were pouring into the country, and were being sent to the front as fast as the inadequate river transport would allow. The Russian detachment to which I have alluded had not at this time made its influence felt.

Our Naval forces were likewise being increased, as the new "small China" type gunboats were being reassembled as rapidly as possible at Abadan with materials prepared in England. The *Butterfly*, *Cranefly*, and the *Dragonfly* were at the front by the end of the year, the *Gadfly* was on her way there, while the remainder of the new craft followed soon afterwards. The "large China gunboats," the *Mantis* and the *Gnat*, were also *en route* from England, with the *Tarantula* and the *Moth* scheduled to follow shortly afterwards.

Steps were also being taken, with the approval of the Admiralty, to establish a Naval base at Basra for the repair and docking of the river gunboats and seaplanes. I had also asked for a floating repair depot, and, with Admiralty approval, a sternwheel steamer of useful design was built by Messrs. Yarrow. This specially constructed craft was eventually commissioned as H.M.S. *Scotstoun*.

As stated previously, the river transport—which was under the Royal Indian Marine—was at the end of the year already beginning to reveal its inadequacy. Although efforts were being made to increase the number of river-steamers, it was not until well on in 1916 that, with a more vigorous policy, the river transport was placed under the newly created Inland Water Transport Department ; under whose management, with ample funds at its disposal, numbers of river-steamers were added, adequate wharfage provided, and railways constructed on a scale of liberality hitherto unknown—and undreamt of in that country.

I have already related that within a week of the first

arrival of the Expedition at Basra, in November 1914, the advisability of constructing railways was brought forward during a conference at General Headquarters. The necessity of a large number of river-steamers, should it be intended to advance to Baghdad, was also emphasized and explained by Commander A. Hamilton, R.I.M., in considerable detail. Both subjects were, however, presumably postponed, probably owing to the fact that at that time the Expedition had no orders to proceed beyond Kurna. The provision of these things requires a long period of preparation. When plans were changed and the scope of the advance was considerably extended, little had been done. Hence the great delay in getting the requisite steamers to the country.

The foregoing provides an outline of the events of the period dealt with in this chapter. The higher strategy of those events it is not my purpose to discuss here.

Kut is undoubtedly an important strategical centre, lying as it does at the junction of the Shatt al Hai and the Tigris. The Shatt al Hai has important Arab towns on it, and although the river channel could be used in high river only by small craft, these towns have also an important land route running between them. The possession of Kut would, therefore, undoubtedly give us considerable advantages in our surveillance of the unruly Arabs of the Marsh districts.

The value of the possession of Baghdad, the central market and capital of the country, the prestige attaching to its capture, and the influence of this on the Mahommedan world at large, are also evident.

It may be noted, however, that the advance to Kut from Amara lengthened our river communications by some 152 miles, which is more by 40 than the total distance from Basra to Amara; also that from Kut to Ctesiphon is about 170 miles by the river route, on which we were depending for our supplies and ammunition, as we then had no railway.

BOOK IV

OPERATIONS FOR THE RELIEF OF KUT

CHAPTER XII

THE ATTEMPTS TO RELIEVE KUT

W E shall now follow the efforts made to relieve the beleaguered garrison of Kut, commencing with high hopes and assurance of success, doomed to the bitter disappointment of the surrender. We shall see the steps taken to retrieve British prestige, and the resumption of our offensive at the end of the year, which was destined to lead to the complete defeat of the Turks and to our occupation of the country.

The British force for the relief of Kut was being gathered together in the vicinity of Ali Gharbi during December. Designated the Tigris Army Corps, as I have explained, it was under the command of Lieutenant-General Sir F. G. Aylmer. Reinforcements by this time were pouring into the Shatt al Arab, to be hurried up the river as rapidly as possible to this concentration, the shortage of river transport for this service, which had been long foreseen by those on the spot, becoming daily more evident. River-steamers were being ordered from all over the world, and arrangements hurriedly made for their construction both locally and in India. The situation was partly relieved through marching the incoming troops by echelons up-country to the front. For this purpose a series of protected marching camps was formed all the way up-river.

On the 1st of January, 1916, the distribution of His Majesty's ships in Mesopotamia was as follows :

The *Espiègle*, the *Odin*, and the *Miner* at Basra, the *Alert* at Abadan, for the very considerable work at the base in connection with manning, storing, and fitting out the gunboats. The gunboats *Butterfly*, Lieutenant-in-Command G. A. Wilson, R.N. ; *Cranefly*, Lieutenant-in-Command A. R. Chalmer, R.N. ; and *Dragonfly*, Lieutenant-in-

Command A. C. Thursfield, R.N., were at Ali Gharbi. The *Gadfly*, Lieutenant-in-Command I. M. Palmer, D.S.C., R.N., had just been completed, and, steaming up-river in her, we arrived at Ali Gharbi on January 2nd, where I conferred with General Aylmer.

This *Butterfly* class of gunboats, of which sixteen were eventually assembled, launched, and commissioned at Abadan for the Navy, were described officially as being of the "small China gunboat" type, in order to conceal the purpose for which they were intended. They were of about 98 tons displacement, 126 feet long, 20 feet beam, and their draught of water was between two and three feet. Their armament was a 4-inch, a twelve-pounder, a six-pounder gun, a two-pounder anti-aircraft pom-pom, and four Maxim guns. Their crew consisted of two officers and about twenty men, and each ship had a good wireless installation. Burning oil fuel, they had a single screw driven by a reciprocating engine, which developed a h.p. of 175, and could give them a speed of about nine and a half knots.

During 1916 the following vessels of this type were also commissioned in Mesopotamia : the *Grayfly*, Lieutenant-in-Command C. H. Heath-Caldwell, D.S.C. ; the *Greenfly*, Lieutenant-in-Command H. O. B. Firman ; the *Mayfly*, Lieutenant-Commander E. H. B. L. Scrivener ; the *Sawfly*, Lieutenant-Commander C. J. F. Eddis ; the *Snakefly*, Lieutenant-in-Command R. P. D. Webster ; the *Stonefly*, Lieutenant-in-Command Mark Singleton, D.S.C. ; the *Waterfly*, Lieutenant-in-Command W. V. H. Harris, D.S.C.

The *Firefly*, as I have described, had been captured by the Turks on the 1st of December, 1915 ; she was fated to be recaptured by us in February 1917, in which year the *Blackfly*, the *Caddisfly*, the *Hoverfly*, and the *Sedgefly* were also added to the flotilla.

These "flies" were useful little craft, but would have been more so if they had had additionally powerful engines and twin screws. Supplying them with only one boiler apiece was also an unwise arrangement, as if this were put out of action by a shell there was no reserve, and the vessel became helpless.

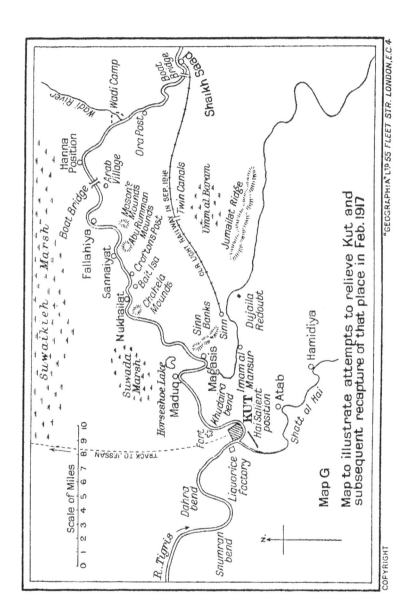

Map to illustrate attempts to relieve Kut and subsequent recapture of that place in Feb. 1917

Map G

Their six-pounder guns were eventually changed with advantage for twelve-pounder, twelve-cwt. ; and in the later vessels I arranged for the 4-inch gun-mounting to be raised above the deck, in order to make possible more elevation on the guns, and thus increase their range. This raising of the mounting also gave more safety to the breech-lever when firing at extreme elevations, though I also had in mind the fact that should any of the new gunboats encounter the *Firefly* they would be able to outrange her.

In addition to these gunboats two steam-launches were, during these operations, placed under the orders of the Senior Naval Officer for mine-sweeping duties, with Lieutenant (temporary) William A. Milne, R.I.M., in command. Arrangements were also being made to establish a Naval depot on shore at Basra, the site at Tanooma, with the old Turkish hospital, being eventually chosen.

During the following incidents I directed operations from the *Gadfly*, until, after being holed by a shell, she had to be sent to Basra for repairs, whereupon I transferred to the *Cranefly*.

Having collected a considerable force at Ali Gharbi, the Tigris Army Corps commenced their advance towards Kut on January the 4th. The army marched up both banks of the river, the gunboats keeping in touch with the advance and rearguards. General Younghusband, commanding the advanced division, accompanied me onboard the *Gadfly* for a considerable time, General Aylmer following with the main body.

We considered that there were considerable opportunities for close co-operation if the General and Senior Naval Officer should be thus together, and we could also take advantage of the all-round view from the gunboat's mast ; the Naval and military signallers and our wireless keeping up communication with the force.

We came in touch with the enemy on each bank on the forenoon of January the 6th, about 11 A.M., when about three and a half miles to the east of Sheikh Saad. Heavy firing immediately developed, and our force made an attempt to turn the Turkish right flank, the gunboats supporting with their 4-inch guns. However, owing to the presence of hostile cavalry and large bodies of Arabs in that direction, this manœuvre did not succeed.

On the morning of January the 7th General Aylmer came up with the remainder of his force, and ordered a general attack, Major-General Younghusband commanding on the left, and Major-General Kemball on the right bank. Very heavy fighting lasted throughout the day, and by the evening the enemy's trenches on the right bank had been captured. Some troops were entrenched opposite the enemy on the left bank, who still clung desperately to their positions. Attempts to turn this flank had been checked by counter-enveloping movements from the north.

Fighting continued throughout the next day, but little progress was made, as the troops were very fatigued. The gunboats were active the whole while ; the *Gadfly* was able during that afternoon to put some shells right into Sheikh Saad. We learned afterwards that the effect of these helped greatly to demoralize the Turks. The extra range was obtained by using some of the *Espiègle's* twenty-five-pound 4-inch shell, which, in the *Gadfly's* Mark VIII guns, had a longer range than her own thirty-four-pounders.

Early on the 9th it was found that the enemy had retreated up-river during the night, so our forces advanced and occupied Sheikh Saad. We at once moved on in the gun-boats, and found a line of mines moored across the river between their trenches at the places where they came down to each bank of the river. Two mines had already broken loose and drifted down-river on the 6th, so we were on the *qui vive*. We soon weighed the remainder, however, without difficulty, and found them to be of the somewhat amateur home-made type which the enemy had used before Kurna in 1915. It was soon ascertained that the enemy had fallen back only about ten miles, to a position near the Ora ruins, and that they had taken up a new position on the left bank of the Tigris, protected on their front by a tributary stream called the Wadi.

It was estimated that the enemy's losses during the three days' fighting at Sheikh Saad had been very heavy, and including prisoners, amounted to some 4500. Our own losses had been 4007, and the results of the premature advance with a hastily collected force were becoming very evident. As regiments arrived in the country they were being hurried to the front, thrown into brigades, often not their own, to find themselves within a short while in action, with lack of guns, munitions, etc., while the Turks during this period had practically command of the air.

The units of the 3rd and 7th Divisions had arrived at Basra in no regular order. When they left France it had been understood that they would be reorganized in Egypt—which they certainly were not. They had merely been packed into steamers as steamers became available. Some units were incomplete. There was a lack of Staff officers, as some of the Staff had not come with the troops from France, while others had not yet arrived. The deficiencies had to be filled by any officers available on the spot and from India. In addition, many of the units had been trained on different lines.

The inadequate river transport in Mesopotamia again resulted in units going up-river at odd times, sometimes without their full equipment. Then, again, land transport at the front was lacking; the Supply and Transport Corps at the Front were under their establishment. High explosive shell was scanty; aeroplanes were too few to allow of regular artillery observation; there were, for a long time, no proper anti-aircraft guns; while many of the guns and howitzers were of old pattern, and the telephone equipment was both ancient and inadequate.

The force was short of sappers and miners; the bridging train material was inefficient; medical *personnel* and equipment was short and sadly restricted. The Generals represented these matters most strongly in the right quarters, but felt bound to expedite the advance, relieve Townshend without delay, and take the risks involved. Pitchforked in and out of transports, packed into barges, and dumped into the desert at what was contemptuously termed a " sideshow "; little glory expected, comforts lacking, with no leave train; this army was pitted against a skilful, entrenched enemy, who was, furthermore, fighting in his own country and under conditions to which he was accustomed. All this gave the troops little to enthuse about.

And the cause of these bad arrangements was the supposed frantic hurry to relieve Kut ; but at that time it was only about a month since Kut had been beleaguered. Considering that the place held out for about four, the hurry seems to have been unnecessary. With a reasonable pause in which to concentrate, and to prepare the relieving force, the confusion would have been obviated. Even apart from the discovery later on of hidden stores of grain in Kut, should it not have been possible at headquarters to estimate a reasonable period during which the garrison of Kut could be expected to live on their supplies, and thus avoid the fatally premature advance of early January ?

The newly commissioned *Flycatcher* (Lieutenant-in-Command H. Lincoln, R.N.R.) arrived at the front on January the 10th. She was afterwards used as a dispatch boat for the Senior Naval Officer, and was frequently at the front. As I have explained elsewhere, she had been a Turkish Thornycroft patrol-boat, was sunk by the *Espiègle* in November 1914, raised and repaired by Messrs. Strick, Scott, at Mahommerah. She was armed with a six-pounder and a Maxim, and proved herself a most useful little vessel.

An unusual incident occurred to the *Gadfly* on the afternoon of January the 12th. Some transport camels were crossing the bridge of boats when two of them slipped in the mud, fell overboard, and were carried downstream. One of the beasts was washed under the *Gadfly's* propeller. The sailor on watch ran to the captain's cabin and reported, " Camel foul of the screw, sir ! " All hands were summoned to clear the screw, and try to save the ship of the desert. But the unfortunate animal was drowned before it could be hauled out of the screw aperture by a rope the bluejackets hitched round its neck.

Heavy rain fell after our arrival at Sheikh Saad, making the so-called roads and desert itself almost impassable ; and it was not until the morning of the 13th of January that General Aylmer, having concentrated his force on the left bank, was able to attack the Wadi position. It was necessary to press forward as soon as possible, for there were reports of the impending arrival of large Turkish reinforcements, and the force in Kut, without access to the right bank, appeared unable to co-operate by active operations. The 7th Indian Division under Major-General Younghusband, with a cavalry brigade on its outer flank, carried out a turning movement from the northward against the enemy's left flank ; at the same time Major-General Kemball, with the 28th Brigade, made a holding attack from the front, the gunboats co-operating from the river with the 4-inch guns, and performing some useful work while engaged with enemy field-guns.

The *Gadfly* and the *Cranefly* moved farther up the river in the afternoon, and fired into a body of enemy troops who appeared to be retiring. But the Turks soon brought down some field-guns, which opened an accurate fire, and successfully kept the gunboats back.

After some hours hard fighting, during which both sides sustained severe casualties, the enemy again withdrew to the west, on the night of the 13th–14th. Having ascertained this, I moved up in the *Gadfly*, with the *Cranefly* in support and endeavoured to harass their retreat. It was soon evident, however, that they had not gone far, but had fallen back on another prepared position. Observing the gunboats coming up the river, they opened a well-directed fire from two guns on the left bank. We immediately replied.

Just before 1 P.M. the *Gadfly* was hit on the starboard side of the upper deck aft by a 4·8-inch projectile, which penetrated the deck, magazine bulkhead, and ship's bottom. Luckily it did not burst, and later was found in the hold. As the ship commenced to make a good deal of water, the ejectors were put on, and the pump was manned. Then, dropping back down-river out of range, she was steered into shallow water, and secured alongside the bank by Lieutenant-in-Command I. M. Palmer, who handled his crippled craft with considerable skill. A leak-stopper was placed over the hole by Shipwright 2nd Class George L. Thomas, to whose stout efforts also was largely due the fact that the vessel did not founder. Later on I transferred to the *Cranefly*, and sent the *Gadfly* down-river. She was most expeditiously repaired at Abadan.

It was found that the Turks on the night of 13th–14th had withdrawn only about five miles to the west, and taken up their strong previously prepared position entrenched across the Umm-al-Hanna defile, which was bounded on the north by a marsh and on the south by the Tigris. However, they were followed up to this position by General Aylmer's force.

Bad weather continued, heavy rain and high, blustering winds adding much to the troops' discomfort. The surface of the desert was turned to oozing mud, of a consistency that made movement by land and river well-nigh impossible, and brought active operations to a standstill. The elements seemed to be fighting on behalf of the Turk, who, snuggly settled in his prepared positions, was affected less by this drastic handicap than our advancing force.

The swollen rivers came down in flood, overflowing their banks ; the bridge across the Wadi was washed away several times, and a sea got up in the Tigris which greatly interfered with the work of throwing a boat-bridge across the river—at this point some 400 yards wide. The bridge was required particularly in order to establish artillery on the right bank of the Tigris, so as to support, by enfilading fire, the attack of our infantry against the Hanna position. It was not until the 19th of January that the necessary guns and troops had been ferried across, and taken up their allotted stations. Our forces on the left bank had meanwhile advanced and entrenched themselves near the enemy's position, while the gunboats moved up into position so as to be able to co-operate with gunfire.

General Sir John Nixon had now been in poor health for a long time, but his sense of duty had kept him going. However, the continued strain and anxiety eventually proved too much for his lowered vitality, and at this time he broke down altogether, and had to be invalided from the country. On the 19th he handed over the command to General Sir Percy Lake, and left Basra. At this stage I might pause to repeat that the Army and Navy were always on good terms with each other in Mesopotamia. From the Army Commander down we found the former always ready to help and to show any kindness to the diminutive Naval force. Among them all General Nixon himself had been a conspicuous friend.

At the time when he arrived in the country, on the eve of the battle of Shaiba, the situation had been very serious. We were threatened on all sides, and our hold on the country seemed insecure. He at once settled himself to tackle the problem with energy, and it was greatly due to the stimulant he provided that the hard-fought battle of Shaiba was won, and the Turks thrown back on the Euphrates. There had been a British reverse in the Karun, but he dispatched the force there which (under General Gorringe) overcame almost insuperable difficulties and drove the Turks westward. Our following successes at Kurna, Amara, Nasiriya, and Kut had all been results of his fiery energy and skilful direction. There is no doubt that sheer bad luck had dogged the force in its later ventures ; and by the breakdown of Sir John Nixon's health he did not get the opportunity to retrieve his failures.

Lord Hardinge, in paying a tribute to Nixon's work to the Mesopotamia commission, said : " It is by men of his grit and stamp that the British Empire has been built up." Myself, I consider him as having been among the greatest of the distinguished and able leaders that I met. Later they had everything needful. Nixon was given the task of making bricks without straw.

However, to return to the state of affairs at the front. Bad, squally weather continued, and the ground became a virtual morass as the result of the continual downpours of rain that was almost tropical in volume. The rivers, sweeping down in flood, destroyed the boat-bridges and delayed operations, thereby giving the Turks further time in which to improve and strengthen their defences.

Bombardment of the enemy's position, in which the gunboats joined, commenced on the 19th of January and continued throughout the 20th, during the night of which our infantry pushed forward to within 200 yards of the enemy's trenches. On the morning of the 21st, under cover of another heavy bombardment directed by all the military and Naval guns, they moved to the attack.

The enemy position was an extremely strong one. Several lines of loopholed trenches, with wire entanglements in front, had been constructed, many with overhead covering, some nine feet deep, and it was necessary for our attacking forces to advance across open muddy ground devoid of cover. On the right our troops were unable to advance nearer than a hundred yards to the enemy's strong position. Our left column, however, consisting of the Black Watch, the 8th Jats, the 97th Deccan Infantry, and the 41st Dogras, seized a position in the front line. Badly needed support failed to reach them, though, and they were obliged by heavy counter-attacks to retire, after having held the position for an hour and a half.

Heavy rain now fell again, and the drenching downpour continued throughout the day, communication becoming slow and uncertain. Although the attack was renewed at 1 P.M., the troops wading up to the enemy's position through a sea of mud, the assault again failed, with severe loss, the troops maintaining their position until dark, when they were withdrawn to their own trenches.

To renew the attack on the 22nd was not practicable. The losses on the 21st had been heavy, and the ground was still a quagmire. Besides, the troops were exhausted. A six hours' armistice was arranged, in order that each side might bury its dead and remove the wounded to shelter. The sufferings of the latter were terrible, for vehicles and stretcher-bearers could scarcely move in the deep mud, and to retain an even balance and avoid stumbling and lurching was impossible.

In the words of General Lake, the troops had shown a spirit of endurance and self-sacrifice of which their country might well be proud. He described the weather as atrocious —and it was all of that. It was a pleasure to welcome dripping Army friends onboard the gunboats, where they could dry themselves and become warm *outside* in our boiler-room, and *inside* with a tot of Navy rum.

During the bombardments the gunboats co-operated with the artillery, who gave all possible assistance. Brigadier-General Gordon, R.A., Major Lynch-Staunton, and Captain McIlwaine of his Staff—and, indeed, all the gunners—did their utmost to help us. Their advice was often sought, and most valuable it proved, particularly that upon the subject of improvised methods of indirect firing, controlled by

o

telephone to forward observer, a procedure which was, of course, comparatively strange to us all. Lieutenant Goodfellow of the R.F.A. was frequently attached to the Navy to help in these matters, until, to our great regret, he was killed in March.

The gunboats' armament had been designed, as usual, for sea-fighting. This included range-clocks, Dumaresq instruments, and similar appurtenances, and I now took steps to obtain dial-sights, clinometers, and telephone wire. The Army lent us everything possible, pending supply from home.

Our gun-sights were of the usual Naval type, and so had a graduation in knots on their lateral bar, which could be adjusted to allow for the speeds of our own ship, and of the enemy, in knots or miles per hour. These sights were a great novelty to the gunners, many of whom had not been onboard a ship-of-war before. I remember one of them, after carefully examining the gun-sights, turning round with a puzzled expression and ejaculating : " But, I say, what the hell are knots ? "

Our ships in the Mesopotamian Division were so small that none of them carried a lieutenant for gunnery duties in her complement ; and although throughout the campaign we did a great deal of firing I never asked for one to be appointed. I thought it much better that the officers and men should puzzle out for themselves the intricacies of their guns and fuses. The conditions, of course, were quite different from those which make necessary the complicated arrangements onboard our big ships, where, naturally, a highly specialized gunnery officer is necessary.

The frequent use of the guns under Service conditions showed to all the necessity of making the best of their weapons. One remembers a newcomer commenting on the unusual sight of officers off duty sitting in the wardroom studying the Service treatises on ammunition, the *Gunnery Manual*, etc., or crowding onboard a new gunboat to examine and criticize her armament.

The very heavy work of ordering from Bombay the ammunition and supplies was, besides other duties, efficiently carried out by Lieutenant C. Hallett, R.I.M.

Advantage was taken of experience gained in the operations to make some useful alterations in the gunboats, Mr. Grant, of the staff of Messrs. Yarrow (now appointed Admiralty Overseer in charge of their construction at Abadan), and Commander Steward, of H.M.S. *Alert*, the depot-ship at that place, being most useful in carrying out what was required. The expeditious completion of the gunboats in the face of the greatest difficulties was largely due to the work of Mr. Grant, who personally took charge of assembling these craft at Abadan, where he employed a very mixed party of Indians, Arabs, Persians, Chinese, and Afghans in his improvised dockyard.

H.M.S. *Grayfly*, Lieutenant-in-Command C. H. Heath-Caldwell, D.S.C., left Basra on January the 13th for the front; the *Mayfly*, Lieutenant-Commander E. H. B. L. Scrivener, R.N., was completed and arrived up-river on February the 14th; the *Sawfly*, Lieutenant-Commander C. J. F. Eddis, later in February, and the *Stonefly*, Lieutenant-in-Command Mark Singleton, D.S.C., R.N., early in March.

The gunboat *Mantis*, Commander Bernard Buxton, R.N., reached Mesopotamia in February, having been towed from England, and arrived at the Tigris front on March the 5th. She is of the "large China gunboat" type, and of these the *Tarantula*, Commander G. H. Sherbrooke, R.N.; the *Moth*, Lieutenant-Commander Charles Cartwright, R.N.; and the *Gnat*, Lieutenant-Commander E. H. B. L. Scrivener, R.N., joined the flotilla during 1916, and proved most useful assets.

With others of their class they had originally been intended to oppose the Austrian monitors on the Danube. They never reached there, however, owing to the collapse of Serbia. Accordingly some were draughted to Mesopotamia, others to the Suez Canal, the east coast of England, and the various other theatres of war. We hear a good deal to-day about their doings up the China rivers, so they have lived up to their name at last! I always considered them a little large, and of too great draught, for the Tigris and Euphrates, but their power, speed, and fine armament were altogether superior to those of the weak little "fly" class. If I had

had my choice I should have chosen something between the two types of gunboat.

The " large China gunboats " are oil-burning, twin-screw vessels of 645 tons displacement, and 2000 h.p., with a speed of fourteen knots. Their length is 237 feet 6 inches, beam 36 feet, draught 4 to 5 feet, and armament two 6-inch, two twelve-pounder, and 6 Maxim guns.

On the Tigris front bombardments of the enemy's positions were continued, and the gunboats joined in these, obtaining some considerable practice in indirect firing, using field-telephones to forward observer. Lieutenant C. G. Hallett, R.I.M., and Lieutenant H. Lincoln, R.N.R., were particularly useful in this dangerous work, and Commander C. R. Wason, of H.M.S. *Odin*, also rendered valuable help.

On the Euphrates lines on January the 7th a mixed force under Major-General Sir G. F. Gorringe, K.C.B., C.M.G., D.S.O., moved from Nasiriya for the purpose of demonstrating towards Shattra, the nearest town to them of any importance on the Shatt al Hai, as it was hoped that the Turks might thereby be induced to weaken their forces opposing General Aylmer on the Tigris by dispatching troops to guard the line of approach along that river. After reaching Butaniyeh, which is about twelve miles to the north-east of Nasiriya, they made a further reconnaissance some six miles farther north of Suwaij, and there attracted large numbers of hostile Arabs, who, opening fire, advanced with a show of considerable determination, and followed our force back as far as the outposts of the camp at Butaniyeh.

These Arabs consisted for the most part of hostile sections of the Khaffaja and Abudah tribes. However, the effect of our retreat from Ctesiphon before the Turkish advance was being revealed by a change in the Arabs' attitude towards us and General Gorringe remarks that doubtless many men from friendly sections were present. The hostile Arabs' feeling was again shown when, on the withdrawal of the force from Butaniyeh to Nasiriya on February the 7th, it was again heavily attacked, especially by the Albu Hamera section of the Azairich tribe, who had been friendly to us for months. On this occasion our troops, owing largely to the unsteadiness of two Indian infantry units, sustained fairly heavy losses.

This treacherous conduct on the part of the Albu Hamera Arabs was punished by a column under Brigadier-General E. C. Tidswell on February the 9th, who, making a surprise attack, burned several Arab villages, blew up a large tower, and inflicted severe losses on the enemy.

Brigadier-General Brooking, C.B., who now succeeded General Gorringe in the command at Nasiriya, reported that the work of General Tidswell's column was well carried out, and that he was of the opinion that this action would produce a good effect, but that the tribes in this district were in a state of ferment on which nothing but the relief of Kut would have any real effect.

Nothing further, however, of importance occurred in the Euphrates or the Karun line during February. On hearing that the relieving force was held up at Hanna, General Townshend had put his force on half-rations, which he calculated would last them for another twenty-seven days. He had not done so before, as it had been his intention to keep his men as fit as possible, in order that they would be able to co-operate with General Aylmer if called upon.

On the 24th of January, however, Townshend again telegraphed that by collecting stores of coarse flour in Kut, by utilizing his horses and mules as food, and by other means he could hold out much longer. He had not commandeered all supplies in Kut until relief was in grave doubt. He had now done so, and rationed the Kut Arabs like the troops. He also thought there was little chance of the Turks making an assault on Kut, and that the floods would further prevent this.

This information, of course, threw an entirely new light on the situation; gave us an opportunity for reorganization, and the collecting at the front of the reinforcements, ammunition, and stores which were now pouring into the country. These, however, were still being greatly delayed in passage to the front by the lack of river transport.

General Lake visited the front on the 28th of January. After a long discussion with General Aylmer, he gave his views of the situation in a report to India, together with an account of the great difficulties under which the Tigris corps had laboured, due to the bad weather and being pressed to advance before properly being organized. This hurry was largely due, said General Lake, to " Townshend's appeals and neglect to state his true position regarding supplies."

After a thorough examination of the state of affairs he then returned to Basra, where at the time he could be more useful and more closely in touch with affairs than at the front.

Considerable anxiety was now being felt in England as to the safety of the force in Kut, and this anxiety was increased by the news of our repulse at Hanna. It was arranged that India should send three more infantry brigades to Mesopotamia, on relief by other troops from home, besides other reinforcements of guns and war material.

It was also decided, now that the Expedition had grown so greatly in importance, and no longer drew resources from India only, but from the Empire as a whole, that the system of control should be changed, and brought directly under the Chief of the Imperial General Staff. This would enable the War Committee of the Cabinet to adjust more effectively the respective requirements of Mesopotamia and the other theatres of war.

This assumption of control by the War Office added greatly to the subsequent efficient conduct of the campaign.

CHAPTER XIII

UNSUCCESSFUL EFFORTS

IT having been ascertained that Kut could hold out so much longer, the force remained in the vicinity of Hanna. The work of reorganization and reinforcement was carried on for some weeks, General Gorringe taking up the appointment of Chief-of-Staff of the Tigris Corps. His great energy and powers of organization were used to enormous advantage.

On the Tigris front the situation at the end of February was briefly as follows :

On the left bank the enemy, having been reinforced, still strongly held the Hanna position, farther in rear being other defensive lines—at Fallahiya, Sannaiyat, Nukhailat, and along the northern part of the Ess Sinn position. All except the last-named had been constructed since the battle of Hanna, on January the 21st, and they were all protected on both flanks by the Tigris and the Suwaikieh Marsh respectively. On the right or southern bank the Ess Sinn position constituted the Turkish main line of defence, with an advanced position near Beit Isa. The right flank of the Ess Sinn position rested on the Dujaila redoubt, which lay some five miles south of the river, and fourteen south-west of the British lines on the right bank.

Reconnaissances were also carried out, and, as it had been confirmed that the Hanna position on the left bank was held in strength, on the night of February the 21st our forces moved up to and entrenched themselves within short range of it. At the same time our men on the right bank had advanced so far that they considerably overlapped the Hanna position.

Lieutenant-General Aylmer now decided to make the

attempt to relieve Kut by turning the enemy's right, or southern flank, and to surprise and assault the Dujaila redoubt as his first objective. Fearing that as soon as the river came down in flood the Turks would cut the *bunds*, and so render all further attempts to relieve Kut impracticable, he decided to make the attempt at the earliest date by which he could take into the field seven brigades, with some 44 guns and 12 howitzers, this being the maximum force for which land transport was available, carrying two days' food and water.

Operations at this time of year depended on the weather, as heavy rains would quickly turn the desert into a morass practically impassable for horse, foot, or guns. Now, as the reader knows very well, a barometer is practically a necessity in weather forecasting—and headquarters soon awoke to the fact that they had not got one ! Then some one who had been down to the sea in ships opined that the sailors would possess this instrument.

After that orderlies used to arrive booted and spurred, carrying polite notes : " With the Army Commander's compliments. Will the Senior Naval Officer kindly let him know the height of the barometer ? "

This was all very well for a while, but as a regular procedure it became rather wearing. There came such a constant procession of orderlies that we had hardly time to do anything other than cope with them. Then I hit upon a bright idea. I had one of the gunboat's barometers packed up, and the next orderly who came on board took it, with a polite note, as a present to the General. He was greatly pleased, I was overwhelmed with thanks, the Navy further increased in popularity, and, what was infinitely more important, we were saved a lot of useless trouble—and the General could sleep with the barometer under his pillow if it gave him pleasanter dreams !

A preliminary bombardment of the enemy's left-bank positions was carried out by the guns and the gunboats, and our forces in front of Hanna displayed activity to divert the enemy's attention ; but operations were once more delayed by rain and mud, and it was not until March the 7th that General Aylmer was able to issue his final instructions. He laid particular stress on the fact that the operations were to be a surprise, and that the first phase—viz., the capture of the Dujaila redoubt—was to be pushed through with the utmost vigour. Should this be successful, the next phase of the operation—namely, that of crossing the Hai—was prepared for, extemporised light pontoons and bridging equipment having been taken to the post at " Ruined Hut," where they could easily be sent for. At the same time the enemy was given the impression that the crossing was to be near Mason's Mounds—in rear of the Hanna position.

The dispositions of our forces were briefly as follows : the greater part of a division, under General Younghusband, assisted by the gunboats, contained the enemy on the left bank. The *Mayfly*, the *Sawfly*, and the *Mantis* were anchored above the bridge of boats in position to assist in the bombardment of the Hanna position, while the *Gadfly* and the *Dragonfly* were stationed below the bridge in a position to command the north-eastern flank and approaches to the camp with their gunfire.

The strong striking force on the right bank, with 4 Cavalry regiments, 28 Infantry battalions, and 68 guns, was to concentrate at a rendezvous some five miles to the south of the Wadi camp at about 8.30 P.M. on the evening of March the 7th. Once there, the force was to be divided into three groups : the first, under General Kemball, was composed of two columns, A and B, the second group was the Cavalry Brigade, and the third—called Column C—was under General Keary.

General Kemball's group, followed by the other two, was to move off to the south-west, diverging after proceeding some six miles. The first two were then to continue about four and a half miles farther, in readiness for Column B to attack the Dujaila redoubt, Column A to cover its flank and attack some more Turkish trenches to the northward. The Cavalry Brigade, farther to the left, was to cover the flank of the two columns. Column C was to attack the Sinnaftar redoubt, and to co-operate to the northward of the attack on Dujaila.

On the 7th the force did not commence its advance from the rendezvous until about 10.30 P.M. It marched off on a fine, clear, starlight night. General Aylmer and Staff remained between the Cavalry Brigade and Column C.

In spite of the darkness the march went well, though somewhat delayed, but dawn was breaking by the time the leading columns had reached their positions. Apparently, however, they were unperceived by the enemy, and this was indeed the case, as we afterwards ascertained. The other columns reached their positions also unperceived, although it was fairly light by that time.

The presence of the force continued apparently unsuspected by the Turks, as Dujaila redoubt seemed to be only lightly held when our columns reached their allotted positions. Time, however, passed in waiting for the guns to register, and in reconnoitring, so it was 9.45 A.M. before troops were deployed and advanced to the attack of the redoubt.

The positions were now found to be strongly held by the enemy, who were pouring in reinforcements. Fighting continued all day, and although at 5.15 P.M. further heavy and costly attacks were launched on the enemy's position, and for a time two battalions of the 8th Infantry Brigade, the Manchesters and the 59th Rifles, and some of the 37th Brigade succeeded in gaining a foothold in the redoubt, they were heavily counter-attacked by large enemy reinforcements, and, under heavy fire from guns near Sinn Aftar, were forced to fall back.

The troops were now much exhausted, having been under arms for something like thirty hours, which included a long night march ; and General Aylmer considered that a renewal of the assault during the night of the 8th–9th could not be made with any prospect of success. Next morning, being short of water, and the enemy's position remaining unchanged, our forces withdrew to the Wadi camp, which was reached that night, the gunboats raising the beams of their searchlights into the air as a guide to the returning column.

In Kut General Townshend had held a force of two brigades in readiness to co-operate, but, while hearing heavy firing, the Kut garrison could observe nothing of the action. He was in touch with Corps headquarters, and said that he would begin to send troops across the Tigris when he saw our turning attack developing south of Dujaila. Nothing was observed, however, and next morning he learned that yet another attack had failed.

From the Wadi camp General Younghusband's force had successfully given the enemy the impression that an assault was going to be delivered against the Hanna position on the night of the 7th–8th. The gunboats had also co-operated in the bombardments, the *Mantis*, the *Mayfly*, and the *Sandfly* above the bridge, the *Gadfly* and the *Dragonfly* below.

The failure of this nearly successful attempt to turn the Turkish right flank, and so to relieve Kut, was a great setback to us. Our losses had been heavy, and, further, reorganization being now required, no other operations of importance took place during March, except minor engagements along the right bank, where our forward positions were slightly advanced.

CHAPTER XIV

THE SURRENDER OF KUT

GREAT was the disappointment felt at the failure to turn the Turkish right and relieve Kut; a disappointment felt deeply by the force on the spot and by Britons at home, in India, and, indeed, all over the world. The question of the relief was becoming everywhere a subject for anxious discussion.

The impending annual Tigris floods introduced another danger to the attacking force. It was still very difficult to get reinforcements, ammunition, and stores to the front, as the available water transport was short of requirements, and the rains had recently made the land route impassable for weeks to come.

The port of Basra was also ill-equipped as a base, and could not cope with the immensely increased requirements of the force. In Turkish days there had been no wharves at Basra, and although we were beginning to construct some, most of the discharging of the vessels had to be done into lighters and clumsy *mahelas*, the supply of which was inadequate. Due to the consequent delay, there was at this time usually a line of vessels some miles in length waiting to discharge. Dockyards and workshops too were inadequate both in numbers and in equipment.

General Townshend telegraphed that he was killing off his animals, and that by reducing rations he could hold out until April 7th, or, on a starvation diet, very little later.

I was asked at this time whether it would be practicable to send by night a powerful tug protected by plating, with a barge on each side of it loaded with supplies, to run the gauntlet to Kut. I replied that I did not consider the idea practicable, since the craft would make such slow progress that it could not fail to prove an easy mark for the enemy in the narrow river, across which also obstructions might be placed. I suggested to General Gorringe that food might be dropped from aeroplanes, and this suggestion was acted upon.

Major-General Sir F. G. Gorringe succeeded General Aylmer in command of the Corps on March the 12th, and it was decided to renew operations as soon as possible after the arrival of the reinforcements then on their way up-river.

Rain again fell; the Tigris came down in heavy, sullen flood on March 15th, causing extensive inundation, some advanced positions having to be abandoned in consequence ; and there was a strenuous struggle with the swollen waters, owing to which an advance on Kut by the right or southern bank from Sheikh Saad was found to be unfeasible.

It was also decided that conditions were now more favourable for an attack on the Hanna position and for an advance up the left or northern bank. Preparations were accordingly made to put this decision into action, while at the same time steps were being taken to arrange for the alignment and construction of a light railway from Sheikh Saad towards Kut on the right bank.

The 7th Division had by March the 28th sapped up to within 150 yards of the Turkish front lines, in spite of being hampered by the flood waters and continually under heavy fire. On April the 1st the 13th British Division, which had just arrived, under Major-General Maude, moved up from Sheikh Saad and took the place of the 7th Division in the front-line trenches.

There was some heavy rain, but by the evening of the 4th of April this had passed, and the ground had dried sufficiently, so that at daylight on the 5th the 13th Division attacked and captured the Turkish first and second lines, in quick succession. Our artillery and machine-guns, with the gunboat flotilla, consisting of the *Mantis*, the *Mayfly*, the *Sawfly*, the *Waterfly* and the *Flycatcher*, co-operating, at once opened on the third and rear lines, and by 7 A.M. the whole position was in our hands.

The Turks had evacuated the position partly on account of the floods, leaving only a weak rearguard with machine-guns to hold their front line. Meanwhile on the right bank the 3rd Division had advanced and captured the enemy position on the Abu Roman Mounds and beaten off a counter-attack.

It was considered an urgent matter to capture the Fallahiya and Sannaiyat positions, three and six miles respectively west of the Hanna position, before the river, which was again rising considerably, rose so high as to make it possible for the Turks to open the *bunds*, and flood the country between the forces. The advance was therefore continued, and, preceded by bombardment, in which the gunboats again co-operated, the 13th Division attacked the Fallahiya position after nightfall. Although stubbornly held, it was carried ; by 9.30 P.M. it was completely in our hands and consolidated. The 7th Division, which had hitherto been in support, now moved forward, and, passing through the 13th, took up a position about two miles east of Sannaiyat, ready to attack the northern part of that position at dawn on the 6th.

It was, however, a very dark night ; the troops were so much delayed in crossing numerous and deep cross-trenches that lay between, and by units and wounded from Fallahiya passing through them, that at dawn, when the assault was to have taken place, they were still some 2300 yards from the enemy's position. General Lake pointed out in his report that this delay was fatal to the chance of success, as the ground was perfectly flat and without a vestige of cover, and in these circumstances, he remarked, it would have been wiser to have postponed the attack at the last moment. But the advance was ordered, and brought to a standstill by heavy fire about 700 yards from the Turkish lines, which were evidently fully prepared for the attack. Eventually our troops, after suffering very severe losses, fell back to the supporting third line, and dug themselves in about 1000 yards from the enemy.

Again the Tigris rose, and further attack had to be postponed, while our troops, working under fire, constructed *bunds*—or embankments—along both banks of the river and the edge of the great Suwaikieh Marsh. Some of our trenches were flooded and had to be evacuated, and many of the guns were likewise surrounded by flooded areas. The situation became for a time extremely critical, communication with troops on the right bank being extremely difficult. Food, stores, and munitions were ferried across the river to them after dark in barges under the command of officers from the gunboats.

During the night our forces on the right or southern bank had advanced far enough to be able, firing across the river, to enfilade the Sannaiyat entrenchments, and were thus able to assist our advance on the left bank during the 7th to within a thousand yards of that position, the gunboats and artillery supporting by bombardment.

General Gorringe now decided again to assault the Sannaiyat position, at dawn on the 9th, with the 7th and 13th Divisions. Meanwhile a bombardment of the enemy trenches, in which the gunboats took part, was carried out at 9 P.M. on the 7th, causing the Turks to man their trenches and to open a heavy fire.

When the moon had set, two hours later, the 7th Division advanced their entrenchment some two to three hundred yards nearer the enemy. Our night patrols had ascertained that the front of the enemy position was covered by barbed-wire entanglements, and that there were also floods and water-cuts from the Tigris in front of it.

The 8th was spent in registration of guns, wire-cutting, and similar preliminary operations, and this day, in the face of many difficulties, a new bridge over the Tigris at Fallahiya was completed. During that night the 13th Division replaced the 7th in the trenches, and advanced to the attack at 4.20 A.M. on the 9th. On this, as on previous occasions, I went to stay with General Gorringe at advanced headquarters during the attack. I did this in order to be in close touch with him, hear news immediately it came through, and to be able to get away in pursuit without delay if an opportunity showed itself.

The evening before I arrived at G.H.Q. for dinner, which was quite cheerful ; Gorringe was not like some generals, who, on the day before a battle, are rather like the head-keeper on the day before his big covert shoot, when a duke is expected.

The next day it was " early to rise " with a vengeance, as we all got up, dressed, shaved, and had breakfast about half an hour before zero-time. The General and Staff looked as smart as if they were just going to pay a call at the War Office, although it *was* 4 A.M. Of course, this was the only practical way of beginning the day, as they could not tell where they would be at the end of it.

After advance began there came minutes of suspense, everyone anxiously awaiting what the advanced telephones would tell. At last we heard that there was an initial success. The General discussed it, and we decided that I might proceed up-river to follow and harass any enemy retirement.

So I got hastily onboard the *Mantis*. ˙ We steamed away, and were hoping that things were going all right—as, of course, we should not have been well placed if they were not !—when I got an urgent wireless message from G.H.Q. to stop. Then we were told the disappointing real state of affairs. It appeared that the 13th Division had been discovered when within 300 yards of the front line of the Turkish position. The enemy had sent up Very lights and flares, and had at once opened a heavy fire on them.

Our leading line penetrated the centre of the enemy's front-line trench ; but, in the glare of the lights, our second line lost direction, wavered, and fell back on the third and fourth lines. Our troops who had reached the enemy's trenches were thus unsupported, and, being heavily counter-attacked by superior numbers, were driven back to from 300 to 500 yards from the enemy's line, where they stubbornly dug themselves in.

Being informed of what had happened, General Townshend again reduced his scanty scale of rations, and reported that he could hold out until April the 21st ; but, a certain amount of supplies in the meanwhile having been dropped by aeroplane, he later reported that he could hold out until the 29th—the extreme limit.

The Tigris, as well as the Turks, was giving the force a great deal of trouble, bursting embankments and causeways and isolating some of the troops and batteries. Altogether there were a great number of causes for anxiety. Of the plagues in Mesopotamia we had experienced intense heat, bitter cold, mud. Now arrived the flies ; and, living in the neighbourhood of recent battles, and the weather proving somewhat milder, we were soon tormented by these pests.

It was decided that the urgency of Kut's relief would not allow of the delay of sapping up to Sannaiyat, so another attempt to force the enemy's right near the Sinn Aftar redoubt on the right or southern bank was decided upon.

Heavy rain again fell, but in spite of floods the 3rd Division advanced across the belts of inundation on the right bank on April the 12th. Some of the troops, well above their knees in water, drove in the enemy pickets east of Beit Isa, and occupied their outpost line, consolidating their position during the night.

Several of the enemy's advanced trenches were also captured, and counter-attacks were repulsed on April the 15th and 16th. Under cover of an intense bombardment the 7th and 9th Infantry Brigades of Major-General Keary's force seized the Beit Isa position on the 17th, inflicting heavy loss on the enemy.

Orders were issued for the 13th Division to come up and relieve the 3rd, but at three o'clock in the afternoon the enemy established a barrage in the rear of the 3rd Division, and counter-attacked in great strength about an hour later. This was followed by further heavy attacks throughout the following night, but our line held firm, and at dawn the Turks retreated, having suffered losses estimated at between 4000 and 5000 men.

Although they had suffered such heavy losses, the enemy had checked our advance, regaining that portion of the position nearest the river, which during the succeeding days our forces made some attempt to recapture. On the 19th, Field-Marshal von der Goltz died at Baghdad, of typhus fever contracted on the Tigris front, and was succeeded by Khalil Pasha.

Meanwhile on the left bank the 7th Division had sapped steadily forward towards Sannaiyat, and, as there were some signs of the enemy's forces weakening, this appeared to be

P

another opportunity for making an attempt to capture that position. The 7th Division were preparing for an assault on the 20th when, the wind veering to the north, flooding the trenches and ground in front of them, the attack had to be postponed.

Throughout the 20th and 21st of April the Sannaiyat position was bombarded. After a preliminary bombardment on the 22nd, in which the gunboats joined—the flotilla being about this time augmented by the *Waterfly*, Lieutenant-in-Command W. V. H. Harris, D.S.C., R.N., and the *Greenfly*, Lieutenant-in-Command H. O. B. Firman, R.N.—the 7th Division advanced on a front which had to be reduced to that of one brigade, the extreme width of passable ground being only 300 yards. Besides our artillery fire, massed machine-guns on the right bank covered the advance from across the river, and did great execution in enfilading the enemy trenches. The leading troops carried the enemy's first and second lines in their immediate front, several of the trenches being flooded. Only a few of our men, however, reached the third line, and, large Turkish reinforcements coming up, the enemy succeeded in forcing our troops back, many of whom were fighting up to their knees in a sticky mess of mud and unpleasant-smelling river-water ; some even were unable to use their rifles, which had become choked with mud in crossing the flooded trenches. By 8.40 A.M. our men had retired to their own trenches, having suffered heavy casualties, amounting to about 1300.

By mutual consent parties went out under the Red Cross and Red Crescent flags to collect the wounded ; the Turks, who were evacuating theirs until nightfall, having also apparently lost heavily.

Persistent and repeated attempts on both banks had thus failed, and it was known that, at the outside, not more than six days' supplies remained to the Kut garrison. General Gorringe's troops were nearly worn out. In the words of General Lake :

> The same troops had advanced time and again to assault positions strong by art, and held by a determined enemy. For eighteen consecutive days they had done all that men could do to overcome not only the enemy, but also exceptional climatic and physical

obstacles, and this on a scale of rations which was far from being sufficient in view of the exertions they had undergone, but which the shortage of river transport had made it impossible to augment. The need for rest was imperative.

For some time attempts had been made to drop provisions into Kut from aeroplanes, and a certain number of these flights had been undertaken, but they were not frequent enough to be of material use. It was again suggested that a steamer loaded with provisions might attempt to run the blockade and get to Kut, in the hope that, by putting supplies into the town, General Townshend's resistance might be sufficiently prolonged to enable our forces to break through the enemy's lines. On this subject the Army Commander consulted the Naval Commander-in-Chief of the East Indies Station, Vice-Admiral Sir Rosslyn Wemyss—now Admiral of the Fleet, Lord Wemyss—who, having just arrived with his Staff in Mesopotamia on a visit of inspection, had come up to the front in the new gunboat *Snakefly*, Lieutenant-Commander Webster. The Admiral agreed to an attempt being made. The new river-steamer *Julnar* was selected for this special service, volunteers for a crew were called for, and this meeting with liberal response from officers and men, she was commissioned by Lieutenant Firman, R.N., in command, with Lieutenant-Commander Cowley, R.N.V.R., second-in-command, and her own engineer, Engineer Sub-Lieutenant Lewis Reed.

Lieutenant-Commander Cowley, R.N.V.R., had been for long a captain of Lynch's river-steamers, and had performed magnificent service in command of the river-steamer *Mejidieh* throughout the campaign. He had never hesitated to take his ship into difficult situations, and his local knowledge of the river had been of inestimable value, and had led to his selection when he volunteered for this forlorn hope.

The work of fitting out the *Julnar* with protective plating, 'etc, for this duty was carried out most expeditiously by Engineer Lieutenant-Commander S. W. Cooke, R.N., of H.M.S. *Proserpine*, and staff from the fleet, under the superintendence of Captain (now Vice-Admiral) Burmester, R.N. At 7 P.M. on April the 24th, carrying 250 tons of supplies, the *Julnar* proceeded up-river from Fallahiya, her departure being covered by all artillery and machine-gun fire which could be brought to bear, in the hope of distracting the enemy's attention. She was, however, discovered and shelled. At 1 A.M. General Townshend reported that she had not arrived and that at midnight a burst of heavy firing had been heard at Magasis, some eight and a half miles from Kut by river, which had suddenly ceased.

Next day the aeroplanes reported that the *Julnar* was in the hands of the Turks at Magasis.

It was found out afterwards that she had been stopped here by hawsers stretched across the river, and a heavy fire had been concentrated on her, Lieutenant Firman being killed, and the remainder of the gallant party of officers and men, of whom five were wounded, taken prisoners.

General Gorringe remarks : " This attempt to succour Kut, although unfortunately unsuccessful, was universally considered in the Tigris Corps to be worthy of the finest traditions of His Majesty's Royal Navy." Lieutenant Firman and Lieutenant-Commander Cowley were afterwards awarded posthumous V.C.'s, and decorations were given to the crew.

After this there was no further hope of extending the food limit of the garrison at Kut.

To quote again from General Lake :

> Everything that was possible with the means to hand had been attempted. The troops only desisted from their efforts when, through battle losses, sickness, and exhaustion, the limit of human endurance had been reached. On April 29th Kut surrendered.

Four months of strenuous fighting had ended in bitter disappointment.

What ill-wind had blown us to this shore—to this dreary, inhospitable country, the home of the treacherous Arab and cruel Turk ? In summer hot even for Indians, to the English cold in winter, even the elements had fought against us, as we struggled through mud or barren desert.

The operations which had originally contemplated the capture of Baghdad had involved the British Empire in over 40,000 casualties, including our force captured at Kut. A

total of close on 12,000 men went into captivity, where over
4000 of them died, many of them under conditions and in
circumstances (I quote from our *Official History*) which
must for ever form a blot on the Turkish reputation.

With the fall of Kut the little Naval force there, consisting
of the armed tug *Sumana*, with Lieutenant-in-Command
L. G. P. Tudway, D.S.C., her crew, and the four 4·7-inch
guns and crews, of whose bravery and excellent behaviour
General Townshend speaks very highly, fell into the hands
of the Turks.

The gunboats' *rôle* on the Tigris front had been lately
that of moveable batteries in the river, and no opportunity
had come for using their latent possibilities of movement, nor
had there been any chance of attacking enemy shipping.
We lived in hopes of better times, and meanwhile had
considerably improved our methods of indirect firing.
Gunboats were also doing useful work on the river lines of
communication, and up the Euphrates.

As has been the case in other unsuccessful operations,
there has been a great deal of criticism of the events which
occurred during the period just described.

Among points for consideration are : whether from the
point of view of the World War there was good reason for
the 1915 advance from Kut to Baghdad ; whether General
Townshend's action in halting and defending Kut was
sound strategy ; and, if so, whether his arrangement of the
defensive position was the best, especially with regard to the
influence which the river Hai would have on the relief of his
force by the right bank. His co-operation with the relieving
army must also be considered, particularly in the matter of
giving them information as to how long provisions in Kut
could hold out, upon which subject could not headquarters
at Basra have checked his estimates ?

The strategy and tactics of the army attempting to relieve
Kut brings up another series of questions. As to alterna-
tives of attack on either bank. Whether the attempt to
assault the Dujaila redoubt in the operation early in March
was necessary, and why the attempt to do so failed ; also
whether General Townshend and his force should have been
extricated and Kut evacuated at a period before the eyes of

the world were turned on the situation developing at this little unknown Arab town.

The question of supply by aircraft also offers an interesting field for consideration and surmise as to whether it should not be possible to supply from the air a beleagured force of moderate size, who are behind adequate defences and have an ample water-supply.

But whatever mistakes the critic will find in the British strategy, a great example of an opportunity lost was surely shown by the enemy immediately after the battle of Ctesiphon. If the Turks had not disclosed their reinforcements, and had Townshend with his force been lured into Baghdad, as it has been said the Germans advised, the British army could have been surrounded by the enemy in the great hostile city, far from their base ; and with Army Commander, Generals, troops, gunboats—indeed, nearly all the Expeditionary Force—compelled to surrender. As General Townshend said himself, " Had I been given two Divisions and got into Baghdad we should not have got out again."

Our hold on the remainder of the country and Basra would then have been a slender one.

After the surrender of Kut had been officially decided upon I obtained the concurrence of the Army Commander, and sent the following telegram to General Townshend on behalf of the Naval forces :

> We, the officers and men of the Royal Navy who have been associated with the Tigris Corps, and many of us so often worked with you and your gallant troops, desire to express our heartfelt regret at our inability to join hands with you and your comrades in Kut.

BOOK V

OPERATIONS LEADING TO THE CAPTURE
OF BAGHDAD

CHAPTER XV

EVENTS AFTER THE FALL OF KUT

AFTER the fall of Kut no operations on a large scale were undertaken until the return of the cool weather, towards the end of the year. His Majesty's Government explained their policy fully to India, who instructed General Lake accordingly.

Policy in Mesopotamia was to be defensive, but it was considered advisable to keep occupied those Turks who were opposed to the Tigris Corps. This was in order to minimize and to counteract the effect of the fall of Kut, and in order to assist the Russians.

For these reasons as forward a position as could be kept secure was to be maintained, and advantage taken of any weakness shown by the Turks. Should the latter be reinforced General Lake had full authority to fall back, the security of the force being of primary importance. The Tigris Corps therefore still maintained close contact with the Turks at Sannaiyat and Beit Isa. During the foregoing period nothing of importance had occurred on the Euphrates or the Karun. In the neighbourhood of the oilfields, as well as in the country to the west and south of Basra, all remained quiet.

Owing to Russian and British action, the situation in Persia had somewhat improved. Successful minor operations were carried out from the 14th to the 24th of April by the 23rd Cavalry, under the command of Lieutenant-Colonel L. N. Younghusband, on the Kharkeh River, near Disful, in Persia, against a force of Bakhtiari tribesmen, who had been operating against the Russians, and were moving back from the Pusht-i-Kuh to their own country.

At Basra H.M.S. *Proserpine* had arrived and taken over

the duties of Senior Naval Officer's ship on March 22nd, it having been found that the little *Espiègle* did not afford enough accommodation for the rapidly growing administrative work, offices, and so on. The *Espiègle* left the Shatt al Arab on March the 23rd, Lieutenant-Commander Seymour, Lieutenant Harden, Lieutenant Hallett, and myself having transferred to the *Proserpine*.

Two Naval twelve-pounders, which were accompanied by gun-crews from H.M.S. *Juno*, fitted on improvised mountings as anti-aircraft guns, had also been sent to the front, and remained as a useful protection to the camp until some military ones were sent out from home.

The gunboats were distributed at the front and on both rivers in such a way as would enable them to move rapidly forward and attack any enemy force raiding the communications ; or to support the military posts with their gunfire, and to convoy transport past the dangerous areas. Small steamcraft were also stationed occasionally in the vicinity of Amara and the Hammar Lake, under the control of the gunboat in that particular vicinity, for use in patrolling the smaller channels. These were given some armour-plate protection, armed with Maxims, and were manned by a mixed crew of seamen and soldiers, with a Naval officer in command.

The gunboats at the front had to rough it a good deal, but on the whole were kept well supplied with food and ammunition. This was largely owing to the splendid administrative work of Captain Wason at Basra, where his valuable powers of organization were given full play, as well as to the hard work of the officers and men at the base.

The *Flycatcher* and the gunboats proceeding up and down the river brought supplies, and we lived fairly well, although not on quite the lines of the Grand Fleet. We were the envy of the Army, however, who often fared nothing like so well. An amusing verse in the " Mesopotamian Alphabet," published about this time in the *Basra Times*, runs thus :

N's for the Navy, banked in here
With plenty of food, and plenty of beer.
I wish that I'd joined the Navy before
I came to Mesopotamia !

The officers and men of the ships at Basra used to take turns in coming up to the front for duty as required, forward observing for the guns, or replacing casualties, and they invariably enjoyed the change from the monotonous work at the base.

On the Tigris line, with the exception of those actually in the trenches, the troops at the front were, as far as was possible, resting during the hot months, and consolidating positions. Fatigue duties were heavy. The intense heat of the desert summer came on rapidly, and there was a good deal of sickness. Every effort was, however, made to exert pressure on the enemy by means of bombardments, in which gunboats co-operated, and this pressure was never relaxed. During May the enemy withdrew considerably along the right or southern bank, leaving it clear as far as the Hai, with the exception of rearguards and bridge-heads on that river. The Sannaiyat position, on the left bank, was, nevertheless, still strongly held. This withdrawal on the right bank was believed to be a result of the Russian advance from Persia *via* Kermanshah towards Baghdad. The proximity of the Russian forces at this time was shown by an interesting visit of a strong Cossack patrol, who safely executed an adventurous march from the neighbourhood of Karind through the Pusht-i-Kuh hills, and reached Ali Gharbi on May 20th, staying for a few weeks, and then successfully returning to their main body. The fall of Kut, however, released strong Turkish forces from our front, and by July General Baratoff had been compelled to evacuate Kermanshah and to withdraw into Persia.

Near our camp at the Tigris front there occurred on the 10th of June an incident which led to a serious loss of ammunition. The Turks suddenly opened fire at 6 A.M. with 5·9-inch guns, which they had secretly brought to an advanced position at Sannaiyat, on three barges heavily laden with military ammunition. These barges were moored at Fallahiya ; and their position, it was believed, had been given away by some exchanged prisoners, whose barge had passed near by on their way up the river. The shooting, which was directed by a small aeroplane dropping smoke-bombs, guarded by a fighting-machine with wireless, was most accurate, other enemy batteries diverting attention at the same time. Captain McIlwaine, Staff Captain to the Brigadier-General, Royal Artillery, hurried to the spot, and, assisted by Seaman Gunner Barnsley, who brought a tug alongside, made a gallant effort to save the barges ; but they were unable to slip the cables and move the barges in time, as the eighth round hit the eastern barge. Her grass matting caught fire, and she exploded within a few minutes, setting fire to the other two, which also exploded, and came down in showers of shrapnel and *débris*. This went on burning and exploding for a few days. Luckily Captain McIlwaine and everyone near had taken cover in time in a *nullah*, and the only casualties were one man and two mules. But 800 tons of ammunition, the ordnance store of two Divisions, were lost. The *Sawfly*, which was lying near, was also hit by several fragments, a sixteen-pounder shell coming down on her deck and piercing it, but fortunately without doing serious damage.

The enemy's retention of the Sannaiyat position prevented the passage of our supply-ships up the river. Our force on the right bank had therefore to depend on a long-drawn-out line of land transport, and General Gorringe's gradual occupation of the positions evacuated by the enemy therefore largely depended on his supply system, and could only be gradual. For the first few months these difficulties of supply owing to our lack of transport, by both land and water, were very great ; but energetic steps were at last taken to rectify this deficiency, and by August, when the floods had abated, we had advanced to positions from which we could dominate the Hai, deny its passage, and, if necessary, bombard Kut itself.

Reinforcements of guns and men gradually arrived at the front ; our supply of aeroplanes was also put on a more satisfactory footing ; and the *Tarantula*, the *Moth*, and the *Gnat* joined the flotilla at this time.

On July the 11th General Gorringe was succeeded in command of the Tigris column by General Maude. This officer, whose name is now well known throughout the British Empire, had already had a brilliant and hard-working career. Ever since, as a young man, he joined the

Coldstream Guards, he had held many responsible and Staff positions ; and during the Great War had served with distinction on the Western Front and at the Dardanelles. Thence he brought his famous 13th Division to Mesopotamia. On taking over command he at once commenced working out the plans which were to have such great results. Field-Marshal Sir William Robertson says of General Maude, whom he selected for the Mesopotamia Command :

> I know that Maude possessed a high standard of honour ; I knew also that he was careful in the interests of his men, held sound views on tactical and strategical questions, recognized the value of good organization, and in every way seemed to be the ideal man to clear up the Mesopotamia muddle and give the Turks a good thrashing in the bargain.

It must, of course, be also remembered that General Maude had circumstances in his favour not enjoyed by his predecessors. Besides the personal advantage of comparative youth, and not having passed the long years of debilitating Indian service which other Army Commanders had done, he had a much larger and better equipped army than they had. The nation had at last realized the futility of the half-hearted, happy-go-lucky way in which this expedition had been managed and equipped ; and, spurred by the loss of Kut, was at last becoming more generous in the supply of weapons and general materials of war, which hitherto had been lavishly supplied to every front but this.

Operations on the Euphrates at this period were confined to raiding expeditions, carried out in order to punish hostile Arabs, who from time to time attacked our ships on the rivers, damaged telegraph-lines, and raided those tribes which were allied to us. Ibn Rashid, the leading hostile desert Arab chief, was driven away southwards in July with much diminished prestige. A very successful raid against Ajaimi, the principal *sheikh* hostile to us on the Lower Euphrates, was carried out on August the 15th. These operations were well organized by Major-General Brooking.

At this period two gunboats were always stationed on the

Euphrates, with headquarters at Nasiriya, and where possible they took part in operations. They also did some very useful work in the examination of the northern part of the Hammar Lake, with the shallow Quataniah and Talaiya Lakes, as well as of the channels between it and Shattra, on the Hai. Some very useful surveying of this part was done by Lieutenant Harding, R.N.V.R.

It was very opportune for the gunboats to visit these out-of-the-way places occasionally. Besides the useful effect on the political and military situation, it was of great value to afford the officers and men practical experience in the use of their armament under difficult conditions. There is nothing like actual use under fire to afford confidence and skill in the employment of guns and rifles. These are not likely to jamb and missfire often in the hands of men who, under fire themselves, are forced to realize the necessity of keeping down that of the enemy.

The *Cranefly*, the *Dragonfly*, the *Snakefly*, the *Greenfly*, the *Grayfly*, the *Gadfly*, and the *Mayfly* were frequently engaged with the hostile Arabs of Badra village and other places in these vicinities.

Among other small operations the *Greenfly* and the *Snakefly*, convoying troops in the sternwheeler *Muzaffri*, proceeded on June the 9th to the vicinity of Badra to punish the inhabitants for destroying our telegraph-line. The village was shelled, and the enemy, whose strength was some twelve to fifteen hundred, replied from concealed positions behind the sandhills with heavy rifle-fire, the ships coming into action with all guns and rifles. C.P.O. J. Paddon and Stoker P.O. T. Howard of the *Greenfly* were wounded, but considerable loss was inflicted on the enemy. Both Lieutenant-Commander Seymour and Lieutenant Webster spoke very highly of the coolness under fire of their officers and men on this occasion.

The *Greenfly* and the *Mayfly* were again engaged with Arabs near Khidr, on the Euphrates, in July, when the former had one officer and two men wounded.

The year 1916 was an unusually hot and unhealthy one, and with the sudden rise of temperature in May the numbers of our sick increased rapidly. The intense heat was aggravated by the failure of the *shamal*, or cool north wind, which, instead of, as usual, springing up in June, did not commence to blow until late in July, when the admissions to hospital at once increased. The Naval and military forces had suffered severely, however, and an outbreak of cholera, besides dysentery and other diseases, took its toll of the troops.

The *Proserpine* had been commissioned at the outbreak of war, her crew being largely drawn from the Naval and Fleet reserves, a considerable proportion of whom were men older than our usual active service ratings. These particularly suffered from the intense heat. Out of her small crew there were over seventy on the sick list at one time, sixty-nine had to be sent to Bombay in the hospital ship *Vita*, and lascar stokers had to be borrowed from the *Dalhousie* to help work the *Proserpine* to Bombay.

The *Proserpine* and the *Odin* went in turn to Ceylon to refit, the crews being sent by watches to the Royal Naval camp in the hills at Diyatalawa, to recuperate their health. All the gunboats' crews were also sent in turn by transport and rail to the hills in either Ceylon or India. The change and the hill climate proved invaluable in its beneficial effect on the health of officers and men, and, though a somewhat expensive journey, this procedure undoubtedly saved many lives.

The great value to the Navy of our hill-camp at Diyatalawa was again exemplified. Originally planned to accommodate Boer prisoners, as I have explained, this site is occupied by the Navy at a nominal rent from the Colony as a hill station where the men of the East Indies station may recuperate. They greatly benefit by this change from the hot, steamy climate of those seas. The Admiralty had insisted each year on my sending my officers and men there by turns, and I can say without hesitation that the results the change produced were most beneficial.

The sea voyage to Bombay or Ceylon and back was in itself valuable. The change from the confined life of the delta, and a healthy existence, with plenty of games, exercise, and recreation, worked wonders in the men and was, in effect, a real economy. The sailors were given an easy time in camp, the only duties being morning divisions, church parades, a musketry course, plus the usual camp guards and fatigues, the latter including a party who, enduring much chaff, went round with anti-mosquito sprinklers.

During my absence on board the *Proserpine* in Ceylon, from August to October 1916, Captain C. R. Wason, R.N., carried out the duties of Senior Naval Officer.

A few words as to our recreations in Mesopotamia might be of interest, although there was not much doing in that line ! We used to get a game of tennis—on hard courts, of course—at the club in Basra, or on courts belonging to the merchants, and later in our occupation of the country tennis-courts were constructed at Amara and other places.

For those who were fond of sport there was a good deal of game-shooting, which served as a welcome change and alleviation from the never-ending work in which we were immersed. So occasionally, instead of Turks and Arabs, we had a pot at the sand-grouse. There were partridges, too, on the rivers. I remember a shoot just north of Qualat Saleh in which we had two guns walking on each bank, and the gunboat steaming down the river in the centre, with gun cleared away to overawe the Arabs, who were probably in ambush among the sandhills, and also looking out for a chance of sport !

In certain seasons of the year snipe are abundant in the deltas of the rivers, and waterfowl abound in the swamps and marshes. Gunboat captains used to experiment with all manner of strange charges and missiles in their quick-firing guns, with ammunition not mentioned in the text-books, and the expenditure of which was not entered in the gunnery logs or returns, but with which, it was rumoured, on one occasion at least a great bag of wild geese was made.

Near the front it was found that the constant din had, as a rule, scared game away, but one afternoon I remember we walked in line through some rough ground and got a nice little bag of quail and " various," one of which was a wild dog, while a heavy bombardment thundered not far away.

CHAPTER XVI

REORGANIZATION

THE summer of 1916 was unbearably hot, but the latter half of that year was a period of comparative rest for the troops. Every effort was being made to improve their personal conditions, to reinforce them, to reorganize the base at Basra and put it into such condition as to be able to maintain them reasonably well.

General Maude very soon decided that the headquarters of the force should be moved nearer to the Tigris front, where the main issue would be decided. After inspection of affairs at the base, the oilfields, and along the Euphrates, General Headquarters were accordingly established there towards the end of October.

The force was now reorganized into two Army Corps of two divisions each—Lieutenant-General A. S. Cobbe commanding the first, and Lieutenant-General W. R. Marshall commanding the new 3rd Indian Army Corps.

From the beginning of September there was a steady influx of river vessels, besides reinforcements, into the country, also a large increase in mechanical transport—tractors for heavy artillery, trench mortars, machine-guns, and other similar necessaries.

Stores, ammunition, and supplies on a generous scale were also pouring in.

The efficiency of our Air Force in Mesopotamia was also much increased during this period by the arrival of a number of experienced pilots, besides up-to-date fighting 'planes; and it was not long before British supremacy in the air had been thoroughly re-established.

The shortage of river transport has been referred to several times in the preceding chapters, and early in 1916 made itself very much felt in Mesopotamia. Steps had not been taken in time to construct railways, wharves, and re-pairing-yards, or to provide craft of suitable light draught. With the arrivals of large bodies of troops and bulky materials in the country, all these wants were even more severely felt. Efforts to rush reinforcements and equipment into the country, then up the river to the front, all within a few weeks, had resulted in chaos. Nor had the necessary steps been taken in time to expand the small existing repairing-yards, in order to keep pace with mere running repairs, essential to a port harbouring considerable shipping. How to keep abreast the new demands now became a serious consideration. In addition, there was a large amount of reconstructive work to be done, as a number of small craft, barges and so on, which were too small to undertake the sea voyage, and had been already responsible for many losses, had arrived from India, Egypt, or possibly Europe. They could be shipped out only in sections or plates, and were put together in the river.

As I have explained, the Admiralty had made early arrangements for the " small China gunboats " to be sent out in parts and assembled, by arrangement with Messrs. Strick, Scott, on slips at the Anglo-Persian Oil Company's concession in Abadan, where a small dockyard was formed. An experienced and able foreman, Mr. W. Grant, a member of the staff of Messrs. Yarrow and Co., with assistants carried out the work. He was also Admiralty representative, and under his supervision the work was performed expeditiously as well as efficiently.

At the beginning of 1916 the India Office also made a contract with Messrs. Strick, Scott, for the re-erection of vessels at Abadan, and the Senior Naval Officer was author-ized to give the necessary orders as to priority of construction there. We rendered every help, so as to secure the best results in the interests of all. The Senior Naval Officer was also later directed to decide, after consultation with the General Officer Commanding, the relative urgency of work on war vessels and transport craft.

Owing to the shortage of stores, lack of good supervision, and sickness—this latter largely due to the intense heat—as I have said before—the difficulty experienced by Messrs.

Strick, Scott, in supplying adequate labour, and in over-
coming the limited resources of their yards, caused great
delay in assembling these transport craft, the little dockyard's resources being already overtaxed by the repairs
necessary to running craft.

In July the General Officer Commanding reported to the
War Office that, owing to the complete breakdown of arrangements, the position had become entirely unsatisfactory, and
asked that a suitable officer, staff, and European skilled
mechanics should be sent out. It was pointed out at the
time that, except for the development of the railway to
Amara, the difficulties of the Tigris communications were
not diminishing.

The transport department of the Indian Expeditionary
Force in this campaign had until this time been administered
and manned by the Royal Indian Marine, who serve under
the Indian Government ; and it will be understood how great
were the difficulties that they had to overcome in the enormously increased responsibilities, the varied duties, and the
consequently increased calls on their department. Difficulties were considerably increased, too, by the fact that the
Royal Indian Marine is not—or, at any rate, was not then—
an independent Indian force, but was under, and controlled
by, the Chief of the General Staff of the Indian Army. They
were thus liable to constant interference by the General
Staff on the spot. Also, their head, the Director of Indian
Marine at Bombay, under this arrangement, could also be
influenced, and might not in consequence be able to bring
the necessary independent authority to bear on the financial
department.

Early in February 1916 the War Office had assumed
control of the Expedition, and in July it took over all the
administrative work, becoming solely responsible for the
policy and management of the Expedition. It was at once
decided to place the whole transport department under
the administration of the recently formed Inland Water
Transport Department. Colonel Grey, who had directed
similar work with great success on other fronts, was sent out
from England in July 1916 to take up this command. The
whole of the *personnel* employed on river transport, including

that of the R.I.M., came under his orders as soon as he assumed control. It may be noted, as showing what excellent *personnel* existed in this force, that the officers who became his principal and most responsible assistants had been the permanent officers of the R.I.M. in the late transport department. Strenuous efforts were made immediately to relieve the congestion of shipping held up during the delays in unloading at Abadan and Basra. For by this time the delays were seriously jeopardizing the success of the operations and the health of the troops, and, indirectly, were affecting all theatres of war.

The Admiralty and War Office also decided that for a period the whole staff and facilities at Abadan should be placed at the disposal of Colonel Grey, only work necessary for the actual supply of oil being also undertaken, and the construction of the last four gunboats was deferred for a time.

The Inland Water Transport Department also started an independent dockyard above Basra for the erection of river craft. This yard soon assumed large proportions. With the construction of wharves, slipways, and docks, also by dredging and river improvement undertakings—in which the work commenced and planned by Sir George Buchanan was largely incorporated, besides the management of the sea and river transport—their work soon became of a very large and far-reaching character. It was most ably and energetically organized and carried out, and it may be said to have solved, to a great extent, at any rate, the pressing problems of transport on difficult rivers peculiar to this campaign.

At the end of the year the Senior Naval Officer was able to report that the port arrangements were working satisfactorily, that it was considered they would continue to do so under the existing arrangement, and that no Naval control—which probably would only have added to departmental friction—was considered wise or desirable at that time. It was emphasized, however, that the conditions were peculiar, that they applied to Basra alone, and that the Admiralty should reserve for themselves the fullest right to assume control at any time.

From July 1916 onwards great activity was exhibited ;

much good and lasting work was done in the development of Basra and its vicinity, and up the rivers. Wharves large enough to allow ocean steamers to draw alongside were constructed at Basra and farther up the river. In the vicinity of Magil—the place originally selected as the terminus of the Baghdad Railway, and now the starting-point of our railway to Nasiriya—was also formed an immense base depot for supplies and ordnance.

Great energy was displayed in endeavouring to improve the roads, railways, and other means of communication; handicapped, as these always will be in Lower Mesopotamia, by the difficulties of the flat country, consisting for the most part of arid, trackless desert, intersected by deep creeks and irrigation channels in those parts near the river. Good roads and bridges to carry the traffic over the numerous creeks were constructed between the various camps and Basra; a road was made from Kurna to Amara, crossing over no less than seventy bridges, of which thirty-six miles consisted of a raised causeway, whereon the narrow-gauge railway from Kurna to Amara was eventually placed.

The railway from Kurna to Amara was completed at about the end of November 1916, one from Basra to Nasiriya about the end of the year, while at the Tigris front the light railway from Sheikh Saad reached Imam-al-Mansur just prior to this time. Many important miscellaneous works, together with a large amount of hutting for the troops, were under construction. A very powerful wireless station was installed at Basra, and completed on the 25th of August.

The work of development at the port of Basra, of dredging and improving the communications generally, also owed much to the appointment of Sir George C. Buchanan, before spoken of, to the force as Director-General of Port Administration and River Conservancy.

Approval having been obtained from the Commander-in-Chief and Army Commander, the old Turkish hospital at Tanooma and its grounds on the north bank of the Shatt al Arab, opposite Basra, were laid out as a shore Naval depot and sick quarters, with magazine, storehouses and sheds, repairing-shop, and boat slip, the Indian Marine vessel *Dalhousie* being utilized as a floating Naval depot.

Naval Kite Balloon Section No. 14 arrived during the summer, under the command of Commander Francis R. Wrottesley, moved up to the front, and camped on the right bank of the Tigris, near Arab Village. Their work, which lay almost entirely with the Army, consisted of keeping a look-out for any movement of enemy forces, and in marking for our artillery. They also proved of considerable service in spotting for the gunboats' firing later in the year, when the well-arranged telephone system of the Kite Balloon station was a most valuable connection between the gunboats, the military telephone organizations, and the observing stations.

The gunboats got a great deal of practice during these bombardments, and it was most interesting for a sailor to have this opportunity of studying military methods at short range—and, incidentally, of adopting them where advantageous to our particular circumstances. Several gunboats could be secured near each other to the river-bank, and used like a 4-inch gun battery, as they were directed by telephone from a forward observer either in the Kite Balloon or the observation stations.

In the latter we were very much impressed by the exact method of locating the fall of shot by simultaneous theodolite bearings from two neighbouring positions. These, telephoned to a recorder in a trench near by, could at once be plotted on a graph placed on a map of the enemy's position, and the necessary correction telephoned to the gun.

By the end of November large reserves of supplies, stores, and munitions had been amassed at the front, communications perfected, and our resources greatly developed. Great improvements in the training and health of the troops had also been made, and they had shaken off the effects of the hot, enervating summer months. General Maude therefore considered that offensive operations could be shortly undertaken, and completed the general concentration of his troops upstream beyond Sheikh Saad.

Rain fell during the early days of December, producing the usual muddy results ; but by the 9th, luckily, it had cleared ; and General Maude prepared for the first step in his offensive, which was to secure a position on the river Hai in his immediate front.

CHAPTER XVII

THE ADVANCE ON KUT

IN Mesopotamia the year 1916, which had opened in gloom, and the opening months of which had been one long list of unsuccessful operations and heavy losses, was to close with a brighter outlook for the future.

At the beginning of December the enemy still occupied the same positions on the Tigris front that they had held during the latter part of the summer; and a desultory type of warfare, with intermittent artillery and aerial activity, still continued.

General Maude decided first of all to secure possession of the Hai, and for this purpose the 1st Army Corps, under Lieutenant-General A. S. Cobbe, was assigned the task of holding the enemy to his position on the left bank of the Tigris, and of piqueting the right bank as far as Sinn Banks; while the Cavalry and 3rd Army Corps, under Lieutenant-General (now Sir) W. R. Marshall, were by a surprise march to secure and entrench a position on the Hai.

During the night of December 12th–13th General Marshall's force completed its concentration in the forward area on the right bank, and on December the 13th General Cobbe bombarded the Turkish trenches on the left bank, in order to give the enemy the impression that an attack on Sannaiyat was intended. The gunboats co-operated in this bombardment, with the Naval Kite Balloon section observing and keeping a look-out on enemy movements.

General Marshall's force advanced across the desert and seized a position on the Hai on the morning of the 14th, extending their hold between the 15th and 18th and 20th, when by a successful bombardment they destroyed the enemy's Hai bridge. Among the many remarkable events chronicled in this book must be included mention of the fact that on this Christmas Day a free ration of champagne was issued to the officers of the force, in which we in the Navy shared. It was a noble gift of the late Lord Curzon to the Expedition. A very kindly thought of that great man, to single out for such consideration the expedition which had felt so lost and neglected in the world upheaval. There was plenty of plum-pudding also, I might add, and our friends the soldiers saw that we came in for a goodly share of everything.

During December our forces interposed between the two Turkish trench systems on the right bank of the Tigris opposite Kut, thus severing the enemy's lateral communications on that bank, and obtaining command of the river upstream of the Khaidari bend. The remainder of the month and the first part of January 1917—although we were delayed by heavy rains for a few days—were devoted to consolidating our position on the Hai, and improving our communications by making bridges, constructing roads, and pushing forward the light railway to the Hai.

Before proceeding with further detailed description of the operations on the Tigris, it might be considered advisable to say something about the state of development at this time of our base at Basra.

As explained more fully above, very large and sweeping improvements had been effected in every branch of the Transport Department, and there were greatly increased numbers of river craft at our disposal. The facilities for repairs had also been considerably increased, adequate-sized wharves constructed, and a number of small river-steamers and barges reconstructed at Abadan as well as at Basra ; while the better provision of mechanical transport, the increase in the number of both animals and vehicles, had enabled the land transport to be reconstituted.

There had also been a large addition to the numbers of experienced *personnel* for the Directorates of Port Administration and Conservancy, Works, Railways, Supply, Transport, and Ordnance. Great improvements had been effected in the organization of local and imported labour.

Hospitals and other vitally essential services had been expanded, and the force had thus been put in possession of far greater advantages than it had ever owned before.

The progress of work at the Naval depot at Tanooma, on the northern bank of the river opposite Basra, had also been considerable, thanks to the able and energetic administration of Captain Cathcart R. Wason, C.M.G., R.N., and the staff of officers and men at the base, who were during this while accommodated in the *Proserpine*, the *Dalhousie*, the *Alert* and at the Naval depot.

Early in 1916 it had been proposed to use the southern corner of the Ashar Creek as the Naval depot, and work had already been commenced there when the more favourable site at Tanooma was offered and accepted for the use of the Royal Navy. Although considerably delayed by abnormal sickness during the hot weather, fairly good progress had been made in the work which became more rapid with the advent of the cool season.

At the time of acquiring the Tanooma site all reserves of Naval ammunition, as well as quantities of stores, were housed on board a captured Austrian steamer of 6000 tons, the *Franz Ferdinand*; but the release of this vessel for overseas traffic became a matter of such importance that the verandas of the old Turkish hospital at Tanooma were converted into temporary magazines, and used until a more suitable building could be erected. In the main building of Tanooma were kept stores for the gunboats and Kite Balloon section; the rooms of the second floor were used as offices, and messes when necessary; and on the space outside a workshop, store-shed, and the like were erected.

The workshop, a corrugated iron building 132 feet by 30 feet, was completed in the middle of December, with lathes, drilling, shaping, and other machines in course of erection. A large galvanized iron store-shed, 125 feet by 60 feet, was put up early in 1917, while a brick magazine and shell-room, 150 feet by 30 feet, was completed towards the end of the month.

The depot ground was banked up and raised above the flood-level, and a pier 360 feet long erected, with a T head, and a depth of water alongside it of not less than six feet at low water, in order to accommodate the *Mantis* class at any time. Lines of light railway were to connect the pier with the depot, and a travelling crane was to be on the T head. A boat slip was also constructed, and buoys for the gunboats were laid off the depot.

The *Odin* left for Aden at noon on the 7th of January, as she was more urgently required elsewhere, Captain Wason taking over command of the *Dalhousie* and of the depot, and Commander E. M. Palmer going to the *Odin*.

At this period several of the gunboats were always stationed in the vicinity of our advanced positions at the Tigris front, with others at various points along the lines of communication. Two were also on the Euphrates, in touch with the 15th Indian Divisional Headquarters at Nasiriya. It was arranged that the gunboats should each take a turn at every station, and then refit in rotation at Basra or Abadan. By this means, and by the work of the useful sternwheel repair-ship H.M.S. *Scotstoun*, commissioned at Abadan on January the 4th, with Lieutenant Nicolle in command, they were kept in efficient condition.

The following gunboats were engaged at various times : the *Tarantula*, Commander Henry G. Sherbrooke ; the *Mantis*, Commander Bernard Buxton ; the *Moth*, Lieutenant-Commander C. H. A. Cartwright; the *Gnat*, Lieutenant-Commander E. H. B. L. Scrivener ; the *Butterfly*, Lieutenant-Commander G. A. Wilson ; the *Sawfly*, Commander G. F. A. Mulock, D.S.O. ; the *Snakefly*, Lieutenant R. P. D. Webster ; the *Greenfly*, Lieutenant-Commander A. G. Seymour, D.S.O. ; the *Gadfly*, Commander E. K. Arbuthnot ; the *Grayfly*, Lieutenant C. H. Heath-Caldwell ; the *Stonefly*, Lieutenant M. Singleton, D.S.O. ; the *Mayfly*, Lieutenant R. H. Lilley, D.S.C. ; the *Waterfly*, Acting-Commander C. T. Gervers ; the *Firefly*, Lieutenant-Commander C. J. F. Eddis ; the *Flycatcher*, Lieutenant Hugh Lincoln, R.N.R. ; the *Scotstoun*, Lieutenant S. E. Nicolle. The *Cranefly*, Lieutenant-Commander A. R. Chalmer, R.N. ; and the *Dragonfly*, Lieutenant A. C. Thursfield, R.N., also did good work on the Euphrates during the period.

To return to the Tigris. By the 1st of January, 1917, the

British Army in Mesopotamia has, as we have described, just commenced the successful operations under General Maude. These were to result in the defeat of the Turkish forces and two months later the advance on and capture of the city of Baghdad ; and I cannot do better than quote the words of that brilliant leader regarding the principles which guided him in the operations which are described in the following pages. He states in his dispatch of the 10th of April, 1917 :

> The area over which the responsibilities of the Army extended was a wide one, embracing Fallahiya, on the Tigris ; Ispahan (exclusive), in Persia ; Bushire, on the Persian Gulf ; and Nasariya, on the Euphrates. Briefly put, the enemy's plans appeared to be to contain our main forces on the Tigris, whilst a vigorous campaign, which would directly threaten India, was being developed in Persia. There were indications, too, of an impending move down the Euphrates towards Nasiriya. To disseminate our troops in order to safeguard the various conflicting interests involved would have relegated us to a passive defensive everywhere. It seemed clear from the outset that the true solution of the problem was a resolute offensive, with concentrated forces on the Tigris, thus effectively threatening Baghdad, the centre from which the enemy's columns were operating. Such a stroke pursued with energy and success would, it was felt, automatically relieve the pressure in Persia and on the Euphrates, and preserve quiet in all districts with the security of which we were charged.

He goes on to group the operations into eight phases as follows :

1. Preliminary preparations from August the 28th to December the 12th.
2. The consolidation of our position on the Hai.
3. The operations in the Khaidari bend of the Tigris.
4. Operations against the Hai salient.
5. Operations in the Dahra bend on the Tigris.
6. The captures of Sannaiyat and passage of the Tigris.
7. The advance on and capture of Baghdad.
8. Operations subsequent to the fall of Baghdad.

We have dealt with the first and second phases, and now on the 1st of January, 1917, our forces were consolidating their position on the Hai, as the result of the occupation of which we had (*a*) secured a position whence we could control the waterway, and directly threaten the enemy's communications west of Shumran; (*b*) rendered Nasiriya safe against a hostile movement down the Hai; (*c*) increased the possibility of obtaining supplies from the prosperous districts on the Middle Hai, and rendered it correspondingly difficult for the enemy to do so; and (*d*) interposed between the Turks and their adherents at Shattra.

The month of January 1917 was occupied in reducing the enemy trench systems on the right bank of the Tigris, the 1st Corps under General Cobbe successfully clearing the enemy from the Khaidari bend by the 19th. The 3rd Corps and force under General Marshall commenced preparations for the reduction of the Hai salient on January the 11th, and, gaining ground steadily in the face of strong opposition, the British trenches had reached within 400 yards of the enemy front line on January the 24th. This was captured on the following day, and after further heavy fighting the salient fell into our hands on February the 4th. The Cavalry meanwhile on January the 11th occupied Hai town, and remained there for some days.

The next stage of the operations was designed to clear the enemy out of the Dahra bend. After careful preparation and bombardment the enemy was first compelled on the nights of February 10th–11th to evacuate the liquorice factory, and withdrew to an inner line across the Dahra bend, in which he was finally enclosed by February the 13th. After most severe fighting the bend was cleared of the enemy by the morning of the 16th.

I have described only very shortly the magnificent efforts by which the Army had gained the recent successes and driven the enemy from the right bank of the Tigris in the neighbourhood of Kut, as the details, after all, belong more to a military than to a Naval history.

As the official historian says:

The capture of the Dahra bend terminated a phase of fighting which had lasted continuously for two months, which had entailed an advance through a network of hostile trenches extending for about twelve miles along the Tigris bank and some miles along the Hai, and had called for fighting qualities of a high standard from the troops engaged.

The Turkish defence of their right-bank positions had been gallant in the extreme, and worthy of our highest admiration.

The Turkish historian offers the opinion that their defence, though it may have weakened our strength, completely broke the powers of resistance of the XVIIIth Turkish Army Corps. The weather had also been much more in our favour than had been the case in the year before.

All these and the following operations were most carefully and skilfully planned and directed step by step by the Army Commander, General Maude, for whom no detail was too insignificant. He worked hard at all hours. I often had opportunities of conferring with him, was kept well in touch with affairs, and he invariably showed great kindness and consideration to the Navy.

I several times visited him at the advanced headquarters near Dujaila redoubt, going there and back by motor-car. Colonel Tennant, commanding the Air Force, flew me over once, and we had a good view of Kut and the Turkish lines at Sannaiyat, howbeit we were fired at as we went over. On that occasion I remember Tennant landed quite near G.H.Q. I changed the airman's head-covering I had been wearing for my Naval cap, and rather surprised them all by suddenly appearing in the camp in Naval uniform! The Army Commander was sitting in his tent, and showed me on his map the latest developments, news of which was then coming in.

The gunboats were doing useful work by joining in the bombardments. By constant practice we had become much more familiar with the methods of indirect firing, our efficiency having been greatly advanced by the energy and perseverance of both officers and men. Commander (now Captain) Sherbrooke of the *Tarantula*, my next senior officer, showed particular zeal, and took great trouble in work in this connection. We also received a great deal of help from Commander Wrottesley, who was in command of the Kite Balloon section. The efficient telephone service of this unit was of inestimable value to us.

Supplied, as we were, with all the latest maps as used by our artillery, we were able to direct our fire on any part of the enemy position when asked by telephone to do so.

Those gunboats which were moored nearest to the enemy position made, by reason of their masts and funnels, such a conspicuous mark that General Cobbe warned me one afternoon when I saw him in camp that the Turks might move a gun closer, and unexpectedly open fire on us. Sure enough, they did so shortly after, and we had to move back hurriedly to a less unhealthy position. The *Gnat* had been there for some time, and had quite a farmyard on the river-bank alongside her, and it was an amusing sight to see her sailors among the hurry and falling shells, rushing onboard with all their much-prized cocks and hens !

On the 15th of February General Maude issued a very complimentary order of the day, congratulating the forces, among whom the Navy received flattering recognition on the recent successes. It concluded by saying : " The end is not yet, but with such absolute co-operation, and vigour animating all, continuance of our success is assured."

The enemy having, after two months of strenuous fighting and very heavy losses, been driven entirely from the right bank of the Tigris in the neighbourhood of Kut, was, how-ever, still protected to the eastward, on the left bank, by the strong Sannaiyat position, the Suwaikieh and Jessan Marshes, and from Sannaiyat to Shumran by the river Tigris. He had, at the same time, been compelled so to weaken and to expand his front by the pressure of our troops in the vicinity of Shumran that his attenuated force presumably would be found to present vulnerable points. General Maude therefore considered that the time seemed ripe for our force to attempt a crossing of the river, and to commence conclusions with the enemy on the left bank. To effect this it was important that the enemy's attention should be engaged about Sannaiyat and along the river line between Sannaiyat and Kut, while the vital stroke was being aimed and delivered as far west as possible.

Orders were therefore issued for Sannaiyat to be attacked on the 17th of February ; and after a heavy bombardment, in which the gunboats took part, the first and second lines, on a frontage of about 400 yards, were occupied by two native regiments in a surprise assault on that day. However, they had to be relinquished after several strong counter-attacks. The operation had, nevertheless, served to attract the enemy to the Sannaiyat front, and bombardments, in which the gunboats, as usual, joined, were subsequently carried out daily, in order to accustom the enemy to bombardment unaccompanied by assault. At the same time methodical preparations were made to cross the Tigris near Shumran, and minor diversions planned to deceive the enemy as to the point where it was intended to cross the river.

On February the 22nd another assault was made on the Sannaiyat position, by the Seaforths and a Punjabi battalion, who gained a footing in the enemy position, which they managed to retain in spite of the most furious counter-attacks. Two frontier force regiments then assaulted the trenches held by the enemy in prolongation of those we had already occupied, and after a severe struggle our forces were by nightfall in secure occupation at last of the first two lines of the Sannaiyat position. General Maude pays a special tribute to the brilliant tenacity of the Seaforths, who had figured prominently in the capturing of this hold on the formidable position which had withstood so many attacks, kept our forces at bay for months, and become the grave of so many of our gallant British and Indian comrades.

In connection with the intended crossing of the Tigris, feints were made on the nights of the 22nd and 23rd of February opposite Kut and Magasis respectively, which had the effect of causing the enemy to move infantry and guns, that could not afterwards be retransferred to the actual point of crossing in time to be of use. The site selected for the passage of the Tigris was at the south end of the Shumran bend, where a bridge was to be thrown over, ferrying places being located near. Just before daybreak on the 23rd of February troops began to ferry themselves across, a party of Norfolks being the first to arrive on the opposite shore, and although considerable opposition was met with about three companies of the Norfolks and 150 Gurkhas were on the left bank by 7.30 A.M. In spite of the activity of the enemy's artillery, which was being vigorously engaged by our own, the construction of a bridge across the river commenced, and having been rapidly proceeded with, was ready for traffic by 4.30 P.M.

By nightfall a division of our troops that had crossed was also pushing on and securing a position ahead, acting vigorously against the enemy's advanced detachments ; another division was making ready to follow.

While all this was progressing General Cobbe had secured the third and fourth lines at Sannaiyat and penetrated the fifth. On the 24th of February he pushed forward. Without much further opposition, he cleared the Sannaiyat, Nukhailat and Suwada positions, and along the left bank as far as Kut. The enemy had suffered most severely. Many of their trenches were literally blocked with corpses.

Meanwhile our troops in the Shumran bend resumed the advance early on the 24th, and after a strenuous fight the enemy was again forced back, while the Cavalry, Artillery, and another division crossed the bridge.

There was now every indication that the enemy was in full retreat, and that his losses in killed, wounded, and prisoners, besides guns and equipment, were rapidly increasing.

CHAPTER XVIII

THE CAPTURE OF BAGHDAD

I WAS kept well informed of the changing situation, and early on the 24th of February proposed to General Maude that the flotilla should move up the Tigris. This was agreed to and I passed through the boat-bridge about midday, flying my Senior Officer's pendant on board the *Tarantula*, leading the *Mantis*, the *Moth*, the *Butterfly*, the *Gadfly*, and the *Snakefly*.

We stopped close by the 1st Army Corps Headquarters to obtain further information, and there met General Cobbe, who rode down to the left bank with his Staff.

He informed me that the enemy were all on the move, and that it appeared clear for us to continue up the river. Recrossing the river, I went to the Intelligence tent, and, getting in touch with Army Headquarters, received a message from General Maude asking me to call at Headquarters and discuss the situation with him. Leaving orders for the gunboats to move up-river, and arranging that I should pick them up again farther on, I went to Headquarters by car. After about an hour's drive, during which it had been amply evident that our advance had commenced in earnest, we arrived at Army Headquarters, and there found General Maude. The Headquarters camp had been struck, and he and the Staff were booted and spurred, their horses and escort of cavalry waiting nearby. He was restlessly pacing up and down, pondering every means of accelerating the advance. The Staff were standing round looking rather worried, and as if any diversion, such as my appearance, was a thing to be welcomed.

The Army Commander at once asked whether the gunboats had started, and it was satisfactory to be able to point them out in the distance, threading their way up-river. That pleased him. He kept saying, "I can't get a move on. So and so won't move," etc. etc.

Finally he suggested that the gunboats might go on to a place a few miles short of Kut. At that I thought I might go even one better, with all this talk about getting a move on, and asked whether there was any reason why we should not try to reach Kut itself. We discussed the matter, in detail, and, as the latest information was to the effect that it was unlikely that any enemy guns remained there, decided to try, although, as he remarked, we should probably run into a lot of sniping. I said that we did not mind that very much.

Then I drove down to the river in the car, and the *Mantis* picked me up as she passed Magasis. We steamed until darkness came on, when we were a few miles short of Kut, and I landed with Commander Buxton to ascertain the state of affairs in that vicinity. We learned from some officers in a near-by trench that Kut seemed to have been evacuated by the Turks, and that there had been no firing from there for some hours past.

I decided to go forward, and proceeded with Buxton in the *Mantis*, with the *Butterfly* following. The other gunboats were left as a covering force a little way behind, since it was dark, and because, should serious opposition develop, and we had suddenly to turn and retire, there would have been considerable confusion in the narrow river, whereas, as it was, from the hidden background they could support us with their gunfire.

So we crept along the well-remembered reaches until there came in sight, displayed in brilliant moonlight, and shrouded in ghostly silence, the battered, shell-torn ruin of what once had been a town.

It seemed deserted, so we anchored, and after a time Buxton and I landed with an armed party, covered by the guns of the ships. We hoisted the Union Jack at the centre of the river front, returned onboard, and remained there until daylight.

During next morning—the 25th of February, that is—I collected the gunboat flotilla, and moved up-river, anchoring just below the bridge which our troops had thrown across the Shumran bend in their celebrated crossing of the day before. They opened it to let us through, amid rousing cheers from the soldiers crowding each bank.

I had received further information and messages from the General, and in accordance with these instructions, led the flotilla on at full speed up the Tigris, in order to co-operate with those of our troops pursuing the retreating Turkish Army. We arrived abreast of our leading infantry at about 9.30, when we were some fourteen miles to the west of Kut, and at about the same time came in sight of the Turkish rearguard. We immediately opened up a rapid fire, and must have inflicted heavy casualties upon them. The enemy did not take long to retaliate, and were soon returning our fire from field-guns and large howitzers in prepared positions which had been reached among the sandhills near Imam Mahdi. We were considerably relieved when some of our field artillery galloped up, and eased the situation by opening a shattering fire in our support. All this time, however, our troops were advancing steadily and the battle continued throughout the whole day, the gunboats remaining in the same vicinity, and actively assisting in the bombardment of the enemy's position. We, of course, made rather conspicuous marks in the river, and all the ships were hit by shells during the day, but luckily no serious damage was done. With the exception of Lieutenant John H. Murdoch, R.N.R., of the *Mantis*, who was somewhat severely wounded in the afternoon, there were no casualties. After a severe fight our infantry gained a footing in the enemy's position, taking many prisoners, but our cavalry were checked on the northern flank by a stolid front of entrenched infantry. Our men had tasted of the sweets of victory, however. After some more desperate fighting the enemy evacuated their position during the night.

From information I gleaned in the early morning of the 26th of February I understood that the Turks were probably retreating, so decided, if possible, to push on up the river with the flotilla. I went ahead in the *Gadfly* (Commander Ernest K. Arbuthnot), to reconnoitre ahead of the others, the *Gadfly* being much smaller, more easily handled, and not such a prominent mark for enemy artillery. The other gunboats followed a mile or so behind, but it soon appeared that the Turks were retiring, and I obtained wireless messages from General Headquarters saying that the enemy were in full retreat towards Aziziya, abandoning guns and other encumbrances on the way. Later in the forenoon I received a wireless message from General Maude that the Turkish Army was in full retreat, very much demoralized. He asked me to co-operate in the pursuit, and with our cavalry and advanced infantry to inflict as much damage as possible. I at once signalled the *Tarantula* to close. Then, Arbuthnot putting the *Gadfly* alongside her in a most seamanlike manner without stopping as the ships steamed up-river, I climbed onboard her with my coxswain, avoiding any waste of time. We went on at full speed, with the *Mantis*, the *Moth*, the *Gadfly*, and the *Butterfly* following. Signs of retreat were very soon apparent, and when we came up to the small town of Bughaila, early in the afternoon, found white flags flying over the town, so went on as fast as possible, leaving the *Gadfly* there. Commander Arbuthnot hoisted a Union Jack, rounding up also some 200 prisoners and a number of trench mortars.

Our cavalry were at this time operating on the Turkish northern flank, farther out in the desert, but were withdrawn in the evening, when the Cavalry Division went into bivouac, about three miles north of the Nahr al Kalek bend. The infantry had not managed to get in touch with the Turkish rearguard, although they had made some magnificent marches in the difficult circumstances.

Near Bughaila the gunboats began to overtake numbers of Turkish stragglers on the left bank of the Tigris. They hailed us, and held up their hands in token of surrender; and we hailed them by megaphone, telling them to go back and give themselves up to our troops. It was impossible for us to stop and look after these numbers, for in the distance we had already sighted the smoke of enemy steamers, which I determined to chase and either to destroy or capture. We also saw some abandoned enemy guns, partly submerged in the river near Bughaila. As we continued at full speed the enemy steamers quickly became visible, and soon it was possible to make out from the

Tarantula which they were. We experienced a strange thrill when the familiar hull of the *Firefly* was made out. It will be remembered that she had fallen into the hands of the Turks after we had had to abandon her on the 1st of December, 1915, during the retreat from Ctesiphon. On that occasion, as will also be recollected, we had been surprised and nearly surrounded by the pursuing Turkish army ; her boiler had been pierced by a shell, disabling her. We were naturally most anxious—indeed, it was the most cherished desire of the gunboats' crews—to recapture or destroy her, and through wearisome bombardments and inaction we had long been waiting for this time, and the chance of bringing the Turkish flotilla into action. At last the long-hoped-for opportunity had arrived !

We opened fire as soon as we came into range—this being, of course, greatly influenced by the windings of the river—and the *Firefly* and the *Pioneer* replied, the *Firefly* making good shooting with the fine modern 4-inch gun with which she was armed. She sent hurtling against us our own shell and ammunition, which had been left onboard her.

Steaming on at full speed, we were now entering the long reach which terminates in the hairpin bend of the river at Nahr al Kalek. My coxswain had just called my attention to a team of oxen dragging a big gun through the fugitives from the *débris* of the Turkish army, who were struggling through the desert on our starboard hand. I pointed to a pom-pom, and said, " Give them some of that ! " He soon brought down one or more of the gun-team, and, as the drivers ran away, I suppose the gun fell into our hands later. Turning from this, I looked ahead, and saw that there was some commotion or other on the bank at the head of the reach. Taking up my binoculars, I made out the cause to be khaki-clad soldiers. They could not be ours. They must be the Turkish rearguard. Placed at the apex of that hairpin bend in the river, besides defending the Baghdad road, which passed there, they commanded two long avenues of the river, up which advancing vessels must make their way, and then circle round the bend opposite to them at point-blank range.

If they had placed their field-guns in time they would have probably sunk us, but we now know that they were part of the Turkish XVIIIth Corps, and had arrived only that morning to take up a prearranged position, although no digging had been done there before. (I quote from the *Official History*.) It was as well for us that this was the case. I had the impression that they seemed to be standing crowded together watching our approach.

One had to consider the risks of getting damaged, running aground, or being disabled in this unknown channel, when a ship would be in a most unpleasant position, but at the same time it seemed that we would be a very difficult target for them, particularly when we circled round the bend, rapidly altering our direction, a manœuvre which should bother any field-gunner. Also, we could keep down their fire with our own—the best protection there is !

Considering the situation in this way, it seemed that the risks must be accepted in order to get at the enemy flotilla, retreating shipping, and other forces, so we kept on at full speed, directing some guns on to them while continuing to engage their flotilla, which had passed them, and was now steaming down a reach to the westward, displaying, incidentally, a good target.

The enemy troops soon opened fire with field-guns, machine-guns, and rifles, and as we, in turn, rounded the hairpin bend each ship was hit many times, and each sustained casualties. The *Tarantula's* upper works clanged and rattled as a stream of bullets spattered dully against them. At the head of the bend we were only 400 or 500 yards away from the Turks. We were using all guns, including the 6-inch, which at this point-blank range must have performed great execution. The noise was deafening, and to it was added the shriek of shells from the field-guns and the enemy flotilla, which, judging by their performance, seemed to possess a curious assortment of guns.

In the *Tarantula* we managed to get past without what might be termed serious damage, although bullets seemed to have found their way into every nook and cranny of the ship. Still, some serious casualties were reported, and we now redoubled our efforts in chasing the Turkish flotilla, while the *Mantis*, next in line, negotiated the bend. In the brief interim the enemy seemed to have brought up more guns. They gave her a warmer reception than, in their first surprise, they had accorded us.

Looking astern after we had got clear away, I saw that she was receiving and returning a very heavy fire, after a sudden great outburst of which I was horrified to see her take a great swerve towards the bank. We feared that some damage vital to her steering-gear or engines had been done, and that she might run aground right opposite the enemy position, and were mighty thankful when she suddenly straightened up and came on. The quartermaster and pilot had been killed outright by bullets which entered through the observation slits of the conning-tower, and her captain, Bernard Buxton, had seized the helm. His prompt action had saved her.

The *Moth*, third in the line, who received heavy punishment, was most efficiently handled by her captain, Charles Cartwright, who received promotion for this service. He and all his officers were wounded. She had two men killed and eighteen wounded, which was a casualty list of about 50 per cent. of her complement.

One shell from almost dead ahead hit the fore side of the stokehold casing, piercing the port boiler both back and front but by great good luck missing the boiler tubes. The after compartment was holed below the waterline, while the upper deck and funnels, like those of all the ships, were riddled with bullets.

I was now able to get a wireless message through to the *Gadfly*, ordering her not to follow us round the bend, for she would most certainly have been sunk, as she was so much smaller and slower than the gunboats of the *Mantis* class.

Having got past the Turkish rearguard, and steaming on as fast as we could, we now began rapidly to gain on the enemy vessels. There were also large numbers of the retreating Turkish Army on our starboard beam—that is, on the left bank—so we also opened rapid fire on them with everything we could bring to bear, heavy and light guns, pom-poms, Maxims and rifles, effecting a great execution at this short range. The enemy, except in very few cases, were too thoroughly demoralized to reply to our whittling hail of steel and lead. We also shot down some of their gun-teams. These they quickly deserted, and the guns ultimately fell into the hands of our Army, when it passed over this ground.

The vessels ahead were by now drawing within easy range, and shortly afterwards the little armed tug *Sumana* stopped and surrendered. I ordered her to go down the river and give herself up. She had been, as I have explained elsewhere, one of our gunboats in the early part of the campaign; being in Kut during the siege, under the command of Lieutenant Tudway, D.S.C., she had been of great assistance to the beleaguered force, and had done some excellent work, but had fallen into the hands of the Turks at the capitulation.

At about 5.30 P.M. the river steamer *Basra*, crowded with escaping troops, stopped, ran alongside the river-bank, and surrendered after receiving a few shells from the *Tarantula*. We were afterwards informed that we had killed and wounded some German machine-gunners who were onboard her, that she had some field artillery onboard, as well as a wounded captured British officer, Lieutenant Cowie, and some men of the Black Watch, together with some of our Indian soldiers, all of whom had been wounded in the last fight at Sannaiyat and fallen into the enemy's hands. Directly she surrendered Cowie took over the command, and with his men did most useful and gallant service with us until we were able to return them to their regiment.

The *Firefly* kept up a brisk fire from her 4-inch gun when she could bring it to bear on us ; but our reply gradually began to tell on her, and, after being hit several times, she apparently realized that she had no chance of escaping, so her crew ran her slap into the river-bank. The light was just beginning to fail, and I saw that although she had stopped she was slewing round in the river. Not knowing what she was up to, I again gave orders to open fire. It was soon evident, however, that she had had the fight knocked out of her. We ran alongside her at about

6.15, and discovered that her crew had escaped ashore under cover of the deepening darkness. Curiously enough, this event happened in the north-west part of the Zaljah Reach of the Tigris, to the westward of Um at Tubul, only a few miles from the place where, in the presence of some of us who were now present, she had been abandoned.

I put a prize crew under Lieutenant John P. Bradley onboard the *Firefly*, and the White Ensign was hoisted over her once more.

The breech of her 4-inch gun, still hot from firing, was open, as the enemy evidently had not had time to throw away the breech-block, and plenty of fused shells were lying round it, ready for action. As the Turks did not seem to have been very particular as to which fuses they used, we later on buried some of the most dangerous-looking ones in the desert! It occurred to me that they might have made some attempt to blow her up or to destroy her. Accordingly I instigated an immediate search of the magazines, and, sure enough, we found some cotton-waste steeped in oil smouldering down there! But it was merely smouldering, and we were able to put it out before any damage was done.

Among other effects, we found that the enemy had left their native cook behind on board the *Firefly*. He was discovered hiding in his galley, and was taken over by the prize crew in the same job, and having, I suppose, prepared lunch for the Turks, he was soon busy cooking dinner for the British Navy. I also heard a story that the same deck log-book made a fresh start in English from the place where the Turks had left off.

During the year the *Firefly* had been in Turkish hands they had not disturbed things very much. Some of our officers found their own books still on the wardroom shelves! In one cupboard we found a wooden block for reshaping a *fez*. It was just as well that no *fez* was on it, as some sailor or other would have been sure to wear it; and it would hardly have suited our men's particular style of beauty. In the vicinity there were some barges aground which had been cast off by the other enemy steamers at the time of escaping. In these and onboard the *Firefly* we afterwards discovered a quantity of most valuable papers and documents, evidently belonging to the Turkish General Headquarters. These were promptly dispatched to our Intelligence Department. Among other important details was a Turkish list comprising the various units of our Army in Mesopotamia, with notes and reference marks in red ink against such Indian regiments as were considered doubtful in their allegiance to us.

Looking round the forlorn desert landscape, one could see the masses of the retreating army in the distance, and as darkness came down, the flames from the enemy gunboat *Pioneer*, which had been hit by the *Mantis* and had run ashore a short way ahead, burning fiercely, lit up the scene— the *débris* after the action, the bloodstained, sanded decks. As we were already far ahead of our troops I decided to go no farther. Then the *Mantis* and the *Moth* rejoined, and, seeing the *Firefly* alongside us, burst, fore and aft, into a round of spirited cheering, which showed the unbounded satisfaction of the Navy in Mesopotamia that the long-awaited day of reckoning had come at last. Who could feel tired or anxious in company with men like these ? I caused the gunboats to move away from the burning *Pioneer*, which had a quantity of ammunition on board, that might have exploded at any moment. She was lighting up the river, too, and revealing us as targets for any enemy guns that might be brought down. So we anchored a little to the east, and there carried out the sad duty of burying our dead. Sherbrooke came and told me when all was ready, gave me a Prayer Book, and we landed on the river-bank. Then we groped our way in the darkness to where the small hushed funeral party was gathered. I read the Burial Service by the light of a flickering lantern in a silence disturbed only by rippling river sounds now that the guns were still. So in desert sands, their duty done, our comrades sleep in peace.

The *Tarantula* and the *Mantis* remained in the vicinity throughout the following day, gradually getting into touch with the Army, whose advance continued ; on March the 1st we went on to Aziziya, and met them again. The *Moth*, with the *Firefly* and the other prizes, were sent down to Basra for repairs. By dint of most useful work at the base the *Firefly* was recommissioned with a temporary crew on the 4th of March, and she soon returned to the front in fairly good working order. She had been most expeditiously repaired, and well fumigated—a process of which she was badly in need at the time of her recapture ! The Turks had abandoned more guns near Aziziya, which were discovered by the *Tarantula*, and our army, with whom we were now again in touch, testified to the quantities of guns and material of every description which the Turks had left behind on their scrambling retreat. Indeed, a well-known author, in describing these episodes, states that the Turkish retreat had, by the gunboats' action, been turned into a rout.

It is most flattering to receive a tribute from the enemy. However, Captain Muhammad Amin Bey, of the Turkish General Staff, who was then on Khalil's Staff, in his book, *Baghdad and the Story of its Last Fall*, says that the Turkish XVIIIth Corps had arrived at the Nahr al Kalek bend that morning. He continues :

> In the afternoon it sustained the attack of the hostile cavalry on its left flank and rear, and of the hostile river fleet on its right flank. The courageous attack of the British Naval forces played havoc with the rear of the Corps.

Referring to this action, Mr. Candler says in his book, *The Long Road to Baghdad*, that this, as was the case at Amara, is an example of how a fleet of gunboats can lengthen the arm of a force in a river campaign, doubling its striking power and at the same time paralysing the enemy's communications when he is in retreat.

Since crossing the Tigris the captures of the British forces had amounted to some 4000 prisoners, of whom 148 were officers ; 39 guns, 22 trench mortars, 11 machine-guns ; the *Firefly*, the *Sumana*, the *Pioneer*, the *Basra*, and several smaller vessels ; besides barges, pontoons, and other bridging material ; quantities of rifles, bayonets, equipment and ammunition, explosives, vehicles, and other stores. In addition, the enemy had thrown into the river and otherwise destroyed several guns, besides a considerable quantity of war material.

The gunboats, Cavalry, and Infantry now concentrated at Aziziya ; and while the extended line of communications was being reorganized General Maude consulted with the Home authorities as to a further advance. This, after some delay, he obtained permission to make, and a general move forward was made on the 5th of March. The supply situation had been readjusted, owing to the strenuous efforts and brilliant work of the G.O.C., Communications, General Sir George MacMunn, and of the Inland Water Transport, under Colonel Grey and Major Hughes.

The gunboat flotilla moved forward with the troops on the 5th, and by the afternoon of that day our cavalry had got into touch with the Turkish rearguard at Lajj. A dense sandstorm, however, came on about this time, making it quite impossible for us to distinguish anything more than a few yards distant, so we could not fire from the gunboats. The sandstorm also made it very difficult for the troops. The 13th Hussars, coming across a body of enemy during the afternoon, charged them, only to find themselves in the front line of Turkish trenches. They extricated themselves from this perilous situation after sustaining considerable losses. The suddenness of their appearance, however, resulted in their inflicting great damage on the Turks.

It was afterwards found that in their gallant attack our troops were up against the 51st Turkish Division—*i.e.*, about 2500 infantry and 16 guns entrenched. This strong rearguard held up our cavalry and advanced forces all day.

This situation was most unsatisfactory from the point of view of us onboard the gunboats, as we could hear a good deal of firing not a great way off ; but the sandstorm so thickened the air that it was quite impossible to make out anything clearly or for us to assist with the heavy guns our people engaged against the Turks. During the evening a Staff officer rode down to the river-bank, so we sent in a boat for him and in this way learned what was progressing. This officer appeared to be under the impression that things had gone very badly with the British, and was inclined to advise me to fall back with the gunboats. At this, however, I demurred, as it seemed that we were in little danger from the Turkish forces, and could have received only a temporary setback. He had had no food all day, but we persuaded him to stay to dinner, and by the time he left he was taking a more rosy view of affairs. So we stayed where we were, and at daylight, the sandstorm having blown itself out, we found that the Turks had retreated during the night. They presumably thought that they had been outflanked, and had not had time in which to occupy their strong Ctesiphon position, which we passed during that day (6th of March).

We steamed undisturbed up the various reaches of the river in this neighbourhood, where we had seen so much fighting in 1915, and, passing the arch of Ctesiphon, anchored for the night in that locality. We now know from subsequent Turkish accounts that Khalil Pasha had first thought of standing at the Ctesiphon position, but, after wasting six valuable days in working on its fortifications had finally decided—one gathers reluctantly—that he could not hold it against this spirited and determined drive of the British forces. Time and the state of the Tigris did not admit of inundating the country in strategic places, as he would have wished ; nor did time allow of the arrival of the Turkish XIIIth Corps, ordered from Persia to reinforce his northern flank.

In order to try to effect a junction with this XIIIth Corps Khalil Pasha concentrated most of the XVIIIth Corps east of the Tigris to defend the line of the Diyala River, a tributary which joins the Tigris at its left or eastern bank, about eight miles below Baghdad, thus leaving the western bank of the Tigris only weakly defended. The Turkish supply arrangements had broken down, and by this time their men were both short of food and demoralized by their recent heavy losses.

Our forces, advancing on the 7th of March, therefore, soon discovered that the enemy had taken up their entrenched position on the line of the Diyala River, and that we were once more in touch with the Turk. The gunboats and artillery immediately went into action, under a heavy, raking fire from the Turkish stronghold, and remained so during the whole of the day, the Turkish artillery making fairly accurate firing, and providing the gunboats with an exciting time. During the night of the 7th–8th of March unsuccessful attempts were made to cross the Diyala River in pontoons, which resulted in somewhat serious casualties on our side ; and it became evident that the enemy line was still defended by numerous guns and machine-guns which had been skilfully placed. The fact that the night of this venture was lit with bright, clear desert moonlight was particularly advantageous to their defence.

A small party now ferried across the Tigris to enfilade the enemy's position with guns from the right bank, and under cover of this enfilade-fire a party of about a hundred of the Loyal North Lancashires managed to get across the Diyala in pontoons during the next night. They found themselves in a very awkward position, however, but managed to retain what they had won for the next twenty-two hours, when reinforcements were got over to them. Until these arrived the isolated detachment put up a wonderful defence, stubbornly driving off determined counter-attacks with very heavy losses, and being the while under constant close fire—both reverse and enfilade—from the surrounding buildings, trenches, and gardens.

By the 8th, however, the pontoon bridge had been brought up and was thrown across the Tigris half a mile below a place called Bawi. Here the Cavalry and part of General Cobbe's 1st Corps crossed to the right bank during that day and the next. Although suffering much from scarcity of water, these troops gallantly drove the enemy from his position, now reinforced near Shawa Khan and other places which covered Baghdad from the south and south-west.

Meanwhile on the left bank of the Tigris General Marshall's force had got more men across the Diyala early on the 10th, and by 7 A.M. of that day the East Lancashires and the Wiltshires had linked up with the detachment of the North Lancashires who had so heroically held their hard-contested ground. By noon the Diyala was bridged. Our troops pushed on, and, driving the enemy from the little roadside villages, finally faced the enemy's last strongly held position, on the Qarara-Tel Muhammad ridge, having captured more prisoners, arms, and ammunition in this latest drive forward.

An attempt had also been made to land troops from two

motor-lighters, under the charge of Naval officers, above the mouth of the Diyala River on the night of the 10th ; but one of the lighters had broken down, and the other had grounded in the shallows within gun-range of the enemy. The *Tarantula*, Commander Sherbrooke, and the *Snakefly*, Lieutenant-Commander Webster, rendered valuable assistance by extricating the second of the motor-lighters from this dangerous position before daylight. The *Tarantula* once again proved the enormous value of this powerful type of river gunboat.

Meanwhile, at about 5 A.M. on the 10th, the enemy on the right bank were reported to be falling back before the front of General Fane's force. The British at once advanced, and were soon again heavily engaged with the Turks, who were holding a line some way nearer Baghdad.

By noon, however, the wind had increased, and, a sandstorm blowing up, it was impossible to see more than 150 yards away. Anyone who has been in one of these sandstorms will remember acutely the combined discomfort of the hot, burning wind, the stinging dust, the thirst and gritty feeling in one's mouth and throat. Sometimes one was under shellfire as well ! The only consolation the troops had was that the storm was blowing in the face of the Turks. The gale continued for the greater part of the night, but by 2 A.M. on the 11th it was learned that the enemy position had been vacated, and that it was now occupied by British troops. Meanwhile our cavalry reached points to the westward of Baghdad, in spite of great privations and lack of water, and their rapid flank movements caused the Turkish command great anxiety.

The Turks, with the sandstorm blowing in their faces, were finding even greater difficulty in observation than us. This fact probably added to their fear of being outflanked on the west and surrounded. Reports from the left bank of the Tigris also showed that the British advance could not be held there, while the Turkish ammunition supply was faulty. Soon after sunset on the 10th Khalil Pasha held a council of war, at which a speedy withdrawal and the abandonment of Baghdad, their famous possession for centuries, was decided upon.

During the night, therefore, the Turkish Army retired by both banks to the northward of Baghdad, which was evacuated in considerable confusion, amid the flashes and explosions of demolition and the wild, elemental fury of the storm. In all conscience a fitting setting for such a drastic stage in the campaign ! Early on the 11th our forces on both banks found the positions in front of them evacuated. These we now occupied, and an advance was made on Baghdad. Just before 6 A.M. a patrol of the Black Watch, under second Lieutenant Houston, occupied Baghdad railway Station, on the right bank ; and the 1/5 Buffs were the first battalion to enter Baghdad, Captain Harrison crossing the river and hoisting a Union Jack over the city. The Cavalry Division was directed on Kadhimain, with orders to pursue beyond. Meanwhile the 13th Division pushed forward along the left bank, their advance guard entering the city during the morning.

So on Sunday the 11th of March the Christians' armies closed on the ancient city, the golden domes of Kadhimain looked down on British cavalry, and the gunboat flotilla steamed triumphantly up the sluggish-flowing Tigris. Finding no mines to impede our progress, we soon reached the outskirts of Baghdad, having in company our Army Commander onboard his steamer.

The great river led us into the centre of the city, where people were cheering and waving us welcome from the river-banks and house-tops. Showing its best face to the Tigris, Baghdad there displays a frontage diverse and picturesque. There the Government, official, and better houses have so many years looked on the river, and farther back these merge into a yellow tangle, where buildings and great bazaars jostle with mosques with minarets of blue and green and gold, piercing the dazzling sky.

Sending the *Tarantula* on with some of the gunboats, I anchored near the citadel at about half-past three, in order to get in touch with the situation and projected movements. General Maude, looking very cheerful—and well he might —came alongside in his motor-boat, and over afternoon tea we discussed the situation. That was a visit which I shall always remember with pleasure.

The pursuit of the enemy up-river was then continued, and two barges were captured a few miles farther on, while the *Tarantula* again performed valuable service with the advanced squadron of gunboats. These had some exciting brushes with the enemy, whose rearguard tried to entrap and cut them off on several occasions by bringing down guns among the sandhills below them.

One interesting feature of the gunboats' entry into Baghdad was that the reconditioned *Firefly* accompanied the flotilla, flying the White Ensign over the Turkish, and with Lieutenant-Commander C. J. F. Eddis, her original captain, again in command. Subsequently she was thoroughly repaired, a new crew was sent out from home for her, and Lieutenant (Acting) G. Taylor of the *Proserpine* took over the command.

The little *Flycatcher*, which came up to Baghdad a day or so later, was also a source of interest to the inhabitants, who had known her in former days as a Turkish patrol-boat. The British forces entered the city amid demonstrative manifestations of satisfaction on the part of the inhabitants, who cheered the troops as they marched in and us as we steamed in single line up-river through the town. The last Turkish train had left at 2 A.M. and in the interim before our arrival Kurds and Arabs had been looting and firing buildings at different points. Upon our entry, however, order was soon restored.

I must not omit to recount one story I heard shortly after entering the town. It was to the effect that the first of our forces which *really* arrived in Baghdad were some soldiers who stumbled upon an Arab coffee-house in the duststorm, and, while refreshing themselves, asked what the name of the place was. To their astonishment they were politely told Baghdad !

Baghdad, living in the glamour of history and fable, looks best under the dim, early grey morning, when bathed in a desert sunset's fading splendour, or when limned in silver moonlight—but shows every year of disreputable old age in glaring sunlight or through a murky sandstorm. I do not know that we, who had served in the country so long, expected anything very wonderful, and have never seen any

s

reason why so many should have been disillusioned with what they finally beheld—except perhaps those only very recently out from home.

The best towns that we had seen in the country—Basra, Mahommerah, and others similar—had not left us expecting anything very wonderful of Baghdad—especially when one bore in mind the fact that the Turk had been in possession so long ! Of course, there are some fine mosques in the city, but the Government buildings and the arsenal were rather shabby-looking edifices. Otherwise Baghdad seemed to contain only rather shabby, tumbledown houses, straggly narrow streets, and many wonderful smells.

A new thoroughfare, called Khalil Pasha Street, in memory of that Turkish commander's Kut victory, had been driven right through the town, chipping off bits of houses and buildings in the process, which, being not yet repaired, looked very untidy, as if they had just been sawn off. Apparently there was as little in the way of sanitary arrangements as in other Arab towns.

One wonders what sort of a place it was in the " magnificent " days of its Caliphs. What their army and navy looked like. Whether they had duststorms then. Muhammad Amin says that this was the thirtieth time Baghdad had fallen to a conqueror, and that never before had the event passed off so quietly. Of course, in the good old days there would have been a grand massacre of the inhabitants shortly after our arrival, and, all things considered, I am not so sure that I entirely blame some of those old conquerors, judging by what we saw of the inhabitants.

For over a fortnight before the arrival of the British the enemy had been removing stores and destroying property which he could not remove, but, for all that, an immense quantity of booty remained. This included guns, ranging from old brass smooth-bores of the Middle Ages to modern quick-firers ; rifles and pistols of every type, from flintlock to the latest-pattern Colt ; munitions of every description, and machinery for liquid fire—which had, however, been carefully put away and never used. In one corner of the arsenal was a great heap of iron cannon-balls of every calibre, in another a pile of new German mines, and, as a sad reminder, the guns of General Townshend's force. These included our Naval 4·7-inch guns. All had been rendered useless before they fell into the enemy's hands at the capitulation of Kut. There was also an enormous quantity of other material, rolling-stock, railway workshops, pumps, cranes, signal and telegraph equipment, and the like.

Baghdad's great new wireless installation had been wrecked on the morning of the 11th. The transmitting-gear had just been completed in time to tap out a few messages to Berlin, telling of our approach on the city. The Turks had also, before leaving, made arrangements for blowing up the citadel. The wires, however, were found and extinguished by our troops.

Some of the old smooth-bore cannon in the arsenal must have been of great age, and, being of considerable size, one imagines that no other town in those parts could have possessed such formidable weapons. In the days when they were cast events moved slowly, and slow must have been the majestic movement of such guns across the sandy plains and deserts. One can imagine rebellious *pashas* asking mercy, warring *sheikhs* suing for peace, at the news that the great guns had left Baghdad. Their arrival on the field of battle must surely have decided the issue.

CHAPTER XIX

EVENTS AFTER THE OCCUPATION OF BAGHDAD

THE immediate object of the British was now to consolidate their position and to co-operate with the Russians in establishing themselves on the Tigris about Mosul. The Russians, however, were delayed by lack of reinforcements and by dense snow in their efforts to effect a junction with the British and to advance on Kirkuk and Mosul. Beyond engagements with the Turkish rearguard they were able to do little, and the Russian Revolution, which commenced the day after we reached Baghdad, exercised more and more effect, resulting in their exerting little further influence on the campaign.

The Turkish XIIIth and XVIIIth Corps, defeated and deprived of their base at Baghdad, were retreating to the west and north. It was necessary for General Maude, therefore, to drive these out of the vicinity, to destroy them if possible, and also to prepare for the advent of Turkish reinforcements.

Partly as a set-off to the Russian breakdown the British Commander-in-Chief of our Egyptian force was at this time told to adopt an offensive *rôle* in Palestine, and later to exploit his successes as much as possible. This attitude led ultimately to our capture of Jerusalem.

Operations subsequent to the fall of Baghdad, from March the 12th to the 31st, 1917, consisted in the main of the necessary advances in order to defend and to obtain control of the river *bunds* upstream of the city. General Cobbe, operating on the right bank, with gunboats co-operating by shelling points in the Turkish line with very good effect, carried a strong position south of Mushaidie have been made in the arrival, disembarkation, and initial operations of the campaign if the *Emden*, that stormy petrel of the War, had entered the river, and brought to the Turks the assistance of her trained crew, with long-ranging 4·1-inch guns.

In order to describe the Naval co-operation with the forces it has been necessary in most cases to give a brief description of the military side of the operations discussed ; even military operations in which the Navy could not directly take part have often been outlined, so as to give continuity to the history of the campaign. In these cases I have quoted largely from the official dispatches and from the excellent *Official History*.

In conclusion, it is a great pleasure to me to place on record the cordial relations which existed between the Army and Navy in this campaign. It will be remembered that many former combined operations have failed owing to friction between the two Services ; but we in Mesopotamia were happily free from this, and, in spite of the effects on one's temper of the trying climate and other plagues of the country, the Navy, Army, Air and Political Services always pulled happily together.

The small detachment of the Navy was indebted to every rank of the Army, from the Army Commander downwards, for many kindnesses, and it is impossible to quote the names of the many officers of the Staff, Infantry, Artillery, Supply and Transport, Ordnance, Inland Water Transport, Red Cross, Nursing Sisters, and Medical Services who so many times gave the Navy such generous and open-handed assistance.

Let me also record our gratitude to friends in Bombay and Ceylon for presents of every kind of useful thing and luxury, which alleviated greatly the lot of both officers and men. Captain (now Admiral) Lumsden, Director of Indian Marine at Bombay, took a practical hand in this, and our friends in Ceylon—particularly in Colombo—looked upon us as their special children. They showered good things and useful gifts upon us.

Lastly, let me pay a tribute to the fine spirit and bravery of the sailors and soldiers—British and Indian—to whom the success of the Expedition is so largely due. On this far-away campaign, in countries which many of them had never heard of, in the blazing heat of Arabian deserts, the arid wilds of Mesopotamia, or bitter cold of the Persian mountains, through exile, hardship, and reverses, most gallantly they played their part in the Great War, and fought their way to victory.

THE END

railway station, some twenty miles north of Baghdad, and by the 16th the Turks were again in full flight to the north.

On the 14th General Maude established a post on the right bank of the Diyala River opposite Baquba, which town was surprised and captured, as a preliminary to joining hands with the Russian force, who, although delayed, as I have said, were trying to advance through Persia by way of Kermanshah and Kasr-i-Shirin. A gunboat was also sent to, and stationed at, Baquba for some time.

Our troops also occupied Feluja, on the Euphrates, thirty-five miles west of Baghdad, on the 19th of March, driving out the Turkish garrison, which retired up the right bank of the Euphrates, thus giving us control of the Middle Euphrates between Feluja and Nasiriya.

The remainder of March on the Tigris front was occupied in operations against the Turkish XIIIth and XVIIIth Corps to the north of Baghdad, and on the nearer slopes of the Jebel Hamrin Hills ; but by the end of the month the XIIIth Corps had been driven back to Deli Abbas. After operations in which the gunboats again did good service the XVIIIth Corps was driven beyond the line of the Shatt al Adhaim. This period had been devoid of important incident on the Karun.

On the Euphrates a column sent from our force at Nasiriya had inflicted a severe defeat on the enemy in the vicinity of As Sahilan, destroying their towers and fortifications. This lesson had an excellent effect round about Nasiriya, and no further hostilities of importance occurred during the period under review. The Turkish detachment at Samawa retreated to Feluja when Baghdad fell, and were subsequently again " moved on " by our troops.

As the result of further fighting during the month of April the enemy's XIIIth and XVIIIth Corps were driven back with heavy losses, the former into the Jebel Hamrin Hills, and the latter to Tekrit. But the hot weather now came on apace, and, with the exception of punitive expeditions and some operations on the Euphrates, there was little activity.

The *Bee* and the *Scarab* were at this time prepared at Port Said as additions to the force, and shortly afterwards were towed to Basra. The last four of the "small China gunboats" were commissioned on the following dates : the *Blackfly*, Lieutenant-Commander Longstaff, and the *Caddisfly*, Lieutenant-Commander Elwell Sutton, on March 21st ; the *Sedgefly*, Lieutenant-Commander Wheelwright, on March 22nd ; and the *Hoverfly* on April 7th. They were all completed, launched, and went up-river shortly afterwards.

All the sixteen "small China gunboats" having been launched, the Naval work at Abadan ceased, and the *Alert* was brought to Basra early in April 1917, moored off our Naval depot at Tanooma, and employed as a tender to the *Dalhousie*.

Shortly after our arrival at Baghdad the Army Commander placed a house on the left bank of the Tigris at the disposal of the Royal Navy, and this was most useful as a depot for reserve ammunition and stores. Gunboats were able to moor alongside it, and rooms were set aside for the sick, which proved a most desirable arrangement during the excessive heat of the Mesopotamian summer, when the steel gunboats became miniature furnaces. The Admiralty approved of "Navy House," Baghdad, being taken over, and also of the expenditure on necessary repairs.

A short summary only has been given of the foregoing operations, in which the gunboat flotilla participated as far as conditions and circumstances allowed, rendering substantial assistance to the Army. The troops were often now, however, operating far away from the river, which becomes very shallow and difficult of navigation, at no great distance north of Baghdad.

The possibilities for gunboats thus became less and less, although much useful work was at this time done on the Euphrates, and in patrolling lines of communication. It therefore became possible later in the year to reduce the flotilla considerably, thus releasing officers and men for duty in other waters. My period of service, and that of Captain Wason on the station had long elapsed, so we were relieved, and accordingly left for England early in May. The command was again merged in the Naval Persian Gulf Station, under Rear-Admiral Drury St. A. Wake ; and at

INDEX

the same time Captain E. Dugmore took command of the *Proserpine*, with the gunboat flotilla, and Captain G. V. Knox took command of the *Dalhousie* and depot at Tanooma.

As everyone knows, the campaign proceeded to a triumphant conclusion. Ramadie, on the Euphrates, was captured on September 29th, 1917, with over 3000 prisoners, 13 guns, and a great quantity of war material. On November the 5th the Turks were again defeated on the Tigris, before Tekrit, and this important place fell into British hands on the following day. November the 17th was marked by the deeply regretted death at Baghdad of Sir Stanley Maude from an attack of cholera, and General Marshall succeeded to the command of the Army in Mesopotamia.

From this period onwards the Turkish forces in Arabia were thrown back on all fronts, receiving—and not recovering from—blow after blow. While General Marshall continued his series of operations in Mesopotamia and Persia General Allenby in Palestine had forced the Turkish retreat on Jerusalem in November, with a loss of 70 guns and 10,000 casualties. That city fell into our hands on December the 9th. The pursuit of the Turks in Palestine was followed up, and on the 25th of September, 1918, Tiberias and Amman, on the Hedjaz railway, were occupied, about 45,000 prisoners and 265 guns being taken. Our troops entered Damascus on October the 1st. Sidon and Beirut were next occupied, and on the 26th of October Aleppo fell into British hands, completing the conquest of Syria, and cutting the Baghdad railway.

Meanwhile on the Tigris General Marshall advanced and captured Kalat Shergat on the 28th of October. He then engaged the Turks five miles north of that place, and about fifty miles south of Mosul, completely routing them, and taking about 7000 prisoners. Their whole remaining force in the country surrendered on October 30th, 1918.

The campaign was at an end.

With Mesopotamia and Syria in British hands the Turkish Cabinet appealed for an Armistice, and Turkey surrendered unconditionally on the 31st of October, 1918—that is, on the day following the close of the war in Mesopotamia.

In Mesopotamia the Turks, stiffened by a leavening of

Germans, had proved a hard nut for the invading force of British and Indians to crack. The few Germans in the country revealed great fertility of resource; both in Mesopotamia and the neighbouring country of Persia they were a constant thorn in the fleshy side of the British, and probably it was largely owing to their skilled advice that the Turks always chose and fortified their positions so well. The most striking instances of this which we have seen in the preceding pages were the Hanna and Sannaiyat positions, protected on their northern flank by the marshes and on their southern by the Tigris. These natural features enabled them to hold the Hanna defile for months.

As we have seen, the work of the small Naval detachment was varied : sometimes patrolling the river or convoying river craft, or exploring new waters, often taking part in combined operations, with detached military forces, or co-operating in battles or bombardments of enemy positions with the military. Occasionally, as at Ezra's Tomb and at Amara, or during the advance to Baghdad we were granted the opportunity—always eagerly looked for—of an engagement and a chase of the enemy's forces and river craft, with a chance of taking advantage of the power and mobility conferred by steam or fuel power when other means of pursuit of the enemy were exhausted, owing to the limitations of human effort. Indeed, one of the most complimentary references that I have read about the gunboats' performances was that which stated that the part played by them in the advance of 1917 up the Tigris, in pressing the pursuit of the enemy, resulted in such disastrous consequences to the Turks that it largely determined the fate of Baghdad.

The enemy's fear of gunboat action was amply shown by their frequent use of booms or other obstructions to prevent our advance ; these were employed, as we have seen, below Basra, Kurna, at Rotah Creek, Nasiriya, Kut, and Magasis. It has also been noted how, at different times, the enemy paid considerable attention to mining the river. They also floated mines down, and in this way nearly blew up the *Odin* in April 1915.

It is interesting also to consider what a difference would